PARNELL RECONSIDERED

Parnell Reconsidered

edited by

DONAL MCCARTNEY AND PAURIC TRAVERS

UNIVERSITY COLLEGE DUBLIN PRESS

PREAS CHOLÁISTE OLLSCOILE
BHAILE ÁTHA CLIATH

First published 2013
by University College Dublin Press
Newman House
86 St Stephen's Green
Dublin 2
Ireland

www.ucdpress.ie

ISBN 978-1-906359-70-6

Cataloguing in Publication data available from the British Library

Typeset in UK in Plantin and Fournier by Ryan Shiels
Text design by Lyn Davies
Printed on acid-free paper in England by Antony Rowe,
Chippenham, Wilts.

Contents

Acknowledgements

The preparation of these essays for publication has been facilitated by many people whose assistance we wish to acknowledge. First and foremost, we thank the members of the Parnell Society and the Avondale Trust – Bernadette O'Reilly, Deirdre Larkin, Leslie Armstrong, Bernadette Bianchi, Tony Byrne, Bernadette Crombie, Nuala Jordan, Felix M. Larkin, Eunan McKinney, Frank Murray, Joyce Padbury and Noel Tierney – for their individual and collective support. Publication of the volume has been made possible by a generous grant from the Parnell Society.

We are indebted to our contributors for their engagement, responsiveness and patience; to Theresa O'Farrell for her secretarial skills; to three anonymous readers for their valuable comments and suggestions; and to Noelle Moran and the staff at UCD Press for their customary professionalism.

We gratefully acknowledge permission from the governor of the Central Bank to use Robert Ballagh's beautiful Parnell Ir£100 note as our cover. We also acknowledge the assistance of Jean Costello of Avondale House, Coillte Teo, the librarian and staff of the Gladstone Library, St Deiniol's, Hawarden, the National Library of Ireland, and the director and staff of the National Archives of Ireland.

Finally, we are happy once again to acknowledge our indebtedness to Peig McCartney and Mary Moore.

DONAL MCCARTNEY
PAURIC TRAVERS
Dublin, May 2013

Notes on Contributors

D. G. Boyce is Emeritus Professor at the University of Swansea. A graduate of Queen's University Belfast, he is a fellow of the Royal Historical Society. His monographs include *Englishmen & Irish Troubles* (1973); *The Revolution in Ireland* (1988); *The Irish Question in British Politics* (1988); *Nineteenth Century Ireland* (1990); *Newspaper History from the Seventeenth Century to the Present Day* (1978); *Nationalism in Ireland* (1995). Edited collections include *Parnell in Perspective* (1991); *The Making of Modern Irish History* (1996); *Defenders of the Union* (2001); *The Ulster Crisis* (2005); *Gladstone & Ireland* (2010).

Dr Myles Dungan is an author and broadcaster. A graduate of UCD and TCD, he has been a Fulbright scholar in UC Berkeley. He is the author of seven books on historical themes – *Distant Drums* (1993); *Irish Voices from the Great War* (1996); *They Shall Grow Not Old: Irish Soldiers and the Great War* (1997); *The Stealing of the Irish Crown Jewels* (2003); *How the Irish won the West* (2006); he edited *Speaking Ill of the Dead* (2007); *Conspiracy: Irish Political Trials* (2009); *The Captain and the King: William O'Shea, Parnell and late Victorian Ireland* (2009).

Felix M. Larkin is a historian and former public servant. His postgraduate research work was on the history of the *Freeman's Journal*. A graduate of UCD, he is currently chairman of the Newspaper and Periodical History Forum of Ireland. He is the author/editor of two books – *Terror and Discord: the Shemus Cartoons in the Freeman's Journal, 1920–1924* (2009) and *Librarians, Poets and Scholars: A Festschrift for Dónall Ó Luanaigh* (2007) – as well as several chapters in books and scholarly articles.

Donal McCartney is Emeritus Professor of Modern Irish History at UCD and President of the Parnell Society. His monographs include *Dawning of Democracy* (1987); *Cardinal Newman and the Catholic University (1995); W. E. H. Lecky, Historian & Politician* (1994); *UCD: A National Idea* (1999). Edited collections include *Parnell and the Politics of Power* (1991); *The Ivy Leaf: The Parnells Remembered* (2006); *Words of the Dead Chief* (2009).

Pat Power is a local historian from Arklow. He is a leading expert on the history of Wicklow and in particular of the Parnell family. He has published several articles and pamphlets in this area.

Dr Pauric Travers was founding director of the Parnell Summer School and is chair of the Parnell Society. His publications include *Settlements & Divisions* (1988); *Eamon de Valera* (1994); *Dublin Burning* (1996); with MacDonagh & Mandle, *Culture & Nationalism in Ireland 1750–1950* (1982); with John O'Brien, *The Irish Emigrant Experience in Australia* (1991); with Donal McCartney, *The Ivy Leaf: the Parnells Remembered* (2006) and *Words of the Dead Chief* (2009).

Dr Fionnuala Waldron is Dean of Education and Director of the Centre for Human Rights and Citizenship Education at St Patrick's College, Drumcondra where she specialises in history education. A graduate of UCD, her doctoral research focused on the social and political role of the drinks trade in Dublin at the time of Parnell. Recent articles include 'Statesmen of the street corners: Labour and the Parnell split in Dublin, 1890–1892', *Studia Hibernica*, Vol. 34 (2007). Edited collections include *Perspectives on Equality* (2005); *Human Rights Education: Reflections on Theory and Practice* (2010); *Reimagining Initial Teacher Education* (2012).

Dr Margaret Ward is the director of the Women's Resource and Development Agency in Belfast and former director at the Democratic Dialogue think tank in Belfast and research fellow at the Bath Spa University. She is the author of several books including *Unmanageable Revolutionaries* (1983); *Hanna Sheehy Skeffington: A Life* (1997); *Maud Gonne: A Life* (1993); *In their own Voice: Women and Irish Nationalism* (1995), as well as many scholarly articles.

Introduction

Roy Foster in *Paddy & Mr Punch: Connections in Irish & English History* posed the question why Parnell has been the subject of so many different interpretations.[1] He attributes it to a number of factors including the nature of the documentary evidence, Parnell's reticence, his skilful manipulation of the creative potential of ambiguity and the changing contexts and needs of succeeding generations. Whatever the reason, Parnell continues to intrigue historians and those with an interest in Irish history and politics. This book reconsiders Parnell – his political philosophy, his *modus operandi* and his legacy – in the light of his own words, deeds and context. In doing so, it seeks to throw light on the meaning of Home Rule and the changing nature of the nationalist movement in Parnell's time and afterwards. These essays have a particular relevance and resonance given the plethora of centenary celebrations already organised or planned for the years 2012 to 2022 – Home Rule in 1912 and unionist resistance, the labour problems 1913, the suffragettes who followed in Anna Parnell's footsteps, the Easter Rising and the Somme. In the light of this decade of commemorations it is worth reconsidering to what extent Parnell contributed to the Ireland that came after him. To what extent did he try to prevent the emergence of a divided Ireland with two states – one pervasively Catholic and nationalist and the other Protestant and unionist and with its own form of Home Rule? The essays consist of a mixture of research papers and review essays delivered originally at the Parnell Spring Days held at Avondale in April 2010 and Hawarden in May 2011 to commemorate the 1886 Home Rule Bill; at the Parnell Summer School in August 2011 which commemorated the centenary of the death of Anna Parnell, and at other related Parnell Society events.

Parnell had a capacity to be all things to all men. In particular, he harnessed diverse forces in Irish life and forged them into a powerful national movement. But what did he stand for himself? What did Parnell understand by Home Rule? Was he really a separatist at heart, as Pearse suggested? Or did he, in his own words, accept Home Rule as a 'final settlement' in the troubled relationship between Ireland and Britain? How are we to interpret this pronouncement, and others, which seem to strike a different note – such as his famous Cork speech of January 1885, or his dramatic manifesto to the Irish people of 1890? Several of the essays in this collection address these questions.

Donal McCartney and George Boyce sift through the sometimes conflicting evidence. Boyce emphasises the futility of simplistic generalisations about Home Rule and independence. He suggests that while the extraordinary encounter between Gladstone and Parnell (and Gladstone's Herculean attempt to shape the destiny of Ireland) resulted merely in the 'Irish solution that never was' i.e. Home Rule, it reveals surprising aspects of nationalism and imperialism at this crossroads in history and that Gladstone's failure should not detract from his impact on British and Irish politics.

McCartney emphasises the limits of Parnell's goals in his own day, while acknowledging his longer term influence on those who succeeded him. He cites Parnell's *ne plus ultra* speech delivered originally in Cork in January 1885, and it is this speech that is the focus of Pauric Travers's essay which examines the context in which it was first delivered and the very different context in which the words were chosen for inscription on Saint-Gaudens' Parnell Monument. The Cork speech was a self-conscious response by Parnell to the criticism that Home Rule was a dangerously imprecise political goal and, in particular, the accusation that he never defined what he meant by Home Rule. In the circumstances, this speech, in which Parnell asserts both the sovereignty of the nation and the limits on the national demand at that time, represents the clearest statement of his political philosophy.

The press, its importance in Parnell's rise and fall and his impact on its development, are considered by Felix M. Larkin and Myles Dungan, particularly in relation to the *Freeman's Journal* and *United Ireland*. Both these newspapers in their different ways set the dominant narrative of Irish politics which was to be consolidated by later historians. Using the experience of Anna Parnell, Margaret Ward illustrates how the political role of women has often been downplayed or even expunged in the telling of national myth. In reconsidering the story of the Ladies' Land League and the fate of Anna Parnell, she argues that Anna and Fanny Parnell were exemplars of two distinct streams of female action – both of which ultimately fell foul of the dominant male tradition represented by their brother.

Ward's consideration of Anna Parnell throws her brother's conservatism on gender issues, his political ruthlessness and his pragmatism into sharp relief. His style and approach as a pragmatic politician and his adroitness in balancing conflicting interests is well illustrated by his handling of his party's relations with the drinks trade, a topic which is explored by Fionnuala Waldron. Dublin publicans were predominantly nationalist and looked towards the Irish Party to protect their interests. The party, however, was divided on the issue of restrictive legislation and Parnell himself showed some sympathy with the temperance cause. Moreover, Parnell knew that parliamentary support for the drink interest could damage his party's relationship with the Liberals, who were increasingly identified with temperance. Yet, if the publicans were to be kept on board, Parnell had to find a way of protecting their interests without alienating the temperance wing of the party or threatening the Liberal alliance. Waldron suggests that his success in balancing these competing claims is evidenced by the response of the Dublin publicans to the Parnell split and their tribute to him on his death as a friend to the trade. She concludes that the best indicator that Parnell had found a successful formula to marry party and trade interests was that it survived his death.

Parnell was the Protestant leader of a largely Catholic nationalist movement. However the assumption that he himself was uninterested in religion is challenged in Pauric Travers's essay on this subject which reassesses Parnell's attitude to religion and its impact on his life and career. The significance of Parnell's background is also highlighted in Pat Power's consideration of the family connections with Paris, a city described by Walter Benjamin as 'the capital of the nineteenth century'. Paris in the second half of the nineteenth century was a ferment of social excitement and political intrigue. Power considers the surprising importance of Paris in Parnell's personal and political life: the Parnell family had close connections with the city – the Parnell sisters were there on the eve of the Paris Commune and the Franco-Prussian War, and the city provides the setting for key events and critical moments in Parnell's life.

Power's essay emphasises the interplay of the personal and the political in the Parnell story: undoubtedly it is this which partly explains his enduring fascination. According to Michael Davitt, the O'Shea divorce scandal destroyed what had promised to be the most successful political career ever devoted to the cause of Ireland. Long after Parnell's death, other sex scandals were alleged against him, as if his affair with Mrs O'Shea had not been damaging enough. What were these scandals? How true are the allegations? What effect have they had on his reputation? These issues are explored by McCartney in his essay on Parnell and scandal.

Barry O'Brien, one of Parnell's earliest biographers, referred to the enigma of Charles Stewart Parnell. Paul Bew, his most recent biographer, returns to this theme in *Enigma: A New Life of Charles Stewart Parnell*.[2] In the intervening years, Irish historians and writers have struggled with the enigma, interpreting and re-interpreting Parnell from their own perspective and the perspective of their own time. These essays seek to throw new light on that enigma.

Notes

1 R. F. Foster, *Paddy & Mr Punch: Connections in Irish & English History* (London, 1993).

2 R. Barry O'Brien, *The Life of Charles Stewart Parnell* (London, 1898); Paul Bew, *Enigma: A New Life of Charles Stewart Parnell* (Dublin, 2011).

CHAPTER I

Parnell and the Meaning of Home Rule

Donal McCartney

The Act of Union was the most important single factor in shaping Ireland as a nation in the modern world.[1]

When Charles Stewart Parnell formally became a member of the Home Rule League in 1874 and spoke about repealing the Act of Union, many believed his ultimate aim was total separation from Britain, as when he reportedly said in a speech in Cincinnati in1880: 'None of us . . . will be satisfied until we have destroyed the last link which keeps Ireland bound to England.'[2]

Gladstone's first government (1868–74) proved to be the catalyst for the launching of the Home Rule movement. With his avowed mission to pacify Ireland, he disestablished the Church of Ireland; passed the first of his land acts in favour of the tenants; and attempted to solve the university education question to the satisfaction of the Irish Catholic bishops. These reforms, and attempted reforms, had gone too far for many Irish Protestant conservatives who wanted safeguards against the Liberal government and the increasing power of the Catholic and nationalist majority. On the other hand, old Repealers, tenant right advocates and ex-Fenians, perceiving a chink in British armour, were only encouraged to push for further concessions.

Exploiting these nationalist and conservative reactions, Isaac Butt initiated the Home Rule movement. The declared objectives made it quite clear what Butt meant, and did not mean, by Home Rule. He proposed a domestic parliament for Ireland's internal affairs, whilst the Imperial Parliament would control all questions affecting the Crown, the Empire, peace, war and all taxation for imperial purposes. He unequivocally said that he was not seeking separation from Britain. The intention was to perpetuate and consolidate the connection between the two countries. He repudiated the idea of Repeal of the Act of Union which sought the restoration of 'Grattan's Parliament', a parliament supposedly separate from, and equal to, that in London. What he called a 'federal solution', proposed a parliament subordinate to that of the United Kingdom.[3]

The Home Rule League he led was an amorphous and fragile combination. When Parnell became a member on 2 March 1874, he instinctively sided with its radical wing. For him, Home Rule was simply repeal in modern dress. An election address, written for his brother, John Howard, said as much. It read: 'the cause of repeal of the Union under its new name of Home Rule will always find in me a firm and honest supporter.'[4] According to Butt however, Repeal of the Union was precisely what Home Rule was not. But the principles which committed members of the Home Rule League to a limited parliamentary autonomy, were flexible enough to embrace also those who held with its first principle proclaiming 'the inalienable right of the Irish people to self-government'.[5] All members were committed to the amount of self-government specified in the Home Rule programme. For the conservative wing that was the maximum measure of independence sought. And for the radical wing, that merely meant the minimum acceptable.

This allowed people like Parnell the scope when speaking of 'self-government' – a favourite phrase of his – to convey a meaning much wider than any restricted federal relationship between Ireland and Britain. Addressing his constituents at Nobber, Co. Meath on 16 October 1875, Parnell said: 'Much has been said of the difference between Home Rule and Repeal. Well, I could never see the difference. It is a fact that to obtain Home Rule we must first repeal the Union. Nobody doubts that.' – conveniently ignoring the fact that Butt did. He continued:

> As for any difference between Repeal and Home Rule, I have been looking through a mental microscope but I can find none between them. If any difference exists it is merely one in name and no more.[6]

Parnell, the political pragmatist, had no time for the theoretical. This characteristic attitude of mind and ambiguity of speech would allow him to be all things to all shades of Irish nationalism. He was not decided on the details of any scheme of self-government – all options were open while he waited on events to unfold.

When Butt raised the question of Home Rule in parliament on 30 June 1876, the Chief Secretary, Sir Michael Hicks Beach, highlighting the signs of division in the Irish ranks, availed of the opportunity to round on Parnell specifically. He declared: '. . . last autumn the hon. Member for Meath (Mr Parnell) made a speech in which he said that Home Rule and Repeal meant the same thing.' Parnell intervened with: 'What I said was that Home Rule would necessarily entail Repeal of the Union.'[7] Noticeably, he did not deny the accuracy of the Chief Secretary's charge, only admitting to another statement he had also made at Nobber. Some ten years later in a speech at Plymouth in June 1886, Parnell would say: 'It is a favourite device with politicians when they are accused of one thing to say not that they did not do it, but that they did something else.'[8] He might well have given as an example his own reply to the Chief Secretary. Parnell had indeed said that Home Rule would entail repeal of the Union. But he had also stated that, in his opinion, Home Rule and Repeal were the same thing. And when Hicks Beach went on to say that the learned Member for Limerick, that is, Butt, 'repudiates any wish to repeal the Union', Butt endorsed the comment with 'Hear, hear!'[9]

It was in that same speech that Hicks Beach made a reference to the 'Manchester murderers'. Following cries of 'No! No!' from the Irish bench, the Chief Secretary responded: 'I regret to hear that there is any hon. Member in this house who will apologise for murder'. Parnell retorted: '. . . I wish to say as publicly and directly as I can that I do not believe, and never shall believe, that any murder was committed at Manchester.'[10] Scarcely a year in parliament, Parnell had already become a marked man in the eyes of British politicians. Of more immediate significance, however, was the interest and support he had aroused among Fenians at home and in America.

A speech in Liverpool in November 1876 seemed to indicate that his understanding of what Home Rule meant was far more than Home Rule was intended to provide. 'There is,' he declared, 'no reason why Ireland under Home Rule will not be a nation in every sense and for every purpose that it is right that she should be a nation.'[11] Then, describing a militia review he had seen in New York, he added: 'while they would never wish to trespass upon the integrity of the English Empire,'[12] the English knew that Ireland was determined to be

> an armed nation, and they fear to see her so, for they remember how a section of the Irish people in 1782, with arms in their hands, wrung from England legislative independence. Without a full measure of Home Rule for Ireland no Irishman will ever rest content.[13]

The implication that Home Rule could lead to an 'armed nation' was clearly not what Butt had intended.

The famous 'new departure' message sent by John Devoy to Parnell on 25 October 1878 declared that the 'Nationalists here [in America] will support you' provided he accepted certain conditions. The first of these conditions was: 'Abandonment of federal demand [and] substitution [of] a general declaration in favour of self-government.'[14] This had always been Parnell's policy, studiously avoiding endorsing federalism as the solution. And instead of talking about Repeal or Home Rule, his demand was henceforth packaged in more general phrases – self-government, legislative independence, the restoration of Grattan's Parliament, and Ireland's place among the nations of the world.

However, with his detailed scheme of federal Home Rule, Butt had revealed his hand too soon. Twice – in 1874 and 1876 – he had brought a Home Rule motion before Parliament, and twice it had been over-whelmingly defeated. It was a time when Imperialism had taken hold of the English imagination; and Britain was in no mood to allow Ireland to opt out of the Union for fear of striking at the very heart of the Empire and weakening its defences.

Given the overwhelming opposition from both Conservatives and Liberals to any idea of Home Rule, Parnell saw no point in bringing it once more before parliament. Reasoned argument alone would not suffice. He decided he must wait until he had the numbers to force the issue. Until then he would concentrate on the more immediate, pressing problems – the worsen-ing agrarian crisis of the late 1870s and the coercion that accompanied it. He was elected president of the revolutionary Irish National Land League at its founding meeting on the 21 October 1879, and advocated the destruction of landlordism, which he continued to describe as the chief prop of the Union. With its much more effective organisation, the Land League replaced the decrepit Home Rule League.

Some of Parnell's most inflammatory remarks were made during the period of the agrarian agitation. In the words of his colleague, William O'Brien, Parnell seemed caught in 'the contagious heat of the revolution surging round him'.[15] Such fiery speeches had prompted Gladstone to declare that the Land Leaguers 'were marching through rapine to the dismember-ment of the Empire',[16] and led, eventually, to the jailing of Parnell and the proclaiming of the Land League as 'unlawful and criminal'.[17] Throughout, however, Parnell never lost sight of his ultimate goal – an Irish Parliament. 'Victory,' he proclaimed in Roscommon on 17 November 1879, a month after the founding of the Land League,

> is even now dawning in the West . . . Before long you will be . . . possessors of Ireland . . . entitled to make laws for your country, entitled to own the land on which you live, and having the proud privilege of asserting the great Irish nation in her future years of honour and glory amongst the nations of the earth.[18]

And in Galway on 24 October 1880, he announced: 'I would not have taken off my coat and gone to this work [the land agitation], if I had not known that we were laying the foundations by this movement for the recovery of our legislative independence.'[19] But 'legislative independence' – another favourite phrase of his – was a principle, not a fully worked out scheme. It was an aspiration, not an elaborate constitutional proposal. The formula was vague, and the net wide enough to enable separatists, agrarian agitators, moderate nationalists, and eventually even bishops, to come together under Parnell's leadership.

After the Irish National Land League was suppressed by the government, Parnell established the Irish National League in 1882. The disappearance of the single word 'Land' from the title of the new movement was more than just O'Connellite sleight of hand to avoid legal proceedings. It indicated a highly significant change of direction and emphasis. The objective of the Land League had been the destruction of landlordism (with its evil consequences) and the establishment of a peasant proprietorship. Self-government did not figure in its declared objectives. Indeed, one of its resolutions stated that none of the League's funds were to be used to further the interests of any candidate for election to parliament. In contrast, the objective of the Irish National League was: 'the restitution to the Irish people of the right to manage their own affairs in a parliament elected by the people of Ireland.'[20] Just as the Land League had earlier displaced the Home Rule League with its change of focus, so now did the National League replace the Land League – and so marked the transition back to parliamentary constitutionalism and away from quasi-revolutionary agrarianism. However, Parnell's National League was led by his former land agitators, giving it a radical language and complexion. This development in Irish politics frightened English politicians. Speaking in Dublin on 24 August 1885 at the outset of the election campaign he said:

> It is not now a question of self-government for Ireland; it is only a question as to how much of the self-government they will be able to cheat us out of . . . how far the day, that they consider the evil day, shall be deferred. [He went on to announce] a programme and a platform with only one plank, and that one plank National Independence.[21]

The 'National Independence' speech was denounced widely in the British press. Ominously, two leading members of Gladstone's front bench, Lord Hartington and Joseph Chamberlain, condemned it. Chamberlain said that such claims went far beyond anything previously 'known or understood by Home Rule . . . and if . . . conceded we might as well abandon all hope of maintaining a united kingdom.' He feared 'We should establish within thirty miles of our shores a new foreign country animated from the outset with unfriendly intentions towards ourselves.'[22]

The passing of the Representation of the People Act of 1884 increased the number of Irish voters from 226,000 to almost 738,000.[23] The general election which followed resulted in exactly what had been feared – a Parnellite party of 86 members, holding the balance between Conservatives and Liberals and thus holding the British Parliament to ransom. As Gladstone later acknowledged, Parnell's 'ascendency over his party was extraordinary . . . The absolute obedience, the strict discipline, the military discipline . . . was unlike anything I had ever seen.'[24] With Conservatives and Liberals now bidding for his support, Parnell's strategy was to get the best deal he could in these changed circumstances. The announcement of Gladstone's conversion to Home Rule decided the matter.

In response to a request from Gladstone, Parnell sent him a draft of 'A Proposed Constitution for Ireland'. It was the first time he had had to spell out, in detail, what he understood by Home Rule. In this document he proposed an elected Irish Parliament of 300 MPs with responsibility for all domestic affairs including revenue, customs and excise, police and the judiciary. Special arrangements were to be made to ensure Protestant minority representation proportionate to their numbers. The Irish Parliament would have no power over any Imperial matter, or over the rights of the Crown. Parnell's proposals amounted to the restoration of a reformed 'Grattan's Parliament', but without the Irish House of Lords, and without the controls that had been imposed on that parliament by Dublin Castle.

The Government of Ireland Bill which Gladstone introduced to Parliament on 8 April 1886 offered less than Parnell had proposed. Gladstone said that none of the terms such as 'national independence', 'legislative independence', 'an independent Parliament', or even a 'federal arrangement' quite accurately described what his bill offered.[25]

This First Home Rule Bill was a disappointment to Parnell. It was not Repeal; not the restoration of Grattan's Parliament, which as Gladstone pointed out had been independent and co-ordinate with the Parliament in England. What this bill offered was a subordinate parliament, with certain functions devolved from Westminster for the purposes of purely domestic matters. It was devolution, with supremacy still residing in the Imperial Parliament. Clearly it was not what Parnell had sought throughout his political career. Yet he recognised that it had some advantages over Grattan's Parliament. Notably it removed the old Irish House of Lords; and, what was central to the difference between Home Rule and Grattan's Parliament, Irish Ministers – not Dublin Castle – would have responsibility for the administration of the country. He was prepared therefore to make the most of it. He lavished praise on Gladstone for his genius, talent, extraordinary ability and energy devoted to the cause of Ireland. Yet he also drew attention to great faults in the measure. He was willing to accept the compromise proposed regarding the customs, but with the reservation that it could be amended to meet Irish views fairly. He likewise argued that the proposed contribution by Ireland towards imperial expenditure was too high in relation to the country's poverty. He criticised the withholding from an Irish

Parliament of the direct control over the police and the appointment of judges. He saw how little confidence there was in Ireland in the police and judiciary, viewed as they were as a weapon, used by England, for the coercion of the people. Nor did he approve of the veto which Gladstone proposed to give to the 'first order' of the Irish Parliament for the security of the minority.[26] If, however, these concerns could be satisfactorily remedied in Committee, he would accept the bill as a final solution to the long-standing dispute between Ireland and England.[27] The irony was that this first Home Rule Bill was closer to Butt's scheme of a subordinate Irish Parliament than to Parnell's idea of the restoration of Grattan's Parliament. It was, however, an acceptable instalment. And Parnell was willing to give it a fair trial.

A pragmatist, Parnell had come to realise that Gladstone's bill conceded all that was possible in the circumstances given the passionate reaction in Britain to his modest proposal. *The Times* of London labelled it the 'Separation Bill'.[28] The bill was lost by thirty votes (341 to 311) when some 93 Liberals, under Chamberlain, voted with the Conservative opposition against it. But, as Parnell acknowledged, Gladstone 'had touched the hearts of the Irish nation.'[29]

Parnell's statement that he accepted the 1886 bill as a final solution was never to be put to the test. But had he forgotten what he himself had declared at Fintona, Co. Tyrone in September 1881?: 'Remember there is no finality in politics, and that the politician who tells you to stand is effete. The progress of the people is ever marching on.'[30] And surely he had not forgotten the most famous and oft-quoted of all his words, delivered at Cork on 21 January 1885?

> It is given to none of us to forecast the future . . . no man has a right to fix the boundary of the march of a nation. No man has a right to say 'Thus far shalt thou go, and no further;' and we have never attempted to fix the *ne plus ultra* to the progress of Ireland's nationhood, and we never shall . . . while we leave these things to time, circumstances, and the future, we must each one of us resolve in our own hearts that we shall at all times do everything that within us lies to obtain for Ireland the fullest measure of her rights . . . and while we struggle today for that which may seem possible . . . we shall not do anything that may hinder or prevent better men who may come after us from gaining better things than those for which we now contend.[31]

Two months later, at the St Patrick's Day banquet in London, and only one year prior to Gladstone's 1886 bill, he expressed the very same sentiments and in much the same language.[32] His whole pragmatic approach to politics and his *modus operandi* can be encapsulated in the words spoken on those three separate occasions. And if he had forgotten, or chosen to ignore, these earlier speeches, he was reminded by several unionist opponents of these and similar statements he had made. But he who once had famously said to Mrs O'Shea 'never explain, never apologise', was not about to waste his time extricating himself from his past speeches and tactics in any vain attempt to answer intransigent opponents of Home Rule. The furthest he would ever go would be to deny he ever said what his critics accused him of having said, or that he had been wrongly reported.

Was, then, the First Home Rule Bill really the final solution? Yes, but with some mental reservations, and only to the extent of what was then possible and available. However, after his encounter, with Cecil Rhodes, the imperial federalist, Parnell appeared to be coming round to a strong belief in the idea that Ireland might have a future to play within an imperial federation. But whereas O'Connell was denigrated for seeking no more than repeal through peaceful methods, and Redmond was to be for accepting the third Home Rule Bill in 1912, Parnell was made to appear in the canon of Irish nationalism as a separatist – which he had never claimed to be. Quoting from those speeches in Cork and at London's St Patrick's Day banquet, Pearse summoned 'the pale and angry ghost of Parnell to stand beside the ghosts of Tone and Davis and Lalor and Mitchel', and could claim that: 'His [Parnell's] instinct was a Separatist instinct'.[33]

Following the defeat of the 1886 Home Rule Bill, Parliament was dissolved. The subsequent general election was decisively lost by Gladstone. After the defeat, Parnell was Gladstone's honoured guest at Hawarden on two occasions, March 1887 and December 1889. They discussed what the next Home Rule Bill might contain whenever Gladstone returned to power, but without making any detailed commitments. Only five days after Parnell's second visit to Hawarden, Captain O'Shea filed for divorce. The resulting scandal poisoned the relationship between Parnell and Gladstone, as well as the whole political atmosphere of Home Rule. The stark choice for his Party, and his people, was: Parnell or Home Rule? Fighting for his political survival, Parnell may have seemed to have resorted to his more militant self; and once again the question was raised: Was his ultimate objective total separation from England? – as his many English critics, Irish Unionists, and later, Irish nationalists believed? Or was some connection with England and the Empire his preferred choice?

Michael Davitt was perhaps getting close to the answer when he said: 'Mr Parnell never went in thought or in act a revolutionary inch, as an Irish nationalist, further than Henry Grattan.'[34] John Devoy was even more perceptive. The Clan na Gael chief along with John O'Leary, head of the IRB, had arranged to meet with Parnell in Boulogne on 7–8 March 1879 to discuss the possibility of an alliance. Devoy later reported that Parnell was prepared 'to go more than halfway to meet us', but, he continued:

> He did not say definitely, and we did not ask him to say, whether he would prefer total separation, repeal of the union, or some form of legislative independence involving some connection with England, but the impression he left on me was very distinct, that he had not his mind made up as to which was the best, or the one most likely to be realised, but that he would go with the Irish people to the fullest limit in breaking up the existing form of connection with England.[35]

Devoy seems to have shrewdly assessed his man. It seemed to contemporaries, as well as to historians since, that Parnell always kept his cards close to his chest. But if he did, it was because his cards were blank, and had yet to have their value added. His final destination remained undetermined, and a mystery even to himself. But it was a journey he was ready to fight every inch of the way. One is reminded of a saying attributed to Cromwell to the effect that no man goes further than he who knows not whither he is going. So Home Rule, or as he preferred, self-government, remained undefined – until it became a realistic option in his dealings with Gladstone.

From the commencement of his political career, Parnell had used Home Rule as a battle-cry, and as a catch-all for the many Irish grievances. During his first attempt to win a parliamentary seat, Parnell said that Home Rule was 'a question embracing and embodying every other; for when they obtained it they would then have the power to make their own laws upon every matter.'[36] Parnell had also used Home Rule as a bargaining-counter: justice to Ireland or self-government. For as long as Irish self-government was without any hope of being granted by Westminster, Parnell increased the militancy of his remarks whenever he considered it beneficial to his cause.

Once, however, he did give an indication of his own preference. In a speech in Belfast on 15 October 1879 he said:

> Whether they were to have the restoration of the Irish Parliament of 1782, or whether they were to have a plan of federalism such as that which was formulated by the great Isaac Butt, or whether in the course of the year and in the march of events the Irish nation should achieve for itself a complete separation from England, was a matter which must be left to the course of events for solution.[37]

He himself, he said, believed England and Ireland should live together in amity connected only by the link of the Crown. 'That was Grattan's idea and his dream'.[38] Repeal of the Union did not, then, in Parnell's eyes, necessarily involve a total dissolution of the marriage between Ireland and England. But in the eyes of British and Irish Unionists it could only lead to a total separation. And, of course, Parnell was never heard to pledge his undying loyalty to the monarch in the manner of O'Connell to his 'darling little Queen'.

The attempt to discover what Parnell meant by Home Rule gives an insight into his characteristically ambiguous political style. It allows us, too, to form some impression of his formidable skills in balancing, consolidating and directing all shades of nationalist opinion. From an English and Unionist point of view, however, his public utterances were always open to the interpretation that whatever he meant was far more threatening than Butt's federalism. And while publicly he held the sword of Damocles over the heads of English politicians, in private negotiations he surprised Gladstone and Conservative Chief Secretary, Lord Carnarvon with his moderation and reasonableness.

Gladstone described him as one of the best men with whom he had ever done business; and reported after their first Hawarden meeting in 1887 Parnell's thinking that an Irish Parliament, 'even with insufficient powers . . . might be accepted.', with Gladstone adding: 'I understood him to mean might be accepted as a beginning.'[39] Carnarvon considered of great significance Parnell's acceptance of the principle of gradualism in any transfer of power from London to Dublin. Even that arch-critic of Gladstone's first Home Rule Bill, Joseph Chamberlain, recognised – though admittedly after Parnell's death – that he was 'a good man to make a bargain with'; and that 'He knew that you cannot always get your own way, and that you must sometimes take the best thing you can get at a given moment. There was nothing irreconcilable about him'.[40]

The Home Rule episode was not to have a happy ending for either Parnell or Gladstone. But like the plot in a ballet or grand opera, the story was of much less importance than the performances of the leading characters. And it was the dedication, the skills, and the achievements on the way that mattered most.

No one had done more than Parnell to bring Home Rule to the fore in Anglo-Irish relations and make it a distinct possibility. He had turned it into a glittering prize, seemingly within grasp. The temptation for the majority of his party and people could not be resisted; and that which in the end was no more than a glittering illusion brought about Parnell's downfall. He had made Home Rule seem not only possible but even inevitable; and Home Rule had turned upon its own master craftsman. Tragically, he was undone by his own creation. Revolutionary in language and tactics, he was essentially a constitutionalist who succeeded in bringing with him in his train the inheritors of the tradition of 1798, 1848 and 1867 whose idealism and suffering he had always admired, but whose methods he refused to follow.

His career was a link in the chain leading from Grattan through O'Connell, through Butt and finally to the establishment of a democratic Dáil Éireann. And it was this parliamentary emphasis and legacy that Parnell has ultimately given to the concept of Home Rule.

★★★

Parnell's attitude to Irish representation in the Imperial Parliament, in the event of the establishment of an Irish Parliament, is also revealing. Whether in the event of Home Rule Ireland should continue to be represented in the Imperial Parliament was an issue on which, initially at least, Parnell had an open mind – he could see advantages and disadvantages in both the exclusion and inclusion of Irish MPs in Westminster. If he were to follow strictly the model of Grattan's Parliament, exclusion would have to be his choice. His flexibility in this matter, however, surfaced in a secret meeting in London on 1 August 1885 with Lord Carnarvon. Carnarvon reported back to the new Conservative Prime Minister, Lord Salisbury, that in the event of a Home Rule settlement, Parnell would 'regret' any exclusion of Irish members from Westminster, but added 'suggestively' that surely it could be arranged to 'forbid' Irish MPs from speaking or voting on some subjects. As L. P. Curtis has put it: 'If, however, removal was "a necessary condition" of Irish self-government then he had no choice but to accept it.'[41]

The Liberals, too, were anxious to find out what Parnell might insist upon and where he might be prepared to compromise. Gladstone asked his friend J. T. Knowles, editor of the liberal *Nineteenth Century*, to approach R. Barry O'Brien, to write some articles on Home Rule which would tell its readers, not O'Brien's own views, but what Parnell was prepared to accept as a solution: 'We want to get Mr Parnell's mind on paper'. At a subsequent meeting on 5 November 1885 between Knowles and O'Brien, O'Brien outlined the points on which he thought Parnell would insist and those on which he would be prepared to give ground. On the issue of whether the Irish members should remain in the Imperial Parliament or be excluded from it, O'Brien said that Parnell would not insist on their remaining. He added that 'The Catholic Church would certainly be in favour of their retention in order that Catholic interests might be represented, but the bulk of the Irish Nationalists would not really care one way or the other.'[42] O'Brien wrote an article on this basis and sent it off about 20 November. It did not appear until the January issue of the *Nineteenth Century*, entitled 'A Federal Union with Ireland'.

Parnell's open-mindedness on the subject was confirmed in his 'A Proposed Constitution for Ireland', submitted to Gladstone through Mrs O'Shea, at the Liberal leader's own request, on 30 October 1885. In this he stated: 'The representation of Ireland in the Imperial Parliament might be retained or might be given up. If it be retained the Speaker might have the power of deciding what questions the Irish members might take part in as imperial questions, if this limitation were thought desirable.'[43]

This presentation of Parnell's attitude left the way clear for Gladstone to propose that which he thought least likely to provoke opposition from his own supporters. Both he and the Irish leader were fully aware that Parnell's Party had made itself an irritating nuisance, and become intensely disliked, because of the obstruction tactics practised and the interference by Irish members in what was considered purely British legislation. With the increase in the number of Irish Nationalists in parliament it was feared that in the future they would be in a position to make and unmake governments of the United Kingdom.

Introducing his Home Rule Bill in 1886, Gladstone referred to the problem that his proposal of excluding Irish members from a Westminster Parliament that was to control Irish customs and excise would be a breach of the age-old principle of 'no taxation without representation'. It was hardly forgotten that this principle had played a major role in the loss of America (the Boston lawyer, John Otis, had declared, when objecting to the taxes imposed on the colonists by an English government: 'Taxation without representation is tyranny.'). But Gladstone argued that 'to give up the fiscal unity of the Empire would be a great public inconvenience, and a very great public misfortune . . . for Great Britain; and I believe it would be a still greater misfortune for Ireland'. Therefore he felt obliged, he said, not to propose anything that would endanger the understanding of his measure 'by the people of England and Scotland, which might be the case were the fiscal unity of the Empire to be broken.'[44]

Parnell drew attention to defects in these fiscal arrangements which he hoped could be remedied at the Committee stage of the bill, but he raised no objection to the clause excluding Irish representation from Westminster. Like Gladstone, the advantage he saw in this was that it was likely to have the support of those Liberals who thought that Westminster would be well rid of the troublesome Irish. He also recognised that retention of the Irish members in the Imperial Parliament could provide that parliament with the pretext to interfere in Irish affairs.

The exclusion clause, however, received such adverse criticism from those opposed to the bill that R. Barry O'Brien wrote: '. . . this question of the exclusion or retention of the Irish members became the crux of the whole scheme.'[45] And a more recent historian has written: 'What attracted the sharpest criticism was the provision barring the Irish representatives from Westminster.'[46] While objections to the 1886 bill were many, varied, and strongly-expressed, it is certainly true that Joseph Chamberlain, who played a crucial role in its defeat, placed a great deal of weight on this aspect of the debate.

Chamberlain's opposition to the bill was based on his belief that if the Irish MPs were retained at Westminster, then some form of his own local government scheme could be devolved to Ireland; but if the Irish MPs were excluded and given their own parliament in Dublin it would be tantamount to independence and the end of the Union. He therefore insisted that it was a cardinal principle of the British constitution that taxation and representation should go together. But his opposition was not to one clause alone, but to the bill as a whole, because, he said, it was 'one for separation, and not for Home Rule.'[47]

The emphasis Chamberlain gave to the argument that the exclusion clause violated the 'no taxation without representation' principle was employed specifically to defeat the bill. He admitted as much in an interview he gave to R. Barry O'Brien some twelve years later in 1898, saying openly, and more than once 'I wanted to kill the Bill'. Adding: 'I attacked the question of the exclusion of the Irish members. I used that point to show the absurdity of the whole scheme.' As O'Brien put it, it was a strategy 'to turn Mr Gladstone's flank.'[48]

During the debate Gladstone announced that he was willing to appease those who opposed his bill on the 'no taxation without representation' principle, by offering to revisit the exclusion clause. He suggested that it could be 'reconstructed' to admit Irish members whenever Irish customs and excise were to be discussed. His offer, however, was to no avail, for the whole bill was defeated on the second reading.

Following the debate on the 1886 bill most of Gladstone's leading colleagues had come round, like their leader, to the idea that under any future Home Rule arrangement Irish MPs would have to be retained in the Westminster Parliament. The question between them was whether all 103 Irish members should remain, as Sir William Harcourt argued, in order to ensure a Liberal majority, or whether their number should be reduced and restricted to imperial matters – including customs and excise – which is what Gladstone advocated.

Parnell, too, was now fully aware that an Irish presence in the Imperial Parliament was necessary to allay Liberal, as well as Tory, fears of 'separation'. And if the 1886 bill were any precedent, Parnell also realised that control by an Irish Parliament over the police and judiciary, and the settlement of the land question, were also likely to be missing from any new Home Rule Bill. To ensure that these matters be dealt with to Ireland's satisfaction, Parnell was going to need the full complement and strength of the Irish Nationalist MPs in Westminster. His anxiety over these matters was later expressed in his manifesto 'To the People of Ireland' of 1890.[49]

In the brief report of the discussion between Gladstone and Parnell during the latter's first visit to Hawarden on 10 March 1887, there is no direct evidence that the question of continued Irish representation in Westminster was aired. But it seems to have been implied or assumed by both leaders that the Irish would continue to have some representation in that parliament. So the following month when Parnell met with Cecil Rhodes, the wealthy South African advocate of 'imperial federation', he was quite ready to accept a donation of £10,000 on the understanding that he and his party would press for the retention of the Irish MPs at Westminster.[50] Already sold on this issue, he did not have to be 'bought'. Nor did he make any secret of the fact in his negotiations with Rhodes that he expected Gladstone's next Home Rule Bill would contain a retention clause. In a letter to Rhodes he wrote:

> I may say at once, and frankly, that you have correctly judged the exclusion of the Irish members from Westminster to have been a defect in the Home Rule measure of 1886, and, further, that this proposed exclusion may have given some colour to the accusation so freely made against the Bill that it had a separatist tendency.

He continued that it was his belief that the Irish people had accepted the measure 'with the same spirit with which it was offered . . . [with] a desire to let bygones be bygones, and a determination to accept it as a final and satisfactory settlement of the long-standing dispute between Great Britain and Ireland.' Furthermore:

> . . . my own feeling . . . is that if Mr Gladstone includes in his next Home Rule measure the provisions of such retention we should cheerfully concur with him, and accept them with goodwill and good faith, with the intention of taking our share in the Imperial partnership . . . I am convinced that it would be the highest statesmanship on Mr Gladstone's part to devise a feasible plan for the continued presence of the Irish members here, and from my observation of public events and opinions since 1885 I am sure that Mr Gladstone is fully alive to the importance of the matter, and that there can be no doubt that the next measure of autonomy for Ireland will contain the provisions which you rightly deem of such moment.[51]

Parnell's letter was tantamount to saying that even if Rhodes were to withhold his donation, the Irish Party would be supporting the retention of Irish representation in Westminster.

When Parnell and Gladstone had their second meeting at Hawarden just before Christmas 1889, they recognised, according to Gladstone's account, that there would be difficulty in defining the form the Irish representation in Westminster would take. They discussed the various options and Gladstone reported that Parnell had no absolute or foregone conclusion on the matter and they agreed to leave it until they had to face the practical particulars in the new Home Rule Bill. In the controversy which followed the O'Shea divorce case and the dispute over the issue of Parnell's leadership of his Party, Parnell asserted in his manifesto 'To the People of Ireland' that Gladstone had proposed to reduce Irish representation in the Commons from 103 to 32 in the next Home Rule Bill. In support of this contention he quoted from a letter he had written to Rhodes on 3 March 1890, nine months before the controversy with Gladstone, informing Rhodes of the proposed reduction.[52] That Parnell, in his discussions with Rhodes in 1888, opposed any reduction in the number of Irish MPs was confirmed by Rhodes in his interview with R. Barry O'Brien when the latter was preparing his biography of Parnell.[53] Parnell's argument had always been that they must not abandon their full strength in Westminster while matters critical to Ireland's welfare were withheld from any Home Rule settlement. (The original bill of 1886 had proposed the exclusion of all 103 Irish MPs from Westminster; Gladstone's second bill of 1893 would limit their number to 80; while the 1914 Government of Ireland Act stated that the number to be returned by Irish constituencies to serve in the parliament of the United Kingdom would be 42.)

Given the strong opposition there had been to the exclusion clause in the 1886 bill, and given Gladstone's indication during the debate that he was willing to reconsider that clause, Parnell was only too pleased not to have to accept a bill that excluded the Irish from the Imperial Parliament while vital matters remained unresolved. He was now more than ever convinced that Ireland's interests could be best safeguarded by the presence of a full cohort of Irish representatives in a British Parliament where the autonomy he looked for under Home Rule was unlikely to be conceded without pressure from a strong Irish contingent. As he had emphasised in that famous speech in Wexford on 9 October 1881 which had led to his arrest and imprisonment: 'And the Irishman who thinks he can now throw away his arms, just as Grattan disbanded the Volunteers in 1782, will find to his sorrow and destruction when too late that he has placed himself in the power of a perfidious and cruel and unrelenting English enemy.'[54]

Given Parnell's views on the need to maintain strong Irish representation at Westminster until Ireland's demands had been fairly met, the contention made at the 2010 Parnell Summer School that Parnell 'had taken a bribe of £10,000' to amend the Home Rule Bill and that his acceptance of the donation by Rhodes was 'a possible one hundred year-old scandal'[55] seems very wide of the mark. Parnell did not change his mind about Irish representation at Westminster because of the money from Rhodes. He had already decided on this policy. Besides, the so-called 'bribe' had been publicly discussed in the correspondence between the two men in the *Times*. Since 1880, Parnell and his principal colleagues had never made any secret of their canvassing in America, Australia, New Zealand and elsewhere for much needed Party and Land League funds. And there is evidence that at least £5,000 of the money from Rhodes was spent on the costly Plan of Campaign championed by John Dillon and William O'Brien.[56]

Rhodes also secretly contributed £5,000 to the Liberals in February 1891, on the condition that if the next Home Rule Bill did not allow for Irish MPs to sit in Westminster, the money would be returned. No such condition had been attached to the Irish donation. It has been pointed out that Parnell got the better of the negotiations with Rhodes since he never agreed to reject a bill which did not include Irish representation at Westminster. And it has been argued by the South African historian, Donal McCracken, that 'The accusation that Rhodes bought the votes of the Irish party cannot be substantiated.'[57]

Prior to his relations with Rhodes, there is little evidence that the Irish leader had given any thought to his idea of imperial federation. While it would be too much to say that Parnell had been converted to this idea, he now intimated that he had not ruled it out absolutely and might be prepared to consider it if its development could be shown to be of benefit to Ireland. His letter to Rhodes of 23 June 1888, (previously quoted above) showed a cautious response to the idea. He wrote:

> It does not come so much within my province to express a full opinion upon the larger question of Imperial Federation, but I agree with you that the continued Irish representation at Westminster immensely facilitates such a step, while the contrary provision in the Bill of 1886 would have been a bar. Undoubtedly this is a matter which should be dealt with in accordance largely with the opinion of the colonies themselves, and if they should desire to share in the cost of imperial matters, as undoubtedly they now do in the responsibility, and should express a wish for representation at Westminster, I certainly think it should be accorded to them, and that public opinion in these islands would unanimously concur in the necessary constitutional modifications.[58]

Here was Parnell with characteristic ambivalence keeping Rhodes on board while at the same time showing himself to be fully alive to the practical and political difficulties that imperial federation was likely to encounter. On the issue of imperial federation, as on his chief concern – the degree and form of Ireland's independence – he was prepared to wait upon events before coming to grips with the constitutional details. Parnell's nationalism is also evident in his letter to Rhodes: he considered his country a distinct entity, a separate nationality, and not just another colony of Britain. Like others later in the Irish Party, especially the Redmonds and John Dillon, he might well have come to see advantages for Ireland in imperial federation as an incipient idea leading on to the British Commonwealth of Nations. But this is pure speculation. The three Home Rule Bills of 1886, 1893 and 1912 proposed to confer on Ireland considerably less autonomy than that attained by the independent colonies of Canada, Australia, New Zealand or South Africa (the future Commonwealth countries). Before 1921 Ireland had never been offered a status of autonomy equal to that of these independent colonies.

There is no way of telling how Parnell's non-violent political methods might have directed 'the progress of Ireland's nationhood'. All that we can be certain of is that he had said that 'no man has a right to fix the boundary of the march of a nation'. But that march presumably could go in any one of several different directions depending on unfolding circumstances. In trying to foresee what these circumstances might be from the vantage point of 1891, one would necessarily have to take into account such matters as the spirit of nationalism which Parnell had encouraged and to which he had contributed. We would also have to remember the divorce scandal and subsequent split in the Party which had destroyed his career and his influence over a people who had once idolised him, and a clergy that had once been happy to give him their cooperation. But the future belonged to a time after Ireland, and indeed the United Kingdom, underwent a massive change in its cultural and political outlook between Parnell's death in 1891 and the signing of the Anglo-Irish Treaty in 1921.

Notes

1 Oliver MacDonagh, *Ireland: the Union and its Aftermath* (London, 1977), preface.

2 F. S. L. Lyons, *Charles Stewart Parnell* (London, 1978), p. 111.

3 For Butt and federalism see David Thornley, *Isaac Butt and Home Rule* (London, 1964); Lawrence J. McCaffrey, *Irish Federalism in the 1870s: A Study in Conservative Nationalism* (Philadelphia, 1962).

4 Lyons, *Parnell*, p. 44.

5 J. C. Beckett, *The Making of Modern Ireland 1603–1923* (London, 1966), p. 382; Thornley, *Isaac Butt*, p. 162.

6 Robert Kee, *The Laurel and the Ivy: The Story of Charles Stewart Parnell and Irish Nationalism* (London, 1993), pp 94–5, quoting *Freeman's Journal*.

7 *Hansard*, 3rd series, vol. 230, col. 803 (30 June 1876).

8 Jennie Wyse-Power, *Words of the Dead Chief* (Dublin, 2009 edn), p. 114.

9 *Hansard*, 3rd series, vol. 230, col. 803 (30 June 1876).

10 Ibid., col. 808.

11 Kee, *Laurel and the Ivy*, pp 126–7.

12 Kee's newspaper source (not given, but possibly the *United Irishman* of Liverpool, 18 Nov. 1876) has Parnell declaring: 'without wishing to do harm to the integrity of the English Empire'.

13 *Nation,* 25 Nov. 1876; Lyons, *Parnell,* p. 57.

14 T. W. Moody, *Davitt and the Irish Revolution 1846–82* (Oxford, 1981), p. 250; Lyons, *Parnell,* p. 80.

15 Quoted in Lyons, *Parnell,* p. 166.

16 This is a Gladstone speech being quoted in the House of Commons by Plunket (the Dublin University MP) in the debate on the Home Rule Bill, *Hansard,* 3rd series, vol. 304, col. 1135 (8 Apr. 1886).

17 Moody, *Davitt and the Irish Revolution,* p. 497.

18 Kee, *Laurel and the Ivy,* p. 210.

19 Lyons, *Parnell,* p. 138.

20 Ibid., p. 236.

21 Wyse-Power, *Words,* pp 105–6.

22 R. Barry O'Brien, *The Life of Charles Stewart Parnell* (London, 1910 edn), p. 364.

23 K. Theodore Hoppen, *Elections, Politics, and Society in Ireland 1832–1886* (Oxford, 1984), pp 87–8. His exact figures are 225, 999 to 737,965.

24 R. Barry O'Brien, *Life of Parnell,* p. 556.

25 *Hansard,* 3rd series, vol. 304, cols 1036–1085 (8 Apr. 1886).

26 The 'first order' or upper house was partly elective and partly based on a property qualification, the second order was to be a wholly elective body.

27 For Parnell's reaction to the Bill see *Hansard,* 3rd series, vol. 304, cols 1124–1134 (8 Apr. 1886) and vol. 306, cols 1168–1184 (7 June 1886).

28 *The Times,* 8 June 1886.

29 Wyse-Power, *Words,* p. 116.

30 Ibid., pp 62–3.

31 Ibid., pp 101–2.

32 Ibid., p. 103.

33 Desmond Ryan (ed.), *Collected works of Padraic H. Pearse: Political Writings* (Dublin, 1924), pp 241–5.

34 Michael Davitt, *Fall of Feudalism in Ireland* (London, 1904), p. 115.

35 Quoted in Lyons, *Parnell,* p. 82.

36 Kee, *Laurel and the Ivy,* p. 60.

37 Lyons, *Parnell,* p. 103.

38 Ibid.

39 Quoted in Lyons, *Parnell,* p. 441.

40 R. Barry O'Brien, *Life of Parnell,* pp 386–7.

41 Sir A. Hardinge, *Life of Carnarvon* (London, 1925), vol. III, pp 178–81; L. P. Curtis Jr., *Coercion and Conciliation in Ireland 1880–1892: a Study in Conservative Unionism* (1963), pp 51–2.

42 R. Barry O'Brien, *Life of Parnell,* pp 364–5, 374–5.

43 Katharine O'Shea, *Charles Stewart Parnell: His Love Story and Political Life* (1914), vol. II, pp 18–20.

44 *Hansard,* 3rd series, vol. 304, cols 1057–8 (8 Apr. 1886).

45 R. Barry O'Brien, *Life of Parnell,* p. 379.

46 L. P. Curtis, *Coercion and Conciliation*, p. 103.

47 *Hansard*, 3rd series, vol. 304, cols 1181–1207 (9 Apr. 1886).

48 R. Barry O'Brien, *Life of Parnell*, p. 393.

49 See Chapter 11, 'Parnell's Manifesto '"To the People of Ireland", 29 November 1890: Context, Content and Consequences'.

50 See *The Times*, 9 July 1888 for their exchange of letters. Apart from imperial federation, Rhodes also saw the opportunity to win favour with the Irish Party and prevent it from opposing in Parliament the revival of his Royal Charter.

51 R. Barry O'Brien, *Life of Parnell*, pp 428–30; O'Shea, *Parnell*, vol. II, pp 154–6. Parnell's letter was dated 23 June 1888.

52 *The Times*, 12 Jan. 1891.

53 R. Barry O'Brien, *Life of Parnell*, pp 426–8.

54 Wyse-Power, *Words*, p. 64.

55 *Irish Times*, 10 Aug. 2010, reporting the address of Dr Elaine Byrne; but see Dr Byrne's more restrained and circumspect view of the £10,000 donation in her article 'Irish Home Rule: stepping-stone to Imperial Federation' in *History Ireland*, xx, no. 1 (Jan./Feb. 2012), pp 25–7.

56 Lyons, *Parnell*, p. 587.

57 Donal McCracken, 'Parnell and the South African Connection', in Donal McCartney (ed.), *Parnell: the Politics of Power* (Dublin, 1991), pp 125–36.

58 R. Barry O'Brien, *Life of Parnell*, pp 429–30.

CHAPTER 2

The Odd Couple? Gladstone, Parnell and Home Rule

D. G. Boyce

William Ewart Gladstone and Charles Stewart Parnell were two of the most extraordinary political leaders of the nineteenth century. Their relationship developed during one of the most volatile periods in the relationship between Great Britain and Ireland, beginning with the 'Land War' of 1879–82, and ending with the fall of Parnell in 1891. Their personalities and careers could hardly have been more contrasting: Parnell rose to prominence and then power through his readiness to manipulate the conventions and rules of the House of Commons to draw attention to Irish Nationalist aspirations; Gladstone revered the traditions and procedures of the Commons. Parnell was willing, or at any rate felt compelled, to lend his name and position to land agitation that often descended into violence, and provoked Gladstone, a Liberal Prime Minister, into resorting to coercive legislation to suppress disorder. Gladstone lived eighty-nine years, serving as Prime Minister four times; Parnell was in his forty-sixth year when he died, embroiled in private and political controversy, leaving behind him only his influential, but essentially hollow epitaph as 'the uncrowned king of Ireland'. Gladstone also had his disappointments. His gloomy prediction in 1890 was that 'Home Rule may be postponed for another period of five or six years. The struggle in that case must survive me, cannot be survived by me'[1] applied to both men. But the alliance that they forged in 1886 endured until the end of the First World War, and continues to have resonance in Ireland and throughout the United Kingdom to this day.

Interpretations of their place in Anglo-Irish relations have aroused controversies no less intense. Two of Gladstone's most influential biographers, John Morley and J. L. Hammond saw him as a noble statesman who might have found the elusive answer to the 'Irish Question'. Colin Matthew, one of his most recent and distinguished biographers, and editor of the Gladstone diaries, belongs to this tradition, though not of course uncritical of the great man's failures. In the 1970s two historians, John Vincent and A. B. Cooke, approached Gladstone's Irish experience from a very different and original angle. They applied their theories of 'High Politics' to reveal a very different Gladstone: an arch practitioner of cant whose Irish policies were derived, not from ethical choice, but on cunning and pragmatic political calculation.[2] There was no sign of Home Rule's long gestation, only a series of disconnected or barely connected choices, brought to a head in 1885–6 by the pressure of immediate political events. Richard Shannon's biography was more subtle: he did not doubt Gladstone's sincerity, based on deeply held religious belief in God's purpose in assisting him to power, but argued that Home Rule was not a workable response to Irish Nationalist demands and that Gladstone was guilty of a monumental miscalculation in thinking that it could be steered through the British Parliament, and that a devolved legislature was not likely to provide a settlement of the national question, whereas a concession of local government reform would have satisfied Parnell and provoked no political crisis. Irish interpretation was, unsurprisingly, more favourably disposed to Gladstone's Home Rule initiative, but was uncertain of where Parnell stood in the pantheon of Irish freedom seekers: was he a constitutionalist or a separatist? A man of violence who came to see the errors of his ways?[3] The validity of these interpretations and their implications for Parnell's relationship with Gladstone were tested in his last campaign between November 1890 and October 1891, when Parnell's rhetoric seemed to undermine what had been the cornerstone of his career and the key to his near success in 1886: the Liberal Alliance.

The period when this drama was played out was one of profound change in the context of British and Irish political and social life. The key question was how the political elite could form and lead public opinion in an increasingly democratic (and in Ireland demotic) age, and reconcile the people with the system of parliamentary government. The poet and writer, Matthew Arnold observed in 1861 that 'the time has arrived . . . when it is becoming impossible for the aristocracy of England to conduct and wield the English nation any longer'. But he came to agree with what de Tocqueville believed was true of France: that if rulers gave to the common people a 'self-respect, an enlargement of spirit, a consciousness of counting for something in their country's actions' this would raise them 'in the scale of humanity'.[4] Gladstone did not spring from the aristocracy, but he believed firmly in the need to mould and form public opinion, to educate and lead those who might be judged fit to partake of the constitution. As Colin Matthew observed, it was one of Gladstone's self-appointed tasks to integrate the great social forces of his time, from landowners to trade unionists.[5] His search for a constitutionally fit electorate, however, was not confined to Great Britain, but in the

1880s was extended to Ireland, finding expression in his acceptance that his Government's franchise reform in 1885 would, in his estimate, increase the 'so called National Party of Ireland' from 'a little over forty to near eighty' seats, and his refusal to reduce the number of Irish seats in parliament, despite Irish over-representation.[6] Gladstone's reward for testing his belief in the Irish electorate and the nationalist party's capacity to exhibit responsible civic behaviour did not come right away, but within a year it was vindicated in Parnell's decision to forge British Liberals and the Irish Parliamentary Party into a 'Union of Hearts'.

The question of the moral basis for the governance of the United Kingdom had long interested Gladstone. He addressed it in his book *The State in its Relations with the Church*, first published in 1838. He located it, the moral basis, in the Anglican Church, whose doctrine must be upheld by the State; and this support must be guaranteed, not only for the Church of England, but also for the Anglican Church in Ireland. Gladstone acknowledged that the Irish Church represented only a minority of the people of Ireland; but believed that despite its association with 'a system of partial and abusive government' the Church of Ireland must remain an establishment. It was beneficial to the Roman Catholic majority, for the imperial legislature had taken 'a sounder view' of religious truth 'than the majority of the people of Ireland, in their destitute and uninstructed state'. Also there was what Gladstone called a 'political consideration': for a 'a common bond of faith binds the Irish Protestants to ourselves, while they upon the other hand, are fast linked to Ireland; and thus they supply the most natural bond of connection between the countries'; thus inhibiting any possible desires of the majority towards 'what is termed national independence'.[7] Gladstone's firm convictions of the 1840s called for some degree of explanation when in 1868, as Prime Minister of a Liberal government, he took up the cause of the disestablishment of the Church of Ireland. But he showed an awareness of the problems posed by a multi-national kingdom, and of the divided loyalties that such a political arrangement could produce. His solution was that of the vast majority of his fellow Englishmen, including that of his great mentor, Sir Robert Peel – the preservation of the Union. In 1854 he wrote to an Italian nobleman, the Marquis of Dragonetti, concerning one of the great issues in international relations of the time: the Italian question. Italian patriots were drawing the attention of the European powers to their plight, which was one not only of local tyranny, but of national freedom. Gladstone admitted that Naples was the worst example of government in Europe, a system that was 'as bad as anarchy'. Rome 'unites the evils of the worst government and the most entire anarchy', so bad that any change might be for the better. But he feared what he called the 'wild opinions of some of your political sectaries', by which he meant Italian nationalist revolutionaries, whose notions made him appreciate the virtues of the existing system.[8]

Gladstone explained that the English, for their part, were not shocked by the 'notion of people belonging to one race and language, yet politically incorporated or associated with another' But this was at least a recognition that there were different 'races and languages' in the Kingdom, that the British people were not homogeneous. Supposing that this Union might be strengthened, not weakened, by some political act with a sound moral basis? This consideration underpinned his decision in 1868 to redress the anomaly that he had so strongly defended in the 1840s: the place of the Church of Ireland as a minority institution in an overwhelmingly Roman Catholic country. On 10 February he outlined to the Fishmongers' Company the measures to be matured in the coming parliamentary session. 'What', he demanded,

> could be an object dearer to the understanding of the heart of man than to endeavour to bring about, through the whole of this vast community, that union of feeling and interest which, even in the degree in which we have hitherto possessed it, has been the source of our strength and glory, but which still presents to view, here and there, some points in which it is unhappily defective, and which we wish to bring up to that condition in which every man will almost forget whether he is a Scotchman, Englishman, or Irishman, in the sense and consciousness of his belonging to a common country.[9]

And in the House of Commons on 1 March he described disestablishment as 'a great measure'. The Irish Church establishment had been 'a great source of unhappiness in Ireland, and of discredit and scandal to England'. 'For my part', he continued,

> I am deeply convinced that when the final consummation shall arrive, and when the words are spoken that shall give force of law to the work embodied in this measure – the work of peace and justice – those words will be echoed upon every shore where the name of Ireland or the name of Great Britain has been heard, and the answer to them will come back in the approving verdict of civilised mankind.[10]

It has to be stressed that 'peace and justice' dovetailed neatly with Gladstone's leadership of his party and his desire to create a unifying and politically advantageous political measure. But in 1870, the year in which the Home Government Association was founded by Isaac Butt, and five years before Charles Stewart Parnell won a by-election in Co. Meath, Gladstone turned once more to his theme of justice for Ireland. In the debate on his Land Act he claimed that for a hundred years

Ireland has been engaged in almost continuous conflict with the governing power –
I will not say of the nation, but with the governing power of this island. She has
been engaged in the conflict with all the disadvantages of a limited population, of
inferior resources, of backward political development, and yet she has been uni-
formly successful . . . The career of Ireland has ever been onward, her cry as ever
been Excelsior! Because she has had justice for her cause and has been sustained
in it by that which is the highest earthly organ of justice, the favouring opinion of
the civilised and Christian world . . .[11]

In 1877 Gladstone ruminated on the way in which minor nationalities might –
or might not – be safely absorbed in a wider imperial context: such as Saxons
and Normans in England.[12] In the autumn of the same year he visited Ireland,
receiving the freedom of the city of Dublin. On 7 November he confessed
that he felt he was 'treading on eggs the whole time' and that he 'could not
be 'too thankful for having got through today as I hope without trick &
without offence'.[13] No offence was taken and it is doubtful if any trick was
needed, for his prestige still stood high in Roman Catholic Ireland after his
disestablishment of the Church of Ireland. Gladstone was aware of the rising
Home Rule movement; the general election of January–February 1874 had,
after all, returned 60 Home Rulers to the Commons.[14] In a House dominated by Conservatives (they captured 350 of the 653 seats) they made little
impact, but the adoption of what Parnell called 'a policy of inconvenience to
'English interests',[15] blocking the normal procedures of the House of
Commons earned him his leader, Isaac Butt's, disapproval, but gained him
useful publicity.

Gladstone was a firm believer in the traditions and power of parliament;
Parnell seemed bent on frustrating both. Gladstone later recalled that his
'real knowledge' of Parnell began with the 1880 parliament.[16] At the time he
seems to have formed an unfavourable opinion of the new man, criticising
the 'crass infatuation of the Parnell members' (who numbered 35 as against
30 who still supported the nominal leader of the Home Rule Party, William
Shaw) who opposed his procedural reforms which were intended to expedite
House of Commons' business. Parnell did not wish to be identified too
closely with obstructionism, preferring to call it 'a policy of independent and
strenuous opposition to the government of the day all along the line in detail
upon every question'.[17] In August 1877 he had written to *The Times* empha-
sising his contribution to debates in the Commons, especially on South
African and prison bills. On 28 May 1877 he set out his constitutional values,
complaining about the government of Ireland by unrepresentative boards,
and arguing that the only remedy would be placing local affairs in the hands
of people who had the confidence of the governed: only through 'local self-
government' would these mistakes be corrected.[18]

Gladstone for his part was not afraid to speak the name of local self-government in Ireland. In his visit to Dublin in 1877 he outlined possible modification in the governance of the United Kingdom, declaring that 'local government, not only in the shape of municipal institutions, but in all those other shapes in which it is known to history, is a thing . . . not to be viewed with misgiving'. Parliament was failing in its duties; government was over-centralised. The three kingdoms, Ireland, Scotland and England, 'should be one nation in the face of the world', but people should be trained in their public duties locally so that they could all the more efficiently carry them out nationally. This was an extension of political liberty.[19] On 9 February 1882, in response to an Irish MP, he remarked 'that he did not think exception need be taken to calls for "an Irish Legislative Body to deal with Irish affairs"', provided the integrity of the Empire was maintained and imperial questions continued to be dealt with in the Imperial Parliament.[20]

Relations between Gladstone and Irish nationalism – or as he preferred to call it 'Irish nationality' – were, then, conducted at a slow and cautious pace, with both men talking about reform of Irish government in rational terms – though Parnell was inclined to use more vigorous and emotional language about the 'march of a nation' when he spoke to his supporters in Ireland. Both men were thrown together, not by the similarity of their views on local self-government, but, paradoxically, by the most turbulent and dangerous agrarian crisis of the age, one that threatened to drive rural Ireland into revolution: the 'Land War' of 1879–82.

From the beginning of his political career Parnell defined the Home Rule movement's goal as one of gaining Ireland as much self-government as possible within the British political system. But when several poor harvests threatened severe distress in the west of Ireland he was confronted with a popular agitation that he could hardly ignore. He declared himself in favour of peasant proprietorship because this would be the means of settling the land question 'on a permanent basis' thus removing 'the great reason that now exists to prevent the large and influential class of Irish landlords falling in with the demand for self-government.'[21] Here again Parnell was close to Gladstone's desire to restore a stable and proper relationship between the Irish Protestants and the Roman Catholic majority, which, after all, was one of the reasons Gladstone had given for disestablishing the Church of Ireland in 1869. Parnell was not invited to the demonstration in County Mayo on 20 April 1879 which launched the land agitation and which soon posed serious problems of law and order. But he felt compelled to lend it his support, not least because it gave him an opportunity to dislodge Isaac Butt's successor as leader of the Home Rulers, William Shaw, which he did on 17 May 1880. His progress to the leadership presented him with danger as well as opportunity. His acceptance of what was known as the 'New Departure' in

June 1879, an informal alliance between the advanced nationalists and the parliamentarians, pushed him to the forefront of the agitation. This placed Parnell, if not outside, then certainly on the margins of the normal procedures and conventions of the British political elite. Yet it was to that elite, or the Liberal part of it, that he looked. The Home Rule movement had swiftly replaced the Liberal Party as the prime representative of Irish Roman Catholics (and Presbyterians), and this left a residue of feeling that, as Parnell himself acknowledged in April 1880:

> Ireland has a far better chance with a large, really Liberal and Radical majority in the House of Commons then she would have if there was only a small Liberal majority . . . as they are strong they will be able to embark on a course of real reform in this country.[22]

As the land agitation deepened in 1880–1 it was clear that no government, Conservative or Liberal, could avoid methods of coercion. When Gladstone became Prime Minister on 23 April 1880 his Cabinet authorised the prosecution of Parnell and other Home Rule MPs. But, just as Parnell never relinquished his hold on parliamentary methods during the agitation, and tried neither to approve nor to condemn agrarian violence, so did Gladstone see the need to balance coercion with legislation to alleviate the tenants' plight. His Land Act (1881) offered resort to the Courts; and Parnell played his part in meeting Gladstone half way by urging tenants to 'test' the new legislation through the mediation of the Land League rather than follow their individual inclinations. This only demonstrated the uncertain relationship between Parnell and the League, for his advice was ignored.[23] Gladstone's patience was now wearing thin; on 21 September 1881 he declared that Parnell 'by his *acts* not motives' was 'an enemy of the Empire.'[24] Gladstone followed this up by arresting Parnell on 13 October and imprisoning him in Kilmainham Gaol. Yet there was still a chink of light in Gladstone's denunciation of Parnell: the distinction that Gladstone made between 'acts' and 'motives' is an important one, for it suggested that Gladstone did not see Parnell's behaviour in the land war as revealing the essence of the man. Nor did it: Parnell had no desire to become a martyr for the cause of the Land League nor, as he told an audience in Edinburgh in 1889, no longer had he any desire to come into contact with 'the butt-end of a policeman's musket.'[25]

This encouraged a new departure in relations between Parnell and Gladstone; or, rather, a resumption of the belief that the British Parliament has the imagination and the power to drive a new bargain between Ireland and England. Gladstone continued to muse on the consequence of the Irish landlords reasserting their influence over the peasantry: a union of property. He believed that 'a more intelligent & less impassioned body has gradually come to exist in Ireland. It is on this body, its precepts & examples that our hopes depend, for if we are at war with a nation we cannot win.'[26]

Parnell for his part had no inclination to engage in a protracted 'war' with the British Government. In 1882 signals were received from Parnell that if the Government offered to deal with tenants in arrears of rent, the Irish Party would support law and order. Lady Frederick Cavendish noted that Gladstone 'greatly rejoiced, saying it looked like a "surrender" on Parnell's part "all along the line" – release now to be justified'.[27] Gladstone praised the 'great sagacity' of Parnell and in Cabinet on 1 May described the 'moment' as 'golden'.[28] The Land League was broken; Parnell was far from sorry that this was so[29] and on 2 May he was released from jail with a tacit understanding that he would work for constitutional methods in Ireland in return for the Government proposing a bill to help tenants in arrears of rent. On 6 May this hopeful development was aborted by the murder of Lord Frederick Cavendish, the new Chief Secretary for Ireland, and his Under-Secretary Thomas Henry Burke. Colin Matthew observed that this murder 'stood out in brutal contrast to the open character of public life on the mainland, where politicians walked at will and unguarded through the streets without a thought for their security.'[30]; but on the contrary, the fact that Cavendish and Burke were walking unguarded in Phoenix Park was a sign that politicians in Ireland felt a similar security. And Parnell's instinctive and sincere denunciation of the crime, and his willingness to resign his seat should this prove helpful to Gladstone, demonstrated that there was plenty of life left in Gladstone's belief that the means of stabilising Irish public life were within his grasp. He pressed on with an Arrears Bill on 15 May. He was now reaching the conclusion that Parnell, who had gathered around himself some of the characteristics of 'Captain Moonlight' during the Land War, could – must – be singled out as the leader with whom Gladstone could do business.

What business could be done? Parnell might not have been Captain Moonlight, but he still had a past to live down, and direct contact between the two men was avoided, with Parnell's mistress, Katharine O'Shea, acting as a skilful go-between. On 20 June 1883 Gladstone took a further and vital step towards identifying Parnell as holding the key to an Irish settlement: 'though Parnell is a sphinx, the most probable reading of him is that he works for & with the law as far as he dare. I have even doubts whether he hates the Government.'[31] The credibility of the Home Rule Party as the only serious representative of the majority of the electorate was further enhanced by the Government's decision to press on with franchise reform which, Gladstone estimated in 1884 would cost the Liberals about 25 seats in Ireland 'with the Home Rulers returning nearly 80 MPs.'[32] He concluded – and it was symptomatic of his awareness of the diversity of the United Kingdom and the need to maintain a fair rule for all its parts – that to withhold franchises from Ireland while giving them to England and Scotland and to proclaim the principle of an unequal union, is the greatest blow that can be struck by any human power at the Act of Union.[33]

The British political tradition has usually been presented – with plenty of evidence in its favour – as one of gradualism and pragmatism. Even the great measure of franchise reform, the Reform Act of 1832, had followed decades of debate since the 1770s, one only extinguished by the emergencies of the French revolutionary and Napoleonic wars. A similar development might well be discerned in the attitude of the British Liberal and Conservative parties in 1885 to the reform of the Irish system of governance, which it was appreciated should be given wider public participation. For the Liberals, Joseph Chamberlain proposed a 'Central Board', whereby county councils would send representatives to a central board which would control various Irish government departments; this was rejected by the Cabinet in May 1885, with Gladstone now unambiguously identifying Parnell as the 'leader of the nation'.[34] The end of Gladstone's Government on 8 June passed the initiative to the Conservatives – should they want to pursue it. They did, though in very discreet style, with Lord Carnarvon meeting Parnell in Lady Chesterfield's empty house on 1 August (a sign that the Irish leader was still regarded with some caution by respectable politicians) and disclosing that a Conservative Cabinet would concede as much local government reform as the Liberals. Parnell indicated that his demands were modest, though he always assured his supporters in Ireland that local government reform was a prelude to, not a substitute, for a national parliament.[35]

How, then, is Gladstone's decision on Irish Home Rule to be assessed against the background of gradualism that seemed to be working yet again in British constitutional debate on Irish Government in 1885? Was it a sudden and massive change, or a not unnatural continuation of his musings of reform of the Irish system of government since his visit to Dublin in 1877? Gladstone, out of office, did not lose interest in the Irish issue, though his dalliance with the notion of retirement from politics perhaps diminished any sense of urgency – for the moment.[36] His son Herbert made a speech in favour of Home Rule in July 1885. Gladstone sketched out some proposals 'on Irish Contingency' shortly after his resignation, and predicted the impact of the 1884 franchise reform on the strength and leverage of the Irish Home Rule MPs, which would 'at once shift the centre of gravity in the relations between the two countries.'; it was necessary for the Liberals to have an 'adequate answer to this question.'[37]

In thinking about these grave matters Gladstone was always mindful of the wider context in which any reform of the Irish system of government must be set. He had never lost sight of his recognition that the United

Kingdom was a multi-national regime; he knew that there were consequences of the special characteristics of the Scottish and Welsh, as well as Irish people, one of them being the question of disestablishment – though he was not persuaded of the force of this argument in Wales, and he warned that any such change must await the formation of a viable legislative proposal in Scotland.[38] Here again there would be no unseemly haste. Irish Home Rule for Gladstone was also a matter of gradualism: various remedies had been tried to settle Ireland, and had failed. Parnell would soon stand before the British Parliament with a substantial following and the undoubted confidence and approval of the bulk of the Irish people. He was pleased with Parnell's response to his request for the Irish leader to give some details of a proposed Irish Constitution which he received on 30 October 1885, and which suggested an elective chamber responsible for Irish affairs but with no power to interfere in imperial matters. This offered flexibility on one of the most contentious issues raised by devolution: should Irish MPs be 'in or out', that is, allowed to speak and vote on all British and Imperial, as well as Irish issues, or be removed altogether from the House of Commons and thus allow the representatives of Great Britain to deal with the larger affairs.[39]

Gladstone declined to publish any possible Home Rule scheme until the result of the general election of November–December 1885 should be declared. The election effectively placed Parnell in the hands of Gladstone, and Gladstone in the hands of Parnell: the Liberals won 335 seats, the Conservatives 249; and the Home Rulers 86 – meaning Parnell could keep either of the British parties out, but only put in the Liberals.[40] On 17 December Herbert Gladstone declared that his father had reached the conclusion that Ireland must have Home Rule. This disclosure did not trouble Gladstone, for he was convinced of the moral rightness of such a proposal[41], and that it must be given legislative form once he took office as Prime Minister (with Irish Home Rulers' support) in January 1886.

Gladstone introduced his Home Rule Bill in the House of Commons on 8 April 1886. His proposals were that there should be two legislative 'orders' in Ireland, the first consisting of 28 peers and 75 others meeting high property qualifications (a minimum of £4,000 or an annual income of £200) elected by voters meeting a £25 qualification. The second order would consist of 204 members elected under the existing United Kingdom franchise. Both orders would normally sit as a single chamber, but either could demand a separate vote on any particular issue and exercise a veto. The first order could exercise its veto for a three year limit. The most contentious aspect of the bill was the exclusion of all Irish MPs from Westminster, which implied a degree of 'separation' likely to alarm Unionists, who feared that Home Rule was a step on the road to the disintegration of the United Kingdom. Parnell, regarded by Unionists as a separatist, was unhappy about this exclusion, but he acquiesced in it on the grounds that Ireland would need all the brains she had for her own parliament; at the same time he would have liked a provision for sending a delegation to Westminster on occasion, 'with reference to some definite Irish questions such as might be expected to arise.'[42]

Parnell's willingness to fall in with this proposal, and Gladstone's retention of customs and excise to Westminster and a continuing Irish contribution to the imperial exchequer might be expected to recall America's cry of 'no taxation without representation'. Parnell may have been half American in his genes but he was un-American when it came to the political economy of an Irish constitution. Gladstone believed that Parnell's character had gradually revealed itself; he had been following Parnell's steps 'in the right direction' for some time.[43] Parnell's pragmatism and political gifts were described by John Morley:

> He measured the ground with a slow and careful eye, and fixed tenaciously on the thing that was essential to the moment. Of constructive faculty he never showed a trace. He was a man of temperament, of will, of authority, of power; not of ideas or ideals, or knowledge, or political maxims, or even of practical reason in any of its higher senses, as Hamilton, Madison, and Jefferson had practical reason. But he knew what he wanted.[44]

This was illustrated in Morley's description of a meeting between Gladstone and Parnell on 5 April 1886:

> Mr Parnell came to my room in the House at 8.30, and we talked for two hours. At 10.30 I went to Mr Gladstone next door, and told him how things stood. He asked me to open the points of discussion, and into my room we went. He shook hands cordially with Mr Parnell, and sat down between him and me. We at once got to work. P [*sic*] extra-ordinarily close, tenacious and sharp. It was all finance.[45]

Gladstone noted on his first meeting with Parnell in March 1888 that 'Undoubtedly his tone was very conservative'.[46] There was plenty of evidence for this as Parnell's tone, at times close to Wolfe Tone when he addressed his Irish and more particularly Irish-American supporters, did not always please Gladstone; but he interpreted it as one that reflected his acts, not his motives. Now that Gladstone had committed the Liberal Party to Irish Home Rule, Parnell threw all his weight behind the great slogan that characterised Liberal policy – the 'Union of Hearts'.[47]

It is difficult from 1886 until 1890 to see any significant difference between Gladstone's passionate call for justice for Ireland and Parnell's responses to this. Indeed, this is discernible as early as December 1883, when Parnell declared that 'if our rights to self-government were recognised by the parliament of Great Britain in a spirit of justice . . . then the strife of centuries might be terminated' and that

> there is no reason why the Irish nation, respecting their rights and defending their rights, should not acknowledge and support loyally, the rights of the larger nation so close to our shores (applause).[48]

In October 1885 he called on English statesmen to

> trust the Irish people altogether, or trust them not at all (cheers). Give with a full and open-hand – give our people the power to legislate upon all their domestic concerns, and you may depend upon one thing, that the desire for separation, the means of winning separation at least, will not be increased or intensified (cheers).

In this speech he followed Gladstone's exploration of overseas examples of divided nations. In August 1885 Lord Granville sent Gladstone, who was considering other examples of Home Rule, 'a full account of the Austro-Hungarian Union'; in October Parnell suggested that 'we can point to the example of other countries; of Austria and of Hungary – to the fact that Hungary, having been conceded self-government, became one of the strongest factors in the Austrian Empire'. Like Gladstone he also considered the example of Canada where there existed a 'different system of English rule . . .'[49] On 20 July 1889 at the National Liberal Club he reflected Gladstone's concept of the education and guidance of public opinion: that the Liberal Party had brought the Irish people 'to look to the law, to the Constitution', and 'to parliamentary methods for the redress of grievances'; this was due to the 'admission of the people to the franchise' which allowed the expression of the true opinions of the country.[50] And, most revealing of all in the context of the 'Union of Hearts' that he and Gladstone had forged,

> the conscience of Great Britain was first roused to the anomaly of the English Church Establishment in Ireland (cheers) by the unfortunate and unhappy attempts that were made in 1865 by some rash men to free their country from the oppression by force of arms (cheers).

The feelings of the Irish people at home and abroad had altered. Since Mr Gladstone introduced his great measure of conciliation the whole nature of Irishmen everywhere had been changed.' Those who before threatened and talked of rebellion, and meant it, too, are now willing to live with you in amity as fellow citizens in a great empire.'

The Irish People in the United States of America were willing to accept his (Gladstone's) concessions in good faith and 'any man who raises his hands to stop this work of goodwill should be put down as a disunionist and as an enemy to his race (cheers)'.[51]

This speech bears closer examination: for Parnell's coining of the word 'disunionist' suggested that the Irish nationalist had become a kind of unionist, since anyone who opposed Home Rule was now a disunionist. Moreover, as Parnell moved ever closer to unionism, in the broad sense of a desire to cement firmly the new citizenship status that Gladstone was about to confer on the people of Ireland, Gladstone found his energies directed in the last decade of his political life, towards considering the implications of what he had noted throughout his political career: that the United Kingdom consisted, as he recalled the words of Lord John Russell spoken in 1870 and which Gladstone repeated in the Home Rule debates of 1886: that 'The true key to our Irish debates was this: that it was not properly borne in mind that as England is inhabited by Englishmen, and Scotland by Scotchmen, so Ireland is inhabited by Irishmen.'[52]

The Home Rule crisis significantly altered the debate about British politics. It now acquired – and for the next 40 years sustained (albeit fitfully at times) – argument about the proper constitutional arrangements for governing the Kingdom. Gladstone was cautious: he stressed that Ireland was a special case; Wales and Scotland were different. Scotland was a fine example of what Ireland could be like, if her people were convinced that the law was not their oppressor but arose from their own needs and traditions. Wales, he announced in Swansea in 1887, could be considered for admission to Home Rule, but he had to be convinced that this was what the people really desired.[53] The same was applicable to Scotland, though Gladstone felt Scottish opinion could not speak with the same unanimity as had Ireland.[54] Welsh and Scottish Liberals saw parallels with Ireland in the need for reform of the landholding system. Despite the imminent arrival on the Irish cultural scene of linguistic nationalism, Gladstone showed no interest in the language question there. But in Wales he changed his opinion from dislike to approval: at a National Eisteddfod held in Wrexham in 1888 he observed that it was once the custom 'to deplore the maintenance of the Welsh language and say "let us have one language, one speech, and one communication"'. Now he appreciated the virtues of duality in speech, but, again he was careful to stress that this need not endanger the United Kingdom: he had not heard that

> Welshmen, when they go to England, ever lose their attachment to their native
> land; and I have not found that they are placed at any undue disadvantage in
> consequence of that attachment, although it embraces and regards as the centre
> of Welsh life the tongue that is spoken by the people.[55]

Gladstone's close connection with Wales was also important in showing how he had altered the boundary of political debate in the Kingdom. The British state was, formally at least, based on the Anglican Establishment, which had substantial disagreements with the English and Welsh nonconformist denominations. Gladstone not only identified the nonconformists of Wales as the 'people of Wales'[56], he won that very Protestant nation over to the cause of a Home Rule settlement that would hand power in Ireland to the Roman Catholic majority. This reflected the moral force that he gave the cause of devolution, one reinforced by his passion for history on which he based his denunciations of British misrule in Ireland.[57] Parnell had no such interest in history, but he was willing to use brief sound-bites from Irish history to support his case for self-government, which would vindicate Ireland's claim to be a nation once again.[58]

Gladstone's powers of moral persuasion struck deeply into the heart of the Welsh nonconformists, accustomed as they were to hearing apocalyptic rhetoric in their religious gatherings. The Liberal MP Tom Ellis was initially hostile to Parnell and his family, mainly because of their connection to agrarian agitation, and denounced the 'utter hideousness of the crimes which are committed by dissolute blackguards in Ireland'. In 1885, provoked by the Conservative-Irish Nationalist alliance that was apparently emerging, he described Parnell as the 'dictator at Westminster'.[59] But he followed Gladstone's example, studied Irish history, and recognised Parnell as 'a remarkable man and I am now only beginning to realise how finely he has led the Irish Liberation movement'. The election results of November–December 1885, he claimed, meant that Home Rule for Ireland, Wales and Scotland were 'writ large across each day's results': the 'centuries of arrogance, and what is worse Saxon arrogance' towards the Celtic peoples was now to be checked.[60] In February 1889 he surmised that 'if Parnell wished he could become the Prime Minister of Britain.'[61] So powerful an influence did the Irish leader exert that contemporaries could offer no higher accolade to Ellis as that of 'the Parnell of Wales'.[62]

The Parnell of Ireland had little interest in Wales nor indeed in Scotland, though Michael Davitt, one of the leading land agitators, did.[63] Parnell's attitude to the land agitation in Ireland was always uneasy. He recognised that he could not afford to ignore it, and certainly not condemn the Land League's actions; but the notion, freely asserted by his Conservative and Unionist opponents that he was associated with crime, including the agrarian variety, was hard to shake off. Parnell saw the land agitation as essentially divisive: landlord was opposed by tenant, tenant farmer by agricultural labourer. Gladstone's first Home Rule bid gave him the chance to unite the nation behind the politics of self-government, and its failure did not deter him from keeping it at the forefront of the nationalist movement. He was distressed when a new land agitation, the 'Plan of Campaign', began just a few months after the defeat of Home Rule in Parliament. He could hardly condemn it (not least because some of his own prominent MPs such as John Dillon publicly supported it) but his dislike of the aims and tactics of the plan – the use of collective bargaining on individual estates for the reduction of rent – propelled him further into the arms of Gladstonian Liberalism. In May 1888 at the Eighty Club, London, he admitted that while the Plan had 'saved thousands and thousands of tenants from eviction' and had 'prevented enormous suffering in Ireland', and had indeed 'pacified the country'; still, there were features of the Plan which 'would have had a bad effect upon the general political situation', that

> . . . the iniquity of evictions in Ireland would be lost sight of in this country owing to the repugnance which would be felt by the people of England and Scotland and Wales to some of the features of the Plan of Campaign (hear, hear). Therefore I should have advised the Irish tenants to suffer a little while, in the firm confidence that 'although their trouble might last for a year or two, yet in a short time they would be put an end to forever by the concession of self-government to their country.[64]

By the time he was able to address the mistakes made by the organisers of the Plan it was too late; but he nonetheless stipulated four conditions that would limit the danger of the Plan spreading to new estates and provoking disorder; one of these was that the Irish Parliamentary Party should not be identified with this Plan. He ended by appealing to the people of Ireland to 'withstand every provocation . . . to suffer 'all things rather than to go outside the law as it exists in this country'. 'I trust', he concluded,

> that they will remember that a great and historic party are committed to their cause, and that they are not standing alone; that they have for allies men who have never ultimately been beaten, and that the party – the great Liberal party of England – never in history have taken up any cause or attempted any reform without winning that cause and that reform in the end (loud and long-continued cheers).[65]

Dr Margaret O'Callaghan regards Parnell's dependence on the winning of a constitution as unlikely to succeed even before his own fall from grace in 1890–1 in the divorce case arising from his adulterous relationship with Mrs O'Shea.[66] But Parnell's stock had never stood higher in Great Britain than in February 1889 when the report of the Special Commission appointed to investigate accusations that Parnell was deeply implicated in Irish political and agrarian criminality was published. This exonerated Parnell, who on 1 March appeared in triumph in the House of Commons where he received a standing ovation. Gladstone proposed that Parnell be given a special dinner, an invitation he readily accepted. In the event the celebration was held in private, but publicised on 2 April.[67] Finally there came the metaphysical crowning of the 'uncrowned King of Ireland' – a visit to Hawarden. Parnell arrived at 5.30 on 18 December. He had '2 hours of satisfactory conversation, but he put off the *gros* of it'. They had two hours more on 19 December. 'He is certainly one of the very best people to deal with that I have ever known', remarked Gladstone, who showed Parnell round the estate and the old castle: 'He seems to notice and appreciate everything.'[68]

Gladstone's tone was that of a concerned schoolmaster who was gratified at the remarkable progress of a pupil whose qualities he had sometimes doubted, and whose behaviour occasionally overstepped the mark. Parnell, like a sensible schoolboy, was willing to go along with this, and indeed to improve his reputation as the justifiable choice to be head boy. This made his fall from grace in 1890 all the more vexatious for Gladstone. He did not judge Parnell's immorality; but he did feel deeply deceived by Parnell's assurances that there was no possibility of his emerging from the affair with any stain on his character.[69]

The issue for Gladstone was simple: the nonconformists of Wales and England, and the Presbyterians of Scotland were the backbone of the Liberal Party, and therefore Parnell must retire from the leadership of the Irish Party if Gladstone were to continue the fight for Home Rule. As John Morley put it, 'Platform-men united with pulpit-men in swelling the whirlwind. Electoral calculations and moral faithfulness were held for once to point the same way.'[70] Confusion arose when Parnell met his party on 25 November and was promptly re-elected leader. Gladstone's message to the party that he insisted on Parnell's retirement was not conveyed to the Home Rule MPs. Gladstone therefore published the letter he had written to John Morley on 24 November in which he set out his reasons why Parnell, 'notwithstanding the splendid services rendered . . . to his country', must go:

> his continuance at the present moment in the leadership would be productive of consequences disastrous . . . to the cause of Ireland [as it would] render my retention of the leadership of the Liberal party, based as it has been mainly upon the presentation of the Irish cause, almost a nullity.[71]

R. Barry O'Brien regarded this as a mistake, citing a 'distinguished Liberal' who said its publication could only have irritated Parnell and which suggested 'English dictation'.[72]

This placed Parnell on his mettle. He faced Gladstone with, as Frank Callanan describes it, 'unflinching audacity to deploy all his authority and mystique . . . to impugn the legitimacy of a home rule settlement sponsored . . .

[by those of his party who were] ready to dispense with his leadership.'[73] His tactics included revealing a misleading account of the conversations he had with Gladstone at Hawarden in 1889 (which won him no favours in Ireland where Gladstone's name still enjoyed great prestige).[74] Ireland, or most of it at any rate, knew that if Home Rule – the entry of the nation into the promised land, the triumph of those who had been cast down but were now able to reverse the course of Irish history since 1690, or at least since 1800 – were to be achieved, then it could only be by the parliamentary methods forged between Parnell and Gladstone. Gladstone's bitterness at what he saw as the result of the 'sin of Tristram with Isault' was expressed in his birthday retrospect for 1890. He wrote that had it not been for that sin, and its consequences for the alliance between the Irish Parliamentary Party and his own, the future would have been clear:

> In Ireland the Nationalists were to hold their ground; in Great Britain we were to convert on the first Dissolution our minority into a large majority and in the Autumn of 1890 we had established the certainty of that result so far as an event yet contingent could be capable of ascertainment.[75]

The mark of the divorce on the Home Rule movement, if that not of Cain, was perhaps that of King David (who coveted Bathsheba, the wife of Uriah the Hittite): it did not annihilate Gladstone's deep and lasting influence on Irish democratic politics. A meeting of the Irish Parliamentary Party on 3 December 1890, which Parnell did not attend, produced a majority of 44 MPs against Parnell and 29 in favour. When Parnell sought a new basis of support for his leadership of the Nationalist movement between 12 February and 6 October 1891, he took up a theme which he had never fully abandoned even in the days of the Liberal Alliance: that the Irish Parliamentary Party must always see the Westminster option as just that: a chosen method of exerting influence on British Governments and pursuing Home Rule, rather than as a defining characteristic of the Nationalist movement. At Creggs, on 27 September 1891, he declared that his release from Kilmainham Gaol in 1882 had given 'solid benefits to Ireland', but was not surrender to Gladstone: 'No, I gave up none of my independence or that of my own colleagues to Mr Gladstone'.[76] A few months earlier in Belfast, he had defended his moving towards Gladstone in the issue of Home Rule because he believed that Gladstone 'would settle the Irish question. He believed he would settle it by the aid of a united Irish party, but not with a disunited party'.[77] Parnell did not argue that parliamentary politics were exhausted, but that a united, independent Irish Party could live to fight another day.[78] Among its goals would be to help the Irish artisan through assisting the 'English Radical party to strengthen the back of the grand old man . . . We can insist that equal justice and equal measures shall be meted out to Ireland as well as England (hear, hear).'[79]

Parnell's last campaign was marked by his bitter and often personal attacks on Gladstone (who, it seems, he had never forgiven for imprisoning him in Kilmainham).[80] But, as Frank Callanan points out, Parnell's attacks on Gladstone only harmed his own reputation, since Gladstone through his Home Rule bid has achieved a level of high moral authority amongst Irish Nationalists; one surely enhanced by the Irish leader and Party's persistent and glowing praise for the Grand Old Man.[81] Much can be made of Parnell's 'appeal to the Hillside Men' (Fenianism) and his criticism of the influence of the Roman Catholic Church in Irish politics, but there was no significant Fenian movement in Ireland in 1890–1, and even less significant anti-clericalism.

Home Rule and the Liberal Alliance would not be abandoned; it was still regarded, for all its flaws and inconsistencies, as the only answer to the Irish Question. Gladstone declared that the retirement of Parnell from public life would be a public calamity; but he made no effort to rescue Parnell from his predicament. Callanan sums up the paradox, Parnell was 'not dismissed by Gladstone so much as made redundant by . . . the "Union of Hearts".'[82] The Liberal commitment to Irish Home Rule, though frequently in abeyance as other more pressing and more politically advantageous issues surfaced, was not abandoned, and came nearest to success between 1912 and 1914; though arguably it was one of Gladstone's failures (one that he shared with Parnell) to acknowledge the depth of Ulster Unionist opposition to Home Rule that sabotaged the project.

Although Gladstone saw Ireland as a special case that must give her priority over other nations and regions of the United Kingdom, his influence on the politics of the Celtic fringe was wider than the Irish Question and its resolution. Gladstone was a cautious Celticist, wary of encouraging too ambitious expectations among the Welsh and the Scots. But he was willing to recognise that different parts of the Kingdom might need varying treatment, and that these differences were social, economic and cultural as well as political. Parnell was a cautious Nationalist. He was anxious to steer the movement away from violence, whether agrarian or political, and he had no interest in Irish cultural aspirations (though in Galway in March 1891 he remarked on his certainty that the Gaelic Athletic Association were longing for a general election in order to show the stuff of which they were made).[83] He was unwavering in his determination to advance the political cause of 'a nation once again'; but he was willing to embrace the 'Union of Hearts' to the extent that he accused anyone who stood in its way as 'disunionist'. It was this very success that undermined his last campaign, when it was Parnell himself who appeared to the majority of Irish Nationalist electors to be the 'disunionist'.

Parnell's speeches in the golden age of the Liberal Alliance between 1886 and 1889 came close to a kind of British unionism with a green shade. The presentation of Gladstone clad in the mantle of Celtic nationalism while Parnell donned the cloak of British unionism is of course a paradox too far. But it raises points of great interest. The first is at the level of 'High Politics'. Gladstone and Parnell forged a close political alliance between 1882 and 1890, and before the divorce case seem even to have established close personal relations. Some historians have seen this in a very different light. When Gladstone met Parnell at Hawarden in December 1889 he noted that Parnell

> appeared well and cheerful . . . Nothing could be more satisfactory than his conversation, full as I thought of good sense from beginning to end in so far as I could judge; nothing like a crotchet, or an irrational demand, from his side, was likely to interfere with the proper freedom of our deliberations when the proper time comes for practical steps.[84]

Theodore Hoppen queries whether this was 'open mindedness' or 'unprincipled opportunism.'[85] Richard Shannon perceived weaknesses in Gladstone's position in the Hawarden encounter:

> All he could do was talk around various possibilities and convince himself that Parnell's encouraging nods and impeccably satisfactory sentiments of loyalty and conservatism constituted some kind of working understanding.[86]

Parnell, he argues 'was quite a different man from the one Gladstone had ingenuously taken him for'.[87]

These are perceptive and weighty assessments. But they must be set in the context of what kind of men the two great protagonists were. Here were two thoroughly professional and experienced politicians, tacticians who probed each other's strengths and weaknesses, as even – as especially – allies must. Parnell knew that necessary ambiguity must be practised, given his rise to power in Ireland and the at times messianic appeal of Home Rule to the Nationalist electorate. Gladstone, no novice at necessary ambiguity, sought to draw Parnell into seeing his, Gladstone's, need to take the lead and lay down the parameters of an Irish settlement; indeed, this was why Gladstone insisted on Parnell's standing down when the divorce crisis broke. There is no doubt that in their relationship Gladstone won and held the initiative. John Morley described how early in 1891 Gladstone went to see *Anthony and Cleopatra*. On leaving the theatre 'he had a little ovation. As he drove away the crowd cheered him with cries of "Bravo, don't you mind Parnell."'[88] George Bernard Shaw in his play *John Bull's Other Island* caught the mood perfectly, when his Liberal-minded character, Tom Broadbent, remarked: 'We owe Home Rule not to the Irish, but to our English Gladstone.'[89] Nevertheless Gladstone and Parnell were alike in that they each had an honesty of purpose – Gladstone to strengthen the unity of the United Kingdom; Parnell to win an Irish legislature. Their aims were, they believed, not incompatible.

The second point is that Gladstone in his Home Rule policy was not only seeking a change in governmental arrangements and the administration of Ireland, but working on a wider and certainly deeper level. This can best be illustrated by reference to a speech which Matthew Arnold gave when in the United States of America in 1883–4. He explained that everyone now knew that there had been conquest and confiscation in Ireland: 'So there has been elsewhere'. The consequence of this was a failure in justice, which was 'a source of danger to States. But it may be made up for and got over, it has been made up for and got over in many countries'.[90] English confiscations and the Penal Laws were 'a thing of the past'. But the Irish did not see it this way, because there had been on England's part a failure in what he called 'amiability' as well as justice: failure in one meant failure in the other:

> As we English are not amiable, or at any rate . . . do not appear so the joint oper-
> ations of two moral causes together – the sort of causes which politicians do not
> seriously regard – tells against the designs of politicians with what seems to be an
> almost inexorable fatality.[91]

The two failures together create a difficulty almost insurmountable. Public men in England keep saying that it will be got over. I hope that it will be got over, and that the union between England and Ireland may become as solid as that between England and Scotland. But it will not become solid by means of the contrivances of the mere politician, or without the intervention of moral causes of concord to heal the mischief wrought by moral causes of division.[92]

Gladstone's moral intervention (Arnold's 'amiability') has been identified, in different terms, by Professor Hoppen. Gladstone, he argues, held that it was time to

> . . . cease making the opinion of one country overrule and settle the questions
> belonging to the others, and to deal instead with the interests of each as nearly as
> we can in accordance with the views and sentiments of the natives of that country.
> He even went so far as to demand a new kind of psychological empathy in which
> each of us might individually make a mental effort to place himself in the position
> of an Irishman . . . under the influence of their traditions.[93]

Gladstone's moral intervention, and Parnell's pragmatic response to it left a legacy that endured, and one still being tested in the contemporary devolved United Kingdom constitution where even the strongly Unionist *Daily Telegraph* can in the same breath speak of 'our nation' and yet acknowledge that 'Britishness is not so much a nationality as a framework that yokes us together through shared institutions, such as the monarchy, the Armed Forces and even the NHS.'[94] Gladstone's purpose was to rebalance the constitution, and explore the political nature of the British nation, to which end he moved outside the confines of Britain and Ireland and investigated examples of multi-national regimes ranging from the Austro-Hungarian Empire to the Dominion of Canada. Despite, or rather because of Gladstone's failure, the debate over the relationship between the United Kingdom, Ireland, the British Commonwealth and Europe continues to this day.

Notes

1   Quoted in H. C. G. Matthew, *Gladstone 1875–1898* (Oxford, 1995), p. 315.

2   A. B. Cooke and J. R. Vincent, *The Governing Passion: Cabinet Government and Party Politics in Britain, 1885–86* (Brighton, 1974).

3   D. G. Boyce, 'Introduction', in Boyce and Alan O'Day (eds), *Gladstone and Ireland: Politics, Religion and Nationality in the Victorian Age* (London, 2010).

4   Matthew Arnold, 'Democracy,' in John Bryson (ed.), *Matthew Arnold: Poetry and Prose* (London, 1954), pp 545–69 at pp 552, 560.

5   Matthew, *Gladstone*, p. 93.

6   Ibid., p. 180.

7   W. E. Gladstone, *The State in its Relations with the Church* (London, 1841), pp 13–15.

8   John Morley, *Life of Gladstone* (London, 1908 edn), vol. I, pp 50–1.

9   David Williamson, *Gladstone: Statesman and Scholar* (London, 1898), p. 251.

10   Ibid., p. 153.

11   Ibid., p. 260.

12   Matthew, *Gladstone*, pp 29–30.

13   Quoted in ibid., p. 186; for Gladstone's visit see Kevin McKenna, 'From private visit to public opportunity: Gladstone's 1877 trip to Ireland', in Mary E. Daly and K. Theodore Hoppen (eds), *Gladstone: Ireland and Beyond* (Dublin, 2011), pp 77–89.

14   Alan O'Day, *Charles Stewart Parnell* (Dublin, 1998), p. 23.

15   Quoted in ibid., p. 31.

16   Richard Shannon, *Gladstone: Heroic Minister, 1865–1898* (London, 1999), p. 260.

17   Alan O'Day, *Parnell*, pp 31–3.

18   Ibid.

19   *Daily Express (Dublin)*, 8 Nov. 1877.

20   Shannon, *Gladstone*, pp 288–9.

21   O'Day, *Parnell*, p. 37.

22 Quoted in ibid., pp 42–3.

23 Ibid., p. 45.

24 Quoted in Matthew, *Gladstone*, p. 196.

25 D. G. Boyce, *Nationalism in Ireland* (London, 1995), 3rd edn, p. 218.

26 Quoted in Matthew, *Gladstone*, p. 199.

27 Shannon, *Gladstone*, p. 294.

28 Quoted in ibid., p. 295.

29 O'Day, *Charles Stewart Parnell* (Dublin, 2012), p. 65.

30 Matthew, *Gladstone*, p. 203.

31 Ibid., p. 206.

32 Quoted in ibid., p. 206.

33 *The Gladstone Diaries*, vol. XI, July 1883–Dec. 1886, H. C. G. Matthew (ed.) (Oxford, 1990), p. 87.

34 Shannon, *Gladstone*, pp 358–60.

35 O'Day, *Parnell*, p. 53.

36 Matthew, *Gladstone*, p. 209.

37 Quoted in ibid., p. 221.

38 Ibid., p. 213.

39 See John Kendle, *Ireland and the Federal Solution: The Debate over the United Kingdom Constitution, 1870–1921* (Kingston and Montreal, 1989), pp 41–2.

40 Shannon, *Gladstone*, p. 390.

41 Morley, *Gladstone*, p. 411.

42 Ibid., pp 408–10.

43 Gladstone to Granville, 10 Oct. 1885, in F. S. L. Lyons, *Charles Stewart Parnell* (London, 1978 pb edn), p. 297.

44 Morley, *Gladstone*, p. 408.

45 Ibid.

46 Matthew, *Gladstone*, p. 311.

47 David Bebbington, 'The union of hearts depicted: Gladstone, Home Rule and *United Ireland*', in Boyce and O'Day, *Gladstone and Ireland*, pp 186–208.

48 *Freeman's Journal*, 18 Dec. 1883.

49 *United Ireland*, 10 Oct. 1885.

50 O'Day, *Parnell*, p. 58.

51 *Nation*, 27 July 1889.

52 Quoted in Matthew, *Gladstone*, pp 212–13.

53 Shannon, *Gladstone*, p. 465.

54 Matthew, *Gladstone*, p. 214.

55 Quoted in Boyce, 'Gladstone and the four nations', in Boyce and O'Day, *Gladstone and Ireland*, pp 256–88 at p. 278.

56 Boyce, *Nationalism in Ireland*, p. 220.

57 Ian Sheehy, 'A deplorable narrative: Gladstone, R. Barry O'Brien and the "historical argument" for Home Rule, 1880–1890', in Boyce and O'Day, *Gladstone and Ireland*, ch. 5.

58 For example, Parnell's speech after the report of the Special Commission, *Nation*, 1 June, 1889, p. 12.

59 Neville Masterman, *The Forerunner: The Dilemmas of Tom Ellis, 1859–99* (Llandybie, 1972), p. 65.

60 Ibid., pp 74–5.

61 Ibid., p. 122.

62 Ibid., p. 17.

63 Boyce, 'Gladstone and the Four Nations', pp 263–4.

64 *Nation*, 12 May 1888.

65 Ibid.

66 Cited in O'Day, *Parnell*, p. 76.

67 Shannon, *Gladstone*, p. 480.

68 Quoted in ibid., p. 489.

69 Ibid., p. 497-8.

70 Morley, *Gladstone*, p. 504.

71 R. Barry O'Brien, *The Life of Charles Stewart Parnell* (London, 1910 edn) pp 473–4.

72 Ibid., pp 475.

73 Frank Callanan, *The Parnell Split 1890–91* (Cork, 1992), p. 27.

74 Ibid., pp 23–4.

75 Quoted in Matthew, *Gladstone*, p. 315.

76 *United Ireland*, 3 Oct. 1891.

77 *The Times*, 23 May 1891.

78 Callanan, *The Parnell Split*, pp 240–3.

79 *The Times*, 11 Dec.1890 p. 12.

80 Callanan, *The Parnell Split*, pp 218–24.

81 Ibid., p. 220.

82 Ibid., p. 21.

83 *The Times*, 16 Mar. 1891.

84 K. Theodore Hoppen, 'Introduction' in Daly and Hoppen, *Gladstone: Ireland and Beyond* pp 15–22 at p. 20.

85 Ibid.

86 Shannon, *Gladstone*, p. 489.

87 Ibid., p. 499.

88 Morley, *Gladstone*, p. 521.

89 George Bernard Shaw, *John Bull's Other Island* (London, 1907 edn), p. 23.

90 Matthew Arnold, 'Discourses in America, 1885', in Bryson (ed.), *Matthew Arnold: Poetry and Prose*, pp 625–42, at pp 633–4.

91 Ibid.

92 Ibid., p. 33–4.

93 Hoppen, 'Gladstone, Salisbury and the end of Irish assimilation', in Daly and Hoppen *Gladstone: Ireland and Beyond*, p. 50.

94 *Daily Telegraph*, 'The United Kingdom is worth fighting for', 7 May 2011.

CHAPTER 3

Anna Parnell

Challenges to Male Authority and the
Telling of National Myth

Margaret Ward

It is in this telling of national myth that the political authority of women has so often been expunged.[1]

While Benton referred to the distortion of the role played by Irish women in the War of Independence, conflicting discourses on key events in Irish national history did not begin in the twentieth century. They are most starkly evident in the contested history of the Land War of the 1880s, where memoirs of that period, published by male colleagues of the Ladies' Land League, served to legitimise women's subsequent exclusion from the political sphere. Women were represented as encouraging and instigating agrarian violence, as not understanding the political process; that they were naïve and easily led. The alternative voice of Anna Parnell struggled to be heard against this condemnation. A similar scenario then occurred in the succeeding generation. With men dominating the telling of national myth, women found themselves excluded from nation-building after the gaining of independence. Why was that? Because their former male colleagues resurrected fears of disorderly women in order to create an independent state based on masculine authority and feminine domesticity.

This gender-based conception of political life has its roots in the history of the Ladies' Land League. It is also rooted in the person of Anna Parnell, whose writings and actions have left Irish women a legacy of direct action, uncompromising public speaking and outspoken challenges to those with whom she disagreed.

We need to understand how profoundly modern Anna Parnell was in order to understand the extent of her challenge and the nature of the resistance it provoked. Danae O'Regan has written a scintillating and original analysis of the very different personas of Anna and Fanny Parnell. They were, she said, 'exemplars of two distinct and typical streams of female action in the nineteenth century.' They mark a watershed for women in the political sphere:

> Both were equally effective activists in their different ways . . . and the two types of female action they represent continued into the twentieth century. Times were, however, changing. The traditional philanthropic middle class woman, of which Fanny was an outstanding example, did not disappear, but it is Anna, prepared to challenge authority, break down barriers between male and female spheres of public life, and pave the way for radical change, who speaks to us most clearly today.[2]

The physical appearances of the two sisters are highly revealing of their different natures. Photographs taken around 1878 show this contrast. Fanny was photographed in a fashionable outfit with a large, flattering, plumed hat; her elbows leaning on some object, her hands under her chin in what O'Regan calls 'an appealing, not to say coy pose'.[3] Anna in contrast, makes no concession to the photographer. She is wearing a simple, everyday walking costume; has taken off her hat which is placed on the table that she is supposed to lean on and which she only lightly rests against, arms firmly folded, in half profile, not facing the camera, unlike the half glance of her sister. For a middle-class woman to go hatless in the nineteenth century was a definite challenge to convention. Anna's body language suggests that she is in the studio under great sufferance. It is the only known portrait of her.

Both Parnell sisters were independently minded. A great-aunt was an executive member of the American Women's Suffrage Association and the Parnells had a much wider experience of the world than the majority of their contemporaries, moving as they did between Dublin, London, Paris and Boston. Fanny, at an early age, was described by her brother John as a 'blue stocking' and 'arch rebel', for her support of the Fenians and her attendance at the trial of O'Donovan Rossa.[4] Historian Martha Vicinus has described the challenge posed by the suffragists in terms that have equal force in Anna Parnell's earlier disregard of convention: 'unescorted upper-class women in the streets spoke of political and sexual independence'.[5] Katherine Tynan, a volunteer for the Ladies' Land League, described Anna 'with her curiously gentle, gliding pace' noting that she would walk between Grafton Street and the League office in Upper Sackville Street unconcerned at being unaccompanied and out late at night.[6]

We have plentiful evidence of Anna's fearlessness and use of public space. In June 1882, at the height of the Land War, the *Evening Telegraph* reported a 'curious incident' in Westmoreland Street, when 'a lady' ran out from the footpath 'and seized the bridle of his Excellency's horse. He immediately pulled up and the lady then addressed some words in reference to the prevention of the erection of Land League huts for evicted tenants.[7]

This was Anna Parnell. She had seized the reins of the Lord Lieutenant's horse to ask him if he had given orders forbidding Land League huts to be erected, having learnt that the erection of shelter for 500 people evicted in Limerick had been stopped. In characteristically modest terms she described the situation in her own way: 'I met Lord Spencer on the way to the Castle and asked him whether this statement was true' – modestly omitting to mention how she actually met the man. Lord Spencer, she said, 'answered that he could not hear what I was saying, but he could hear perfectly well, and I told him so, to which he replied "I cannot" and refused steadfastly to say anything else.' From this she drew the conclusion 'that Lord Spencer was really ashamed of himself.'[8]

Anna Parnell's political writings provide considerable insight regarding her personality and her views on the right of women to take part in political activity. Her first piece of journalism is highly significant in this respect, combining both feminist and nationalist sensibilities in a work notable for its use of satirical humour. In 1875 Anna had moved to London to continue her art studies. After her brother Charles Stewart was elected a Member of Parliament, she visited the Ladies' Gallery in Westminster, listening to the debates, where she was obliged to follow proceedings from a 'mean, dimly lit den' (the only space available to women). From this she wrote her ironically entitled series of articles *Notes from the Ladies' Cage* in which she described the obstructionist tactics of the Irish Party in the sittings of 1877.[9] These articles were written for an Irish-American audience. She was careful to emphasise the point that it was not only women in England, but also women in the United States when observing the House of Representatives, who were unable to mix with the male spectators, and confined to a gallery 'reserved for the un-enfranchised portion of the population.'[10] Beverly Schneller, commenting on Anna's political journalism, says that she barely 'hides her contempt for the real obstructions placed before both women and Ireland' in this satirical, biting essay to which she brought 'worldliness and authority'.[11]

In describing the contemptuous treatment that Irish members were subjected to in the House of Commons, Anna presented it as the victory of the 'smallest parliamentary party known to history' over the British bulldog.[12] As Côté says, 'All is humorous, detached and very effective', as the following examples indicate. A minister, tired and irritated after an all-night session of obstructions 'relieved his feelings by coming up to the Ladies' Gallery to quarrel with his wife'; the Sergeant at Arms 'who was so exhausted after a forty-two hour sitting he accidentally set fire to himself with his postprandial cigar' and an unnamed MP disappeared from sight, only to be discovered one week later by his anxious family, recuperating in a hotel room from the session and 'the means he had taken to recover from it.'[13] These were sophisticated writings. They also reveal a woman with an attractive wit, who could use the weapon of irony rather than the bludgeon of angry rhetoric.

In a lengthy assessment of this first effort at political reporting, Côté concludes that it demonstrated:

> . . . an analytical turn of mind, a fine appreciation of the intricacies of parliamentary rules and procedure, and a well-developed sense of the comic and of the absurd . . . [it] suggest[s] the amused tolerance of a detached observer who is untouched by the events she describes yet is highly entertained by the foibles and posturings of the foolish puppets down below.[14]

How did Anna Parnell move from the role of commentator to that of activist? When the Land League was formed in 1879 – as a heralded 'new departure' – uniting parliamentarians and Fenians in a fight for tenant rights at a time of renewed threat of famine, both Anna and Fanny were in America organising the Land League offices there and raising considerable sums of money to be sent to Ireland to support the tenant farmer's campaign for fair rents. Branches of a Ladies' Land League were formed along the east coast of America. It set a precedent for female mobilisation and demonstrated women's enthusiasm for the cause. Anna moved back to Ireland during 1880, and was a close follower of events as they unfolded.

It was clear that the British Government was not prepared to allow the campaign to continue indefinitely and a Coercion Act intended to facilitate mass jailing of leaders and followers was imminent. The male leadership realising they would soon be imprisoned, agreed to what they termed a 'most dangerous experiment': allowing Michael Davitt to invite Anna to set up a Ladies' Land League in Ireland.[15] It was intended that the women would do no more than organise a holding operation, dispensing charity to evicted tenants until the men were released. Underlying this was the attitude that the women would be incapable of doing more. However Anna, and the team of women she gathered around her, began to work to fulfil aims which the men in fact had already decided were unachievable. The Ladies' Land League, under Anna's guidance, became much more than a group of women dispensing charity. It was a militant force, determined to challenge landlord rule. Anna encouraged rural women to come out of their homes and play an active role in withholding rent, boycotting and resisting eviction.

One example, from an early meeting in Mayo, demonstrates the extent to which her actions had a destabilising influence upon gender relations in the Irish countryside. She pleaded with the men crowding the platform to move back and let the women come forward because 'they have only been able to stand at the outskirts of your meetings, at a respectful distance, and pick up the crumbs from your table.'[16] Reports of her meetings were full of references to the importance of women's role in the on-going campaign and women were increasingly visible. In March 1881, after entering the town of Keadue, Co. Roscommon 'accompanied by a procession of young ladies of not less than three thousand persons', Anna referred specifically to the role played by women: 'Mr Forster [the Chief Secretary] said he got more trouble from the women than from anyone else. I am not surprised . . . It may be that some mothers will give trouble to process servers. All animals, the lion, the tiger, the wolf, run to defend their young. When an Irish mother does the same, Forster calls it brutality.'[17] The *Belfast Newsletter*, reflecting a vastly different political perspective, was appalled at the changes it was witnessing, with 'the ladies thronging around the platform instead of, as formerly, viewing the proceedings at a respectful distance.'[18]

Anna Parnell's uncompromising nature is evident in a report of a meeting in Dunmanway, County Cork in August 1881. She had sent a note to the organisers of the meeting giving the conditions on which the Government note-taker would be allowed to attend. It is worth reproducing the comedic proceedings in full for the vivid picture it provides of a woman determined to ensure that her words would not be misrepresented. Before the proceedings commenced, the Government note-taker in civilian clothes 'was requested to come near Miss Parnell'. The following dialogue ensued, with Anna entering into a book the answers to her questions:

Miss Parnell – Are you a Government note-taker? Yes. Do you intend writing shorthand or longhand? Shorthand. Are you a professional shorthand writer or a policeman note-taker? I am here to represent the Government and I am not bound to answer you any further. You decline to answer? Yes. What's your name? William Irwin.

[A policeman, who was present but hadn't offered himself for interview earlier, was requested to come forward.]

Miss Parnell – Do you intend to take notes of this meeting?

Policeman – Well, I was sent here to take notes, no doubt.

Miss Parnell – What's your name?

Policeman – Daniel O'Brien, ma'am.

Miss Parnell – Are you a constable, a sub-constable or a head constable; what's your rank?

Policeman – I'm a constable.

Miss Parnell – Do you intend taking notes in shorthand or in longhand?

Policeman – I don't think I can take notes in shorthand. I don't want to give any information; have you it all now?

[Miss Parnell then addressed the meeting.][19]

As well as tenacity, she had great physical courage. For example, at one eviction scene, she persuaded a local man to carry her on his shoulders across a river. The man was forced to walk with water up to his chin in parts, enabling Anna to reach cottages under threat before the landlord's agent. A newspaper unfavourable to her politics concluded that 'this action, much more than her orations, explains her influence with the common people.'[20]

Both Fanny and Anna Parnell were adept in using the partisan press of Irish America to support their cause. Editorial comment in their favour was often exuberant, as in the following example from the *Irish World:*

> Miss Anna Parnell, by her cool and energetic management of the Ladies' Land League, has called into life a power greater than the Irish landlords, greater than the Irish police, greater than the English army now in Ireland, greater than any army which England has the power to send . . . Great indeed is the power of this young girl, whose slightest suggestion a nation will obey! A very Joan of Arc is she.[21]

While this hyperbole was propagandistic, written for an Irish-American audience, there is ample evidence of how Anna conducted herself at meetings at a time when people were being arrested, when hundreds of evictions were taking place and occasional hand to hand fighting with landlord's agents was happening.[22] Such evidence leads to the conclusion that this assessment of her impact, although colourful, was correct. Irish papers were also enthusiastic in their coverage, leading Anna to protest against too much emphasis being placed on her role in events during evictions in Mitchelstown.[23]

Fanny Parnell lamented in a poem published in 1880 'I am a woman, I can do naught for thee, Ireland, mother!'[24] which may have signified her frustration at being limited to fundraising. While philanthropy was regarded as a suitable occupation for middle-class women, her sister Anna made it clear that in her eyes the Land League was a political movement and not a charity: 'the money we administer is money subscribed by the people themselves and entrusted to the Irish National Land League . . . We don't want people we help to feel humiliated – They will have the best right in the world to everything they get.'[25] In O'Regan's assessment, there was a crucial distinction between the two conceptions of women's role: activist or philanthropist. The former exemplified that now taken by Anna: 'In her fight for a free Ireland she had come to function in a totally different sphere from that of her sister and had become a modern, militant woman activist.'[26]

The traditional gendered assumptions of passive female and active male were being challenged. Women were encouraged to use their traditional domestic role for subversive aims. Anna Parnell urged women to pay for groceries with cash in order to prevent men from using the money to pay rent to the landlord. The public/domestic distinction collapsed into a political movement, where women were empowered to use their traditional role for political ends, and the leadership of the movement (young, middle-class, urban women in the main) challenged all conventions. Ecclesiastical condemnation saw Archbishop McCabe of Dublin issue a pastoral letter condemning this call to

> the daughters of our Catholic people be they matrons or virgins are called forth to take their stand in the noisy arena of public life . . . asked to forget the modesty of their sex and the high dignity of their womanhood by leaders who seem utterly reckless of consequences.[27]

The course of resistance advocated by the women soon put them at odds with the campaign envisaged by the male leadership. Anna was determined that there would be real resistance to landlordism, not what she considered the sham resistance of paying rent 'at the point of a bayonet'. She argued that:

> one estate that was not paying rent, but going into Land League houses when the evicting 'army' arrived would have constituted a much more alarming object lesson to landlords than fifty estates paying 'Rent at the point of the Bayonet'.[28]

The women argued that the building of huts had to be a priority – they would be 'a permanent sign and symbol that all power did not lie with the foreign enemy in possession of the country.'[29]

By October 1881 the entire male leadership had been arrested and the women were left on their own for the next seven months, to continue to support evicted tenants, to defy evictions, to channel funds to the needy and to ensure that the newspaper *United Ireland* was still published, despite the editor being in jail. Their voluminous dresses became hiding places for contraband literature. It was a unique situation and much international interest was aroused. Women continued to join the resistance. By the start of 1882 there were 500 branches, some with between 100 and 200 members. When they were declared an illegal organisation they defied the edict by holding simultaneous meetings across the country on 1 January 1882. An editorial in *United Ireland* wondered 'Is it easier to cow a nation of men than a handful of women?'[30] Thirteen women did go to jail too – but they were arrested under statutes aimed at curbing prostitution. They were treated as criminals in jail, not as political prisoners.

Henry George, a radical figure in nineteenth century America and an advocate of land nationalisation, was in Ireland to observe the course of the land agitation. He was vocal in his admiration of the women's campaign, writing to Patrick Ford, editor of the *Irish World*, that in his opinion the women had done 'a great deal better than the men would have done.'[31] That was a shocking admission for men to hear. The women were better than they were, and not in the kitchen or the drawing room or the nursery, but in terrain that should have been masculine territory – the battlefields of the Land War.

Michael Davitt later said that the imprisoned Charles Stewart Parnell became concerned that the League was being used 'not for the purposes he approved of, but for a real revolutionary end and aim.'[32] The growing alarm of both Parnell and the British Government led to what was later dubbed the 'Kilmainham Treaty' of May 1882. By this, the Government agreed to release the prisoners and to amend the provisions of the 1881 Land Act, whilst Parnell promised to use his influence to prevent further 'outrages'. The men, however, did not want the women to disband, but to stay in existence – under male control of course – in order to carry on the work of deciding who would be eligible for relief. This task the women refused to do.

In considering male reactions to the women of the Ladies' Land League and to the controversy surrounding the eventual dissolution of their organisation, one important issue concerns the so-called 'extravagance' of the women. The campaign was, of necessity, expensive. When in jail, the men had issued a 'No Rent' manifesto and the numbers of evictions had increased in consequence. There were almost 1,000 men in jail, costing £400 a week in food; and the programme of resistance meant that the women spent a total of £70,000 on various forms of relief. Charles Stewart Parnell tried to transform the Ladies' Land League into an alms-giving operation by refusing to pay their debts unless the women agreed to this subordinate role. For his sister, this would be to provide 'a perpetual petticoat screen behind which they [the men] could shelter, not from the government, but from the people.'[33]

Those who supported the women were the radicals, not the parliamentary colleagues of Charles Stewart Parnell. Henry George wrote to Helen Taylor, step-daughter of John Stuart Mill (who had herself been active in support of the Ladies' Land League), 'the women really feel bitter towards the Parliamentary men. They have been treated badly and their obligations have not been kept, and on several occasions the men got a very frank piece of their minds.'[34] Jessie Craigen, an English working-class suffragist leader, had come to Ireland to work with the women and she also wrote to Helen Taylor:

> I made great sacrifices for the Irish cause. I gave up my situation and threw myself on the world without a penny and without a friend: but it was to fight for the liberty of the people and not to put political tricksters into power.[35]

The women decided that it would be 'morally impossible' to continue working with the men – because of their strong political differences – so they argued to be able to disband. Anna was forced to leave these debates due to the sudden death on 20 July of her sister Fanny, who at the age of thirty-three, died unexpectedly of a heart attack. It was reported that Anna was ill from 'brain fever' as a consequence of the shock, although the *Irish World* reported that she had intended to resign her position 'a few days before she was taken sick.'[36] For the month of August at least she was out of the public eye, and thereafter the bulk of the work of winding down the organisation was done by other members of her executive. However all the evidence is that her strong political differences with the men were shared by the other women.

During the summer of 1882 the various branches of the Ladies' Land League closed down. An editorial in *United Ireland* commented (one suspects with a sense of relief): 'They cease their work where others take it up, and return to brighten and sweeten their own Irish hearths again.'[37] Even the *Irish World* had a headline; 'Ladies' Land League to Give Way to The Men'.[38] As O'Regan says, 'When [Anna Parnell] disappeared from politics her male colleagues must have given a sigh of relief, and society quickly forgot her'.[39] The men formed a new campaigning body to take the place of the Land League. This was the Irish National League – composed of male politicians and described as 'an open organisation in which the ladies will not take part'.[40]

Anna Parnell, utterly disillusioned, later wrote 'However long I might live, I knew that it would never again be possible for me to believe that any body of Irishmen meant a word of anything they said.'[41] Discourses of national struggle are constructed by those who control the writing of history, and when it came to the writing of histories of the Land War, with women disempowered and out of the public sphere, the former male leadership had unrivalled scope to construct their narratives. Anna moved to England and lived in obscurity. Several other activists left Ireland; some moved to America where they were treated with much greater respect than if they had remained at home. In 1905, William O'Brien's *Recollections* patronised the 'sweet girl graduates' of the Ladies' Land League, but the most significant account of the period was Michael Davitt's *Fall of Feudalism in Ireland*, published the year before. Davitt, a supporter of land nationalism, was sympathetic towards the women, and rejected the strategy of the Irish Party; but in his emphasis of the achievements of the women he remarked that they had been more success-ful than the men because they had had less scruples in encouraging violence. Anna was furious about 'one of the most blackguardly books ever written, containing the most impudent libels on me, and specially constructed for the purpose of concealing the fact that the Land League ran away.'[42] She wanted to write her own account of the period but Harper's, publishers of Davitt's work, refused to consider the manuscript even before she had written it.

An exchange of views between Anna Parnell and Máire de Buitléir in the early years of the twentieth century reveals Anna's level of alienation, only compounded further by evidence that some sections of a new generation of activists saw women's role in purely domestic terms. In 1906, de Buitléir wrote a series on women, *The Nationalisation of Irish Home Life*, the purpose of which was to enlist homemakers as nation-makers, reminding women that because they made the home atmosphere they were the chief nation-builders. Anna, writing to the *Irish Peasant*, was outspoken in her bitter reaction:

> If Máire de Buitléir would explain the following sentence in . . . 'Our Irish Homes' of November 24: 'The men by their hard fight during the Land War won these homes', by telling me what the hard fight consisted of, I should be very much obliged to her. My own observation was that they ran away. That observation, however, was confined to the Land League time.

When de Buitléir replied with renewed praise for the Land League, adding:

> I do not forget that Miss Parnell was working for Ireland when I was in the nursery, and if I differ from her I do so in all respect. Let her not think that we young Irish-Irelanders are arrogant and supercilious, patronising our elders, who are doubtless often also our betters.[43]

She made the mistake of recommending Davitt's *Fall of Feudalism in Ireland* for a true account of the Land League – the book which had caused Anna such annoyance and grief when it was published. Anna's reaction was strong because she could see what was happening – a re-writing of history and a distortion of the role played by women. Men were uncritically accepted as the true activists and once again the dominant nationalist discourse was an acceptance of the role of women as the primary inculcators of children's spiritual and moral values, with little further expectation of a role to be played by women in the nationalist movement. To make matters worse, de Buitléir, in a Gaelic League pamphlet, *Irish Women and the Home Language*, contrasted the 'gentle low-voiced women' inculcating nationalism at the hearth with the 'shrieking viragoes or aggressive amazons' who seek a public platform.[44]

The impression of Anna Parnell that comes to us is one of sadness, combined with disillusion. This is supported by the vivid imagery contained in her poem *The Journey* (1890s), in which she describes how:

> . . .a band of thieves beset me
> Quite early in the day;
> They robbed me and then they cast me
> All bleeding by the way.[45]

However, that is not the whole picture of the woman in her later years. In her private letters she was capable of playfulness and still maintained a strong determination to fight for women's emancipation. Her letter to Helen Taylor, who was attempting to be adopted as a Radical-Liberal candidate in the 1885 elections in order to challenge the legal bar against women standing for election, shows her fighting spirit remained intact:

> To me you represent the only English politician, and indeed I think I may say, the only English person I have ever known, who looked on the Irish question entirely from the Irish point of view . . . you came over to Ireland and did not shrink from the most wearisome and distressing drudgery in your efforts to assist the tenant farmers during the extensive evictions carried out . . . the most enthusiastic and self-sacrificing patriot could have done no more for Ireland than you did . . . it would be a mere duty, even if it were not a pleasure, for me to support your candidature by any means that may be in my power.[46]

She was also busy writing her account of the two Leagues in her manuscript 'The Tale of a Great Sham', a riposte to Davitt's account. Her account was self-effacing, avoiding almost all mention of her role, scrupulously avoiding personalities in a belief that 'it does not matter what [a] particular individual does . . . except in so far as he or she represents others.'[47] She failed to find a publisher. Dana Hearne's assessment of the manuscript stresses its gender-based nature: 'It is about power, specifically the power of women to be effective in the presence of men who cannot conceive of their having a legitimate and equal place in the "public sphere".'[48] Was this one reason why publishers showed such a lack of interest?

In 1900 a new generation of nationalist-feminists led by Maud Gonne formed Inghinidhe na hÉireann. There was some continuity with the past: founder member Jennie Wyse-Power, as eighteen year old Jennie O'Toole, had been a member of the Ladies' Land League. Inghinidhe's paper, *Bean na hÉireann*, reveals them to have been modern, young women, scathing of Victorian attitudes towards women and supportive of the 'physical force' tradition within Irish nationalism. Anna Parnell was delighted by the news of their formation. She sent money she could ill-afford towards their Patriotic Childrens' Treat organised to reward those who had ignored bribes to come out in support of Queen Victoria. When Helena Moloney, editor of *Bean na hÉireann*, was sent to prison in 1911 for protesting against a royal visit to Dublin, Anna paid her fine so that Helena could continue the work of editing her manuscript. However, the manuscript disappeared after a police raid on Inghinidhe, only coming to light in 1959. It was published by Arlen House in 1986, but is now out of print, despite its value as a critique of the Land War and an affirmation of women's involvement in it.

Anna Parnell died on 20 September 1911, in a drowning incident off the Devon coast. In a poem published in 1905 she had written these bleak lines:

Middle Age
I am longing to be gone,
Though my years are not two score,
Though my course is but half-run,
I've no wish to travel more.[49]

In the hectic period before the Easter Rising, the struggle by nationalist women for inclusion revived the conflicts of the Land League era. Anna Parnell, when visiting Ireland, had spoken to the new wave of activists and had made sure they knew of her work and of the fate of that past generation of women. Six months before the Rising, Constance Markievicz, in her outspoken fashion, gave a lecture that was a very clear summary of the past history of women, the problems they faced and her advice on how this could be changed. She talked about how the Ladies' Land League, founded by Anna Parnell:

> . . . promised better things. When the men leaders were all imprisoned it ran the movement and started to do the militant things that the men only threatened and talked of, but when the men came out, they proceeded to discard the women – as usual – and disbanded the Ladies' Land League. That was the last of women in nationalist movements, down to our time.[50]

Feminists too have a claim to the legacy of the Ladies' Land League. Father Eugene Sheehy, the 'Land League priest', a strong supporter of Anna Parnell, was also the beloved uncle and mentor of Hanna Sheehy Skeffington, who would become Ireland's best known campaigner for women's suffrage. Her earliest memory 'as a chit of four' was visiting her uncle in Kilmainham Gaol. Father Eugene later encouraged his niece to write a history of the 'illustrious ladies of the land'.[51] In 1912, before her first prison sentence, Hanna made a speech in which she declared she was part of a tradition that included women's defiance of landlordism in Land League times. Now, however, women in the suffrage movement were resorting to violence 'on their own behalf'.[52] This was the feminist response to the troubled history of the Ladies' Land League.

In considering the legacy of Anna Parnell, we have to start with the uncompromising way she destabilised gender categories by her insistence that women had an equal right to participate in the public sphere. Male politicians could never forgive her and tried to ensure that women remained subordinates in future movements. For her part, she struggled to impart the harsh lessons of her experience. She has an honoured place in the history of women in Ireland for that insistence on women's agency. Her history deserves to be much better known than it actually is.

Notes

1   Sarah Benton, 'The Militarisation of Politics in Ireland 1912–23', *Feminist Review* 1995, vol. 50, pp 148–72 at p. 149.

2   Danae O'Regan, 'Anna and Fanny Parnell', *History Ireland*, vol. 7, no. 1, Spring 1999, pp 37–41 at p. 41.

3   Ibid., p.39.

4   For further biographical information, see Jane McL. Côté, *Fanny and Anna Parnell: Ireland's Patriot Sisters* (London, 1991).

5   Martha Vicinus, 'Fin-de-Siecle Theatrics: male impersonation and lesbian desire', in B. Melman (ed.), *Borderlines* (New York and London), p. 179.

6   Katharine Tynan, *Twenty-Five Years: Reminiscences* (New York, 1913), p. 83.

7   Quoted in the *Irish World*, 1 July, 1882.

8   Ibid.

9   Anna Parnell, 'How They Do in the House of Commons: Notes from the Ladies' Cage', *Celtic Monthly*, May–July 1880.

10   Ibid.

11   Beverly Schneller, *Anna Parnell's Political Journalism: contexts and text* (Bethesda, 2005), p. 79.

12   Anna Parnell, Notes from the Ladies' Cage.

13   Côté, *Fanny and Anna Parnell*, p. 96

14   Ibid., p. 95.

15   Margaret Ward, *Unmanageable Revolutionaries: Women and Irish nationalism* (London, 1983), pp 4–39 for a chronology of events.

16   Quoted in Côté, *Fanny and Anna Parnell*, p. 167.

17   *Irish World*, 2 Apr. 1881.

18   *Belfast Newsletter*, 15 Mar. 1881.

19   *Cork Herald*, 8 Aug. 1881.

20   'An enemy's sketch of Miss Anna Parnell', in *London Truth*, 1882, quoted in Schneller, *Anna Parnell's Political Journalism*, p. 240.

21   *Irish World*, 8 Apr. 1882.

22   To give an example from one source, the Irish-American paper the *Irish World*, particularly the reports of Henry George. The 11 Feb. 1882 edition gives reports of 77 evictions and 37 prosecutions, stating 'the ladies are more active and defiant than ever.'

23   The Mitchelstown eviction occurred in Aug. 1882, see Côté *Fanny and Anna Parnell*, p. 194.

24   Fanny Parnell, 'Ireland, Mother', Nov. 1880, in R. F. Foster, *Charles Stewart Parnell: the Man and his Family*, (Sussex, 1976), p. 254.

25   *Irish World*, 12 Mar. 1881, at a meeting in Claremorris.

26   O'Regan, 'Anna and Fanny Parnell', p. 41.

27   *Freeman's Journal*, 12 Mar. 1881.

28   Anna Parnell, *The Tale of a Great Sham* (Dana Hearne (ed.)), (West Sussex, 1986 edn), p. 93.

29   Ibid., p. 151.

30 Quoted inWard, *Unmanageable Revolutionaries* pp 28–9.

31 Côté, *Fanny and Anna Parnell*, p. 217.

32 Michael Davit, *The Fall of Feudalism in Ireland*, (London, 1904) p. 349.

33 Anna Parnell, *The Tale*, p. 155.

34 Henry George to Helen Taylor, 1 Oct. 1882, vol. xvii, item 81, Mill-Taylor Collection, London School of Economics and Political Science.

35 Jessie Craigen to Helen Taylor, 19 Aug. 1882, vol. xviii, item 71, Mill-Taylor Collection, London School of Economics and Political Science.

36 *Irish World*, 12 Aug. 1882.

37 *United Ireland*, 12 Aug. 1882.

38 *Irish World*, 12 Aug. 1882.

39 O'Regan, 'Anna and Fanny Parnell', p.41.

40 *Irish World*, 5 Aug. 1882.

41 Anna Parnell, *The Tale*, p. 164.

42 *Gaelic American*, 29 Dec. 1906, report of correspondence between Anna Parnell and Máire de Buitléir, reprinted from the *Irish Peasant*.

43 Ibid.

44 Mary Butler, 'Irish Women and the Home Language', in *The Field Day Anthology of Irish Writing* vol. 5: Irish Women's Writings and Traditions (Cork, 2002) p. 85.

45 Foster, *Parnell*, p. 283–4.

46 Anna Parnell to Helen Taylor, Dublin, November 1886, vol. xviii, item 82, Mill-Taylor Collection, London School of Economics and Political Science.

47 Anna Parnell to Helena Moloney, 7 July 2010, in Ward, *Unmanageable Revolutionaries*, p. 265.

48 Hearne (ed.), *Tale of a Great Sham*, p. 32.

49 Quoted in Côté, *Fanny and Anna Parnell*, p. 261.

50 Constance Markievicz, *Irish Citizen*, 23 Oct. 1915, in Margaret Ward (ed.), *In Their Own Voice: Women and Irish Nationalism*, (Dublin, 1995), pp 46–7.

51 Margaret Ward, *Hanna Sheehy Skeffington: a life* (Cork, 1997), p. 4.

52 Ibid., p. 85.

CHAPTER 4

Parnell and Religion

Pauric Travers

Well, sir, I was myself born a Protestant, I have lived a Protestant, and I hope to die a Protestant.[1]

Parnell was a Protestant who led a nationalist movement that was predominantly Catholic. What was his attitude to religion? Drawing on the evidence of his words and actions during his public career, this chapter will explore that question and the impact of Parnell's own family background. It is often assumed that Parnell had no personal religious convictions and that his Protestantism was nominal and little more than an accident of birth. The chapter will challenge that assumption and suggest that Parnell's religious views deserve more attention than they have received.

In his article 'Parnell and the Catholic Church' in Boyce and O'Day's centenary collection *Parnell in Perspective*, Dr Christopher Woods concludes unambiguously:

Parnell's Protestantism was purely social. As a boy he questioned religion and as squire of Avondale he never read the lesson in church. Tolerant of the religious beliefs of others, *he was himself an unbeliever* [my emphasis].[2]

As his title suggests, Woods' article is concerned primarily not with Parnell's religious convictions but with his political relations with the Catholic clergy. His comment on Parnell's beliefs is in the nature of a passing reference. However it is striking in its certitude. He cites as his sources for this definitive statement Parnell's brother, John Howard, Katharine O'Shea and William O'Brien – although, some of this evidence is less than conclusive. In weighing its reliability one must go back to Parnell's own words, including his declaration in the House of Commons in January 1886 which forms the epigraph to this chapter. These words provide a somewhat different perspective and suggest the need to look again at the available evidence with a more critical – dare one say 'agnostic' eye.

One of the paradoxes of Irish historiography is that while the importance of religion is widely accepted, relatively little has been written about it. Insofar as historians have addressed the subject, they have tended to concentrate on the admittedly fascinating inter-section of religion and politics – for example the role of the churches in nationalist politics, and the bishops and Parnell. Less attention has been devoted to the social and personal dimension of religion. In particular, almost nothing has been written on what it meant to be a Protestant in the late nineteenth century.

Parnell's social Protestantism, to use Christopher Woods' term, is undoubted. By background and context, the Parnell's were middling gentry of Anglo-Irish stock, steeped in a liberal Protestant tradition. Roy Foster, in particular, has sketched the social *milieu* into which the Parnell's fitted in Wicklow.[3] If the dominant tradition in Wicklow Protestantism was conservative and 'rigidly Unionist' in politics, the Parnells were on the liberal wing. One ancestor, Thomas Parnell (1679–1717) – the poet – was a clergyman. Another, John Parnell, opposed the Act of Union, *inter alia*, because of the damage it would do to relations between Protestant and Catholic. His son Henry supported Catholic emancipation in the House of Commons. Another son, William, Parnell's grandfather, wrote a pamphlet entitled *Historical apology for Irish Catholics*, a sympathetic treatment of, among other issues, inter-denominational religious conflict.[4] It is clear that the Parnell family tradition, as Lyons has suggested, was marked by a number of features, one of which was 'sympathy [for] the wellbeing of the Catholic population which surrounded their little islands of Protestantism'.[5]

While the Parnells were undoubtedly part of the Protestant mainstream, they did show some propensity to stray from what Lyons called 'the Anglican *via media*'.[6] The 'little islands of Protestantism' in Wicklow were strongly influenced by the evangelical revival, a conservative strand within the Anglican Church characterised by a distrust of ritual and clericalism, a sense of sin and an emphasis on scripture as the surest guide to salvation.[7] The Plymouth Brethren also attracted significant support in Wicklow. Lady Powerscourt, Parnell's aunt Catherine, her husband George Vicesimus Wigram and her cousin John Parnell (Lord Congleton) all converted to the Brethren. The Brethren (known as Darbyites in Ireland after John Nelson Darby, a Wicklow curate) grew rapidly from the late 1820s. They rejected traditional symbols and a salaried ministry; there was a strong emphasis on fellowship rather than membership, and meeting together in the name of Jesus Christ, without reference to denominational differences – early meetings included Christians from different denominations.[8]

All this formed a backdrop for the formative years of the Parnell children. While Anna and Charles Stewart Parnell in particular were critical of established religion and rejected evangelicalism, it did have some influence on their development. Parnell later spoke highly of the Plymouth Brethren on at least two occasions – once when he confided to T. P. O'Connor that he was attracted by their 'quietness'; and again at Plymouth in June 1886, during an election campaign, when he recalled with 'the greatest reverence, affection and respect' the 'excellent teaching' he received at his first school in Yeovil, Somerset which was then a Plymouth Brethren school. On the latter occasion, he cited the Brethren in support of the cause of religious toleration.[9]

Charles Stewart Parnell's religious formation, like his education, was intermittent and eclectic. The Parnell children were strictly required to honour the Sabbath day and attended service in Rathdrum.[10] In a family memoir written in 1880, his mother Delia stated that 'religiously my son was a Protestant' and that particular pains were taken to place him 'with manifestly kind and religious people'.[11] He was certainly well versed in Christian doctrine and scripture – whether from Wicklow or Yeovil or Reverend Barton's school at Kirk Langley in Derbyshire. His later political speeches feature numerous religious references and biblical imagery. While it would be wrong to draw too many conclusions about his own religious convictions from such speeches, in particular bearing in mind the need for a political speaker to communicate in language with which his audience is comfortable, the religious references and imagery of Parnell's speeches is striking.

Speaking about the values of self-determination and self-reliance at Tipperary on 21 September 1879, Parnell said 'I feel as convinced of this as of God's existence or my own'.[12] Urging tenants to 'stand fast by their homesteads' in Galway on 2 November, he spoke of Providence having placed 'at your hand an opportunity of securing for yourselves and for your children, and the future of all Irishmen, justice, happiness and prosperity.'[13] In Chicago, in January 1880, he invoked God's help for their struggle'. At Thurles, on 23 March 1880, he described the land question in biblical terms:

> Our people after having passed through a night of terrible length and darkness are at length beginning to see the dawn of day – they are beginning to understand that the land of Ireland was not given to a few men for their benefit, but that it rightfully belongs to those who by their labour have sanctified it, cultivated it, and made it fruitful. If we have courage to stand by these Divine truths we shall win our battle.[14]

In July 1880, speaking in the House of Commons on the Bradlaugh case, he said 'His religion, however, taught him (Mr Parnell) to be just and fear not'.[15] At Ennis in September, he referred to boycotting as 'a more Christian and charitable way'.[16] On another occasion he said it would be easier to get a camel through the eye of a needle than get an evicted tenant reinstated by Gladstone.[17]

Much of the language of the land struggle, including the dominant hold the harvest theme, was strongly religious in tone: the fruits of labour were due to the labourer; their struggle, which was in the nature of a crusade, was 'to make the condition of the labouring classes very much more tolerable and very much more what it should be in a Christian country.'[18] At Tipperary in October 1880, Parnell said:

> When you have a good harvest, then is the time to hold it. You had not had anything to hold last year, and perhaps the necessity for exertion was not so great as to-day. The people of Ireland have at last come to that. When they have sown the seed and reaped the harvest it is their duty also to look after themselves, their wives, and their children.[19]

At Dungannon, on 1 September 1881, he referred to the supporters of Irish nationalist movements through the ages as 'disciples'.[20]

At the time of the Home Rule crisis of 1886, Parnell's speeches again took on a strong religious flavour. On a number of occasions he spoke of the nation's destiny in biblical terms. He looked forward to 'a settlement which will be a lasting one and a final one, which will enable our people to go forward as a nation amongst the nations of the world in the task of regenerating our country, of developing our resources, and of attaining to that position for which, I believe, God has destined her.'[21]

Later still at the time of the Split, Parnell's language became even more strongly biblical: at Thurles, in January 1891, he spoke of the necessity to separate the wheat from the chaff.[22] His favourite image of this time is that of the 'Promised Land' used in Committee Room 15 and in several subsequent speeches – the choice offered to the electorate was of indefinitely wandering through the wilderness or of reaching the promised land. Parnell casts himself in the role of Moses whose leadership is central to the progress of the Irish people.[23] At Athenry, on 31 January 1891, Parnell recalled a prayer from his youth: 'I think there is no more beautiful prayer in the language than that which we sometimes address to the Almighty to have mercy on all slaves and captives!'[24]

Clearly Parnell's speeches reflect a background which was Christian and specifically Protestant. Sometimes he spoke explicitly as a Protestant. In the House of Commons in March 1879, Parnell denied the suggestion by the English MP Lord Claud Hamilton that large sections of the Irish people were bigoted:

I stand here as a sample of this – and I bear testimony to the fact that I, a Protestant, a member of the disestablished Church of Ireland, and a member of the Synod, represent the Catholics of Meath.[25]

The nature of social Protestantism and the social and political context of Parnell's Wicklow were changing rapidly in the second half of the nineteenth century with the emergence of the Home Rule movement and the tide flowing towards democratisation at both local and national level. Parnell identified the two most significant changes impacting on relations between Catholics and Protestants as disestablishment of the Church of Ireland in 1869 and the land agitation. Resolution of the latter would, he predicted, allow a new era of harmony. He told a meeting of the Irish Parliamentary Party in Dublin in 1880:

There is another and a greater reason why I think that land reformers ought to strike at the root of the land evil: that is, the system of landlordism. I speak now from the national point of view in the highest sense of the word. There can be no doubt that one of the reasons, and the greatest reason, next to the religious question, which now I hope no longer exists, the greatest reason why the upper, and many of the middle classes in Ireland – I speak more especially of the Protestant body, to which I belong myself – have remained aloof from the National operations of Ireland, and have refused to give them assistance, has been the institution of landlordism. You cannot expect the landlords of Ireland to strike for the rights of Ireland as long as you supply them with every inducement for the maintenance of the English system of government here by upholding this land system.[26]

Interestingly, given his own education, Parnell from the outset was a defender of denominational education and favoured the maintenance of religious schools and the establishment of a Catholic University.[27] Unlike Michael Davitt, who was a strong advocate of State-run, non-denominational schooling, Parnell supported the orthodox Catholic position, whether because of personal conviction or pragmatic politics. Speaking in a debate on Professors in Mixed Colleges and Universities in 1879, he declared:

Roman Catholics were entitled to their own opinions, and it was not to be expected that though the House might assimilate the system of education, Catholics could conscientiously send their children to mixed colleges . . . The system in Oxford and Cambridge was most sectarian, and he did not see how it was possible with a great variety of branches of knowledge, that teaching could be conducted from any other than a religious point of view. Were they going to have no history at all taught in their universities? Were they going to have no theological or divinity schools in order that they might carry out their peculiar ideas as to university education in

Ireland? He said, by all means let the freethinker's children be taught in accordance with the freethinker's wish, but that the children of Roman Catholic parents be taught in accordance with their wish, and the children of Protestant parents in accordance with theirs.[28]

Parnell's attitude to and relationship with Catholicism is interesting. Clearly much of the impact of his political movement came from his pragmatic engagement with the Catholic clergy and hierarchy. While that alliance only emerged slowly, blew hot and cold throughout the 1880s and ultimately collapsed after the split, it is fair to say that Parnell had no difficulty, politically or personally, in forging such a relationship. Although he was viewed with suspicion by some, he enjoyed warm, personal relations with many Catholic clergymen and, albeit temporarily, even some of the bishops. Even at the height of the split when the full weight of clerical censure and disapproval was unleashed against him, he remained remarkably mild in his statements about the Catholic clergy and restrained in his public utterances about clerical interference.

In the Carlow by-election of 1891 for instance, the Parnellites first action on arrival in the constituency was to seek to enlist the support of sympathetic clergy.[29] When Parnell himself visited Bagnalstown on 3 July, he called first on Fr O'Neill, an outspoken supporter who signed the nomination papers of the Parnellite candidate. He then visited the local Presentation Convent.[30] Despite provocation Parnell personally went out of his way to speak highly of the clergy. He rebuked colleagues, including his own candidate Andrew Kettle who criticised the bishops, and avoided open attacks on them himself.[31] Speaking at a meeting in Carlow on the day of the publication of the Irish bishops' statement condemning his continued leadership, Parnell defended their right to pronounce on the moral question albeit belatedly, but accused them of going beyond the moral issue.[32] In Bagnalstown two days later he said:

> I have received many kindnesses from the priests of Ireland from time to time and no matter how some amongst them may revile me and seek to provoke me at this moment, I shall never say one unkind word of any of them as long as I live (cheers). I know the quality of my colleagues who have stood by me. I know what they are made of, and I know, as you know, that there are amongst them good, honest, and fervent Catholics (hear, hear). I cannot say quite the same of some of the seceders (groans).[33]

Nor was this simply pragmatism, born of necessity. Parnell's public attitude to Catholicism was consistently tolerant, indeed sympathetic. Recalling their decision to have their first child, Sophie Claude baptised as a Catholic in 1882 on the grounds that it would be safer – as far as the outside world was concerned, the child was Captain O'Shea's – Katharine O'Shea added that Parnell 'had no feeling at all against the Catholic religion, considering, indeed, that, for those who required a religion it was an admirable one.'[34] Andrew Kettle in his memoir went even further, suggesting that Parnell secretly admired the Catholic religion and speculating that he might have converted to Catholicism – he provides no specific evidence for this wishful thinking other than that while Parnell was in Kilmainham he expressed an interest in going to mass with his fellow prisoners.[35] The motivation for such an action might have been mere curiosity or solidarity or pragmatic politics – although coincidentally it was at precisely this time that Sophie Claude was born. If he ever expressed a desire to attend mass, he doesn't seem to have followed through on it and the basis for casting him as a nineteenth century Tony Blair seems shaky at best.

Kettle also recounts an encounter during the Carlow by-election between Parnell and a Protestant clergyman, Revd McCree who tried to persuade Parnell to withdraw from the contest. By Kettle's account, Parnell rounded on the clergyman in the strongest terms:

> . . . I must deny your right to interfere in this matter at all. When I was at college I had opportunities of seeing men of your Church and of your cloth, preparing for their profession, and I must say they were no better than they should be, morally or otherwise. But it is altogether different with the Catholic clergy. A Catholic clergyman has to undergo a most severe and searching course of discipline. He has to take a vow of celibacy, and deny himself gratifications that are freely indulged in by Protestant clergymen. I do not blame the Catholic clergy for the part they are taking in this disagreeable dispute, but I altogether deny your right to interfere. Good day, Mr McCree.[36]

How much of this is Parnell and how much Kettle is impossible to establish.

Parnell's role in the infamous Bradlaugh case, one of the most notorious and protracted controversies of Victorian England, is revealing.[37] Born in 1833, Charles Bradlaugh was well known as an atheist and free-thinker. He was editor of the secularist newspaper, the *National Reformer* when it was prosecuted for blasphemy and sedition. In 1877, Bradlaugh and Annie Besant published *The Fruits of Philosophy*, a pamphlet by the American birth-control campaigner, Charles Knowlton which offered the neo-Malthusian solution of early marriage and birth-control to over-population, poverty and social problems.[38] They were charged with publishing material 'likely to deprave or corrupt'. At their trial, the prosecutor Hardinge Gifford, described Knowlton's work as 'a dirty, filthy book, and the test of it is that no human being would allow that book on his table, no decent educated English husband would allow even his wife to have it.'[39] In their defence, Bradlaugh and Besant argued that it was more moral to prevent conception than to murder children after birth through lack of food, clothing or fresh air. They were found guilty of publishing an obscene libel and sentenced to six months imprisonment. This sentence was later quashed by the Court of Appeal in February 1878.[40]

Besant proceeded to write and publish her own book, *The Law of Population*, advocating birth control, while Bradlaugh cashed in on his public notoriety by standing for parliament. He was elected MP for Northampton in 1880 but was expelled from the House when he refused to take the oath as he was an atheist. Bradlaugh offered to affirm rather than take the religious oath but this was refused. His case became, and remained for several years, a *cause célèbre*: when he attempted to take his seat, Bradlaugh was imprisoned for a time in the Clock Tower of the Houses of Parliament. The Northampton seat was later declared vacant but Bradlaugh contested and won it again on four successive occasions. A public petition in his favour attracted hundreds of thousands of signatures. Advocates of free speech including Gladstone and George Bernard Shaw rallied to his side, while he was vigorously opposed by the Conservative party, the Archbishop of Canterbury and leading Anglican and Roman Catholic clergymen. In 1883, Bradlaugh again attempted to take his seat but was fined for voting illegally. A bill allowing him to affirm was defeated. In 1886, he was allowed to take the oath as a matter of form but risked prosecution for so doing – the controversy was finally resolved in his favour shortly afterwards when an Act allowing members the right of affirmation was passed.

Parnell's role in all of this is revealing. Much to the surprise of commentators and against the advice of his colleagues, he voted in Bradlaugh's favour in successive divisions in 1880 on his admission and on his possible imprisonment, and ostentatiously shook his hand when he was arrested by the Sergeant at Arms. In response to an appeal from a colleague, Parnell insisted that although he abhorred Bradlaugh's views, particularly on birth control, he was disgusted by the bigotry of his opponents. These opponents included most of Parnell's colleagues, the Irish Catholic bishops and the nationalist press who saw Bradlaugh as an infidel. The *Freeman's Journal* condemned Bradlaugh as a 'blatant, brazen, howling Atheist'.[41] With feelings running high, a 'civil war among Irish members' threatened.[42] In the event only a handful followed Parnell's lead in supporting Bradlaugh.[43] Frank Hugh O'Donnell, who led the anti-Bradlaugh campaign, claimed that the Irish votes were decisive in defeating Bradlaugh and that it was a crucial and ultimately fatal moment in Parnell's career: the bishops were already suspicious of Parnell – he had associated with known anti-clericals in France and welcomed Georges Clemenceau, radical politician and later prime minister of France, to the House of Commons. His actions now were looked on with 'frank detestation' by the bishops. 'If the bishops had confidence in Parnell,' he argued, 'even the sin of the flesh would have met with more pity than anger.'[44]

Parnell's speeches in the House of Commons debate on the committal of Mr Bradlaugh are particularly revealing. On 29 June 1880, he defended Bradlaugh and responded in particular to his Irish critics:

> He could not believe that the Irish constituencies would desire their members to vote for the imprisonment of anybody. They knew the last time that motion was made it was against the late William Smith O'Brien, who was taken to the place to which he supposed the hon. member for Northampton would be taken. . . . He would conclude, as he had begun, by saying that he did not believe the Irish constituencies would wish even an atheist imprisoned.[45]

On 1 July, he returned to the subject in a long and memorable contribution in which he forthrightly addressed Irish Catholic objections:

> His religion, however, taught him (Mr Parnell) to be just and fear not, and although a man might be placed under a temporary cloud, or a temporary disqualification, he thought and felt convinced that in the long run if he acted according to the just dictates of his conscience every right-thinking man at home and abroad would ultimately come to his support . . .

> An appeal had been made to Catholic Ireland. They had been told that that little island was the last country that had resisted the inroads of Continental infidelity, and that unless they desired that that odious thing should creep into Ireland, they must keep Mr Bradlaugh out of the House. Well, that surely seemed to indicate a fear on the part of the Irish Catholics that their religion might be injured by Mr Bradlaugh's introduction into the House, but were they entitled really to look at it from that point of view? Were they as Catholics entitled to say, 'Because we are Catholics we object to Mr Bradlaugh?' They must recollect that exactly the same argument was used against their own admission. They were Catholics deprived of their civil rights for centuries. Why were they deprived from coming into that House? It was because Protestants feared that the admission of Catholics would injure the Protestant religion, and it was because the majority of Protestants began to see that even if they had that fear, it was an unworthy fear – a fear that they ought not to allow to influence them in considering the civil rights of their fellow-men – that Catholics were at last admitted to the same civil and religious rights as Protestants.

Parnell concluded by nailing his colours to the mast of civil and religious liberty:

They must never forget that in dealing with this subject if they once admit the principle that they were entitled to object to a man because his doctrines were likely to injure their religion, they struck at the very root of civil and religious liberty, and that was why he felt it his duty to do that which was perfectly odious to him. It was a personally odious task for him to undertake to vote for the admission of the member for Northampton, Mr Bradlaugh, to that House, but if he had to walk through that lobby by himself he should feel himself a coward if he refused to do so.[46]

Parnell had met Bradlaugh on a number of occasions. He was known to be 'a strong friend of Ireland'[47] with a record of support for Irish causes including land reform, amnesty for Fenian prisoners and a sympathy for Irish radicals. However, in his assessment of Parnell's stance, Walter Arnstein rejects the view that it was an attempt to woo English or Irish radicals.[48] Given the unpopularity of his actions with his colleagues and with Catholic opinion, there is no reason to suppose that Parnell's actions were not primarily motivated by genuine conviction. Any gloss attaching to his stature as a result is somewhat tarnished by the fact that he voted against an affirmation bill introduced by Gladstone in 1883 which would have allowed Bradlaugh to take his seat. By then Parnell's party had gathered force and focus, at least partly due to the public support of the Catholic clergy. The affirmation bill was strongly resisted by the Catholic bishops who signed a petition against it. On this occasion, it would appear, Parnell wrestled with his conscience and lost; or, at least, pragmatism – some would say opportunism – won out over principle. In his biography of Parnell, Lyons concludes reasonably: 'To vote against the Affirmation Bill was probably repugnant to him as an independent-minded, free-thinking individual, but as a politician seeking to consolidate the forces of the right in his own country he could scarcely avoid it.'[49]

In fairness, Parnell's commitment to civil and religious liberty, to freedom of conscience and to religious toleration was sincere and consistent. It was a personal commitment that sprang from his background – but it also represented in many cases a pragmatic response to the situation in which he found himself as the Protestant leader of an increasingly Catholic movement. He was repeatedly called on to explain how the interests of the Protestant minority would be protected in a Home Rule Ireland. He insisted that once the land question was resolved, the remaining source of friction would be removed and the minority would identify with the wider national. He told the House of Commons in January 1886:

We have been spoken to to-night about the necessity of protecting the loyal minority. Well, sir, I was myself born a Protestant, I have lived a Protestant, and I hope to die a Protestant, and if in the future, after the concession of the Irish claims, any danger were to arise to my Protestant fellow-countrymen, I should be the first to stand up for that liberty of speech and that liberty of conscience, and liberty to live and thrive of every section of the community, whether they were Protestants or whether they were Catholics; and perhaps I may be a more effectual aid to them in times of real danger than some of those gentlemen who talk so loudly and boast so much.[50]

Parnell asserted that if a Home Rule Parliament passed laws which were oppressive of the minority, it would deserve to lose its power. In a speech at Plymouth in June 1886, shortly after the defeat of the Home Rule Bill, he was at pains to reassure the Protestant minority:

They will get abundance of fair play, and they know it well enough; and if fair play were wanting on the part of the majority of Irishmen then I say it should be just and right, if Irishmen so far forgot the honour of their country and the public opinion of the world as to revert to the bigoted and sectarian oppression of the Middle Ages, then I say it would be just and right for Englishmen to step in and take away this great privilege which Irishmen would then be proved to have abused.[51]

This was a recurring theme. In Tralee, in January 1891, in the aftermath of the divisive Kilkenny election, he struck the same note:

Another great difficulty is not English public opinion, but it is Irish Protestant opinion; and, fellow-countrymen, it is of the utmost importance that we should do everything we reasonably can to assuage the alarms of those men who live amongst us in every quarter of Ireland, in greater or lesser numbers, to give them every guar-antee that is possible that they will not be injured in property or sentiment when Ireland recovers the right to rule herself – and not only to give this assurance and guarantee, but to abstain from any action tending to show that any section of the Irish electors allow any religious body to influence their opinions.[52]

Later that year, in his famous Ulster Hall speech, Parnell declared that it was 'the duty of the majority to leave no stone unturned, no means unused, to conciliate the reasonable and unreasonable prejudices of the minority' and concluded that Ireland could never enjoy perfect freedom as long as a min-ority consider that their spiritual or temporal interests were threatened.[53] This recourse to the language of conciliation has been interpreted by Paul Bew as a new departure on Parnell's part at a time of crisis.[54] However, the message recurs throughout his career. In August 1891, in one of his last speeches, Parnell spoke of the need 'in tranquilising the fears of the Protestant section' and to demonstrate to the world that while Ireland 'desires freedom above all things, Ireland also desires to use that freedom with toleration to all.'[55] As well as opportunism, Parnell has been accused by Lyons and others of lacking any real understanding of Ulster Unionism. However, as I have suggested elsewhere, his analysis of the religious and economic fears of Ulster Protestants is perceptive from the perspective of his own time and his vision of an independent Ireland shaped by the balance of the social and religious forces within it is relatively far-sighted.[56]

A central argument in Paul Bew's new biography of Parnell, *Enigma: A New Life of Charles Stewart Parnell* is that Parnell was concerned about the place of Irish Protestants in national life and that this is a neglected clue to his political career.[57] It seems clear that Parnell had a genuine and long-standing commitment to religious toleration. His own personal religious convictions are less clear. Although he abandoned formal worship, displayed a certain scepticism about organised religion and had periods of doubt, it would be difficult to sustain Christopher Woods' claim that he was an unbeliever. Walter Arnstein concluded that it was 'difficult to ascertain Parnell's own religious views'.[58] Parnell's colleagues provide contradictory evidence. T. P. O'Connor recalled that he had told him that he had religious faith, 'he once had, lost it, but that it had come back again.'[59] In contrast, Frank Hugh O'Donnell, not a particularly reliable source, claimed that Parnell once told him that he believed 'the Church to have been the constant enemy of human progress in every country and in every age.'[60] Katharine O'Shea, one of the sources relied on by Woods, said that:

> Parnell had no religious conviction of creed and dogma, but he had an immense reverence, learnt, I think, from the Irish peasantry, for any genuine religious conviction. He personally believed in a vast and universal law of 'attraction', of which the elemental forces of Nature were part and the whole of which tended towards some unknown and unknowable, end in immensely distant periods of time. The world, he considered, was but a small part of the unthinkably vast 'whole' through which the 'Spirit' (the soul) of man passed towards the fulfilment of its destiny in the completion of 'attraction'. Of a first 'Cause' and a predestined 'End' he was convinced, though he believed their attributes to be unknown and unknowable.[61]

When Parnell died, he was buried at Glasnevin, under the great Comedian's tomb – in a cemetery closely associated with Catholic Ireland – rather than at Mount Jerome, the family graveyard. The ceremony included a short service at St Michan's parish church (where Parnell's grandfather and great-grandfather are said to be buried) conducted by Revd Thomas Long, rector and Revd George Frye. Apparently it had not initially occurred to the funeral organisers that the family might wish to have a religious ceremony, itself a comment on their perception of Parnell's convictions. At

Glasnevin, later in the day, the funeral rites of the Church of Ireland were performed by Reverend Vincent, chaplain of the Rotunda and Reverend Frye who read the first letter of Paul to the Thessalonians.

Writing after Parnell's death, Katharine O'Shea recalled a conversation she had had with him:

> . . . Parnell again spoke to me of his belief that the soul after death resumed life in the planet under whose influence it was born. He spoke of his belief in a personal destiny and fate, against which it was useless for mortals to contend or fight and how he believed that certain souls had to meet and become one, till in death the second planet life parted them until the sheer longing for one another brought them together again in after ages. (On the day of Parnell's death, October 6, 1891, a new planet was discovered.)[62]

Notes

1 House of Commons, 21 Jan. 1886, see Jennie Wyse-Power, *Words of the Dead Chief* (Dublin, 2009 edn), p. 108.

2 C. J. Woods, 'Parnell and the Catholic church', in D. George Boyce and Alan O'Day (eds), *Parnell in Perspective* (London, 1991), p. 9.

3 R. F. Foster, *Charles Stewart Parnell: The Man and his Family* (Sussex, 1976).

4 F. S. L. Lyons, *Charles Stewart Parnell* (London, 1978), pp 16–20.

5 Ibid., p. 23.

6 Ibid., p. 19.

7 Jane McL. Côté, *Fanny and Anna Parnell: Ireland's Patriot Sisters* (London, 1991), p. 32.

8 There have been some undocumented suggestions that the building at Avondale currently used as a conference centre (adjoining the 'big shed') was formerly used as a meeting room for the Brethren.

9 T. P. O'Connor, *Life of Charles Stewart Parnell: A Memory* (London, 1891), pp 170–1; Wyse-Power, *Words*, p. 114; *The Times*, 28 June 1886.

10 See for example, John Howard Parnell, *Charles Stewart Parnell: A Memoir* (London, 1916), p. 23.

11 Delia Parnell memoir sent to TD Sullivan, 21 Jan. 1880, Sullivan Papers, National Library of Ireland Ms 8237(6), p. 5; Robert M. McWade, *The Uncrowned King: The Life and Public Services of Hon. Charles Stewart Parnell* (Philadelphia, 1891), p. 50; Foster, *Parnell*, p. 76.

12 Wyse-Power, *Words*, pp 32–3.

13 Ibid., p. 35.

14 Ibid., pp 37, 43.

15 Ibid., p. 48.

16 Ibid., pp 48–9, 50.

17 At Kells, 16 Aug. 1891, ibid., p. 166.

18 At Irish Labourer's League, 21 Aug. 1882, ibid., pp 78–9.

19   Ibid., p. 54.

20   Ibid., p. 62.

21   At a banquet in London, 8 Sept. 1886, ibid., p. 117.

22   Ibid., p. 147.

23   Ibid., p. 142.

24   Ibid., p. 150.

25   4 March 1879, ibid., p. 24.

26   18 May 1880, ibid., p. 46.

27   John Howard Parnell, *Memoir*, pp 133–4.

28   14 March 1879, Wyse-Power, *Words*, p. 25.

29   *Freeman's Journal*, 19 June 1891.

30   Ibid., 1 and 2 July 1891.

31   Laurence J. Kettle (ed.), *The Material for Victory: The Memoirs of Andrew J. Kettle*, (Dublin, 1958), p. 96.

32   *Freeman's Journal* 4 June 1891.

33   Ibid., 6 July 1891.

34   Katharine O'Shea, *The Uncrowned King of Ireland* (Stroud, 2005 edn), p. 142.

35   Kettle, *Material for Victory*, p. 96.

36   Ibid., p. 96.

37   For a short account of the Bradlaugh case, see Walter L. Arnstein, 'The Bradlaugh Case: A Reappraisal', *Journal of the History of Ideas*, vol. 18, no. 2, Apr. 1957.

38   Coincidentally, Annie Besant, women's rights campaigner and long-time collaborator with Bradlaugh, was a second cousin of Katharine O'Shea. There is no suggestion that Parnell's attitude to Bradlaugh was influenced in any way by Katharine O'Shea. Katharine does not mention the connection in her book which is not surprising as Besant became something of an outcast in polite society. Both Besant's parents were Irish. She went on to become a socialist and a Fabian – collaborated with Michael Davitt in calling for land nationalisation, organised the famous Bryant & May match-girls strike, became a Theosophist and eventually was a founder of the Indian National Congress. She died in India in 1933. For a contemporary assessment of Besant's outlook and philosophy, see W. T. Stead, 'Annie Besant', *Review of Reviews*, vol. iv, October 1891, pp 349–67.

39   *In the High Court of Justice: Queen's Bench Division' June 18, 1877. The Queen v Charles Bradlaugh and Annie Besant* (London, 1877), p. 251.

40   For the trial of Bradlaugh and Besant, see Sripati Chandrasekhar (ed.), *Reproductive Physiology and Birth Control: The Writings of Charles Knowlton and Annie Besant* (New Brunswick, New Jersey, 2002), pp 26–54.

41   Lyons, *Parnell*, p. 124; *Freeman's Journal*, 22 May 1880; T. P. O'Connor, *Life of Parnell*, pp 90–2.

42   Henry W. Lucy, *A Diary of Two Parliaments* (London, 1886), vol. II, p. 41 cited in Arnstein, 'Parnell and the Bradlaugh case', p. 219.

43   Of the 103 Irish MPs elected in 1880, 63 described themselves as Home Rulers. *Dod's Parliamentary Companion 1880*, cited in Arnstein, 'Parnell and the Bradlaugh case', p. 213.

Frank Hugh O'Donnell says 10 including Parnell supported Bradlaugh, 30 voted against and 20 abstained. F. H. O'Donnell, *History of the Irish Parliamentary Party* (London, 1910), vol. I, p. 493.

44   Ibid., pp 493–4; Jules Abels, *The Parnell Tragedy* (London, 1966), p. 203. For an extended if hostile discussion of Parnell and Bradlaugh, see O'Donnell, *History of the Irish Parliamentary Party*, vol. I, pp 488–94. For a more dispassionate analysis, see Arnstein, 'Parnell and the Bradlaugh case', pp 212–35.

45   23 June 1880, Wyse-Power, *Words*, p. 48.

46   1 July 1880, ibid., pp 48–9.

47   Arnstein, 'Parnell and the Bradlaugh case', p. 218.

48   Ibid., pp 216–7.

49   Lyons, *Parnell*, p. 253.

50   21 Jan. 1886, Wyse-Power, *Words*, p. 108.

51   27 June 1886, ibid., pp 114.

52   18 Jan. 1891, ibid., p. 148.

53   *Northern Whig*, 23 May 1891.

54   Paul Bew, *C. S. Parnell* (Dublin, 1980), pp 127–32; Paul Bew, *Enigma: A New Life of Charles Stewart Parnell*, (Dublin, 2011), pp 129–30.

55   At the National Club, 2 Aug. 1891, Wyse-Power, *Words*, pp 164–5.

56   See Pauric Travers, 'Parnell and the Ulster Question', in Donal McCartney (ed.), *Parnell: The Politics of Power* (Dublin, 1991), pp 57–71.

57   Bew, *C.S. Parnell*, p. 198.

58   Arnstein, 'Parnell and the Bradlaugh case', p. 216.

59   T. P. O'Connor, *Life of Parnell*, pp 170–1.

60   O'Donnell, *Irish Parliamentary Party*, vol. II, pp 324–5.

61   Katharine O'Shea, *Uncrowned King*, p. 274.

62   Ibid., p. 188.

CHAPTER 5

Parnell, Politics and the Press in Ireland 1875–1924[1]

Felix M. Larkin

Charles Stewart Parnell was first elected to parliament in a by-election held on 17 April 1875. Seven days earlier, Sir John Gray had died in Bath. Since 1841, Gray had been proprietor of Dublin's *Freeman's Journal* newspaper. That newspaper now became the property of his son, Edmund Dwyer Gray – Parnell's almost exact contemporary. It remained in the hands of the Gray family throughout Parnell's political career. The *Freeman* was the main nationalist daily newspaper in Ireland in 1875, the only one published in Dublin. It already had a long and chequered history, having been founded in 1763 to support the 'patriot' opposition in the Irish Parliament in College Green. It survived until 1924, albeit in a much weakened state after the Parnell split.[2] This chapter will explore the power and influence of the press, and the nature of journalism, in Ireland in the late nineteenth and early twentieth centuries by reference to Parnell's sometimes troubled relationship with the press – in particular, the *Freeman's Journal* – and by reference also to the effect of the Parnell split on the newspaper market in Dublin.

I shall begin with the aforementioned Sir John Gray – who is probably best known today for his work as a member of Dublin Corporation in bringing the Vartry water supply to the city, for which achievement a statue of him was erected in O'Connell Street, Dublin. A medical doctor and a Protestant, he supported repeal of the Union, and later the Irish Tenant League movement and Church of Ireland disestablishment. He sat as MP for Kilkenny from 1865 until his death in 1875, and had begun to ally himself with Isaac Butt's Home Rule party in the last year of his life. He was close to Cardinal Cullen, and was widely regarded as Cullen's mouthpiece in parliament. Cullen remarked on the occasion of Gray's death: 'He did the Catholics great services but though he did a great deal to pull down the Protestant Church, he had the misfortune to die a Protestant.'[3]

His son, Edmund Dwyer Gray, was also active in politics – and was first elected to parliament in 1877, two years after Parnell. But for Parnell, he might have led the Irish Parliamentary Party at Westminster. To protect his own political prospects, Gray strongly opposed Parnell's rise within the party. He threw the weight of the *Freeman* unsuccessfully against Parnell's candidate in the decisive Ennis by-election of 1879, and he later smeared Parnell by accusing him of having called certain colleagues in the party 'papist rats'.[4] When, after the 1880 general election, Parnell was elected party leader, Gray was one of 18 MPs who voted against him – out of a total of 43. Thereafter, however, he largely supported Parnell's leadership – partly because he accepted that Parnell was now invincible, but also because in 1881 Parnell established his own newspaper, the weekly *United Ireland*, with William O'Brien (later a prominent Irish party MP) as editor. The threat that *United Ireland* might be turned into a daily publication to rival the *Freeman* copper-fastened Gray's loyalty to Parnell.

United Ireland remained under O'Brien's management until the Parnell split – though from November 1887 it was edited by Matthias McDonnell Bodkin, later county court judge for Clare. At the outset of the split, acting on instructions from O'Brien who was in America, Bodkin followed the majority view in the Irish party and steered *United Ireland* into the anti-Parnell camp. He declared his position unequivocally in the issue of 6 December 1890, by which time the party's protracted debate in Committee Room 15 at Westminster on the question of Parnell's continued leadership was drawing to a close and it was abundantly clear what its outcome would be. When Parnell returned to Dublin four days later, the first thing he did was to re-establish his authority over *United Ireland*, forcing his way into its offices with some associates and ejecting Bodkin. One of the Parnellites present described the scene as follows: 'I went up to Matty Bodkin. "Matty", says I, "will you walk out or would you like to be thrown out?" and Matty walked out.'[5] An attempt by anti-Parnellites, led by Tim Healy, to re-occupy the offices failed.

In contrast to *United Ireland*, the *Freeman's Journal* came out strongly in favour of Parnell when the split occurred. Edmund Dwyer Gray had died at the early age of forty-two in 1888, and the paper was now under the control of his widow – a devout, English-born Roman Catholic. She was the daughter and namesake of the philanthropist Caroline Chisholm, celebrated for her work for female emigrants to Australia but caricatured as Mrs Jellyby in Charles Dickens' *Bleak House*.[6] Through the influence of his wife, Edmund Dwyer Gray had converted to Catholicism in 1877. Despite her religious convictions, Mrs Gray was active in her support of Parnell, and even appeared with him in public in Dublin in early 1891 – dressed, according to Archbishop Walsh, in a scarlet cloak. The archbishop subsequently described her as 'a rock of scandal'.[7] However, once the anti-Parnellites launched their own daily newspaper, the *National Press*, in March 1891 and the *Freeman* began as a result to lose circulation and revenue, Mrs Gray wavered.

Her son, representing the third generation of his family associated with the *Freeman*, now enters the story. Also named Edmund Dwyer Gray and aged 21, he had just returned from an extended visit to Australia and was alarmed to find his inheritance at risk. Under his influence, Mrs Gray resolved that the paper should switch sides in the split. This it did in late September 1891, a fortnight before Parnell's unexpected death. The Parnellites then launched the *Irish Daily Independent* to fill the vacuum caused by the *Freeman*'s defection. This, of course, compounded the *Freeman*'s difficulties: it now had two competitors instead of one. The *Freeman* and the *National Press* later merged in March 1892, with Mrs Gray selling her shareholding as part of the deal. In simultaneous transactions, the *Freeman* company bought the *National Press* newspaper for £36,000 and the *National Press* company bought Mrs Gray's shares for exactly the same sum. The *National Press* then ceased publication, and Mrs Gray's shares were distributed to the shareholders of the defunct *National Press* company. There was no role for Mrs Gray's son in the new dispensation; he emigrated to Australia in 1894 and settled in Tasmania, where he became a journalist and politician of note. He was treasurer and deputy premier of Tasmania from 1934 until his death in 1945, except for six months in 1939 when he served as interim premier.[8]

James Joyce has left us a very harsh assessment of the Grays: in his story 'Grace' in *Dubliners*, one of the characters recalls the elder Edmund Dwyer Gray 'blathering away' at the unveiling of his father's statue, and another comments: 'None of the Grays was any good.'[9] However, it was the Grays who made the *Freeman's Journal* an important newspaper. The repeal in the 1850s of the oppressive duty on advertisements and on the newspapers themselves opened the way for a great expansion in the newspaper market. Sir John Gray exploited this opportunity – increasing the circulation of the *Freeman* from between 2,000 and 3,000 copies per day to approximately 10,000. Under his son, Edmund Dwyer Gray, the *Freeman*'s production capacity was further increased; its circulation grew threefold – to 30,000 copies per day – and it became extremely profitable.[10] So successful was it that in 1887 – the year before he died – Edmund converted the *Freeman* into a public company, while retaining control for himself. William O'Brien – who, before becoming editor of *United Ireland*, had been the *Freeman*'s star reporter – later wrote of Edmund Dwyer Gray that he was 'the most enterprising newspaper man Ireland ever produced'.[11]

The Parnell split had a devastating effect on the *Freeman's Journal*. First, the damage inflicted by the *National Press* was huge: the *Freeman*'s circulation fell by a quarter in 1891,[12] and (as already noted) the merger with the

National Press cost it £36,000 – a huge sum, equivalent to £2.5 million sterling today. Secondly, it had to contend with the ongoing competition from the pro-Parnell *Irish Daily Independent*. Parnell himself, in the final weeks of his life, had made arrangements for the establishment of the *Independent*. It first appeared on 18 December 1891, two months after his death. The name of the new paper emphasised that the Parnellites were 'independent' of any alliance with British political parties, whereas their nationalist opponents were tied to Gladstone's Liberal party and had deposed Parnell at the diktat of the Liberals. The *Independent* survived as the organ of the Parnellite wing of the Irish party until the party's reunification under John Redmond in 1900, when it was purchased by William Martin Murphy. In 1905 Murphy transformed the paper into the modern *Irish Independent*, at half the price of the *Freeman* – a halfpenny, instead of a penny – and with a more popular format and a less partisan editorial policy. He copied what Lord Northcliffe had done in London in 1896 when Northcliffe launched the *Daily Mail*, the first mass circulation newspaper in these islands.[13]

Today, the *Independent* rarely acknowledges Parnell as its founder, but instead locates its origin in the changes effected by Murphy in 1905. Even as reputable a journalist as James Downey asserts in his recent autobiography that 'the *Irish Independent* was founded by William Martin Murphy in 1905'.[14] That is simply wrong – but Downey works for the *Independent* and is following its official line. Presumably the reason for the *Independent*'s persistent misrepresentation of its history is its pro-clerical editorial policy under Murphy and, afterwards, under his son and grandson – before it was acquired by Tony O'Reilly in 1973. Its Parnellite origins at the time of the split do not sit comfortably with its later clericalist tradition.

After its merger with the *National Press*, the *Freeman's Journal* operated first as the organ of the anti-Parnell faction of the Irish party and then, after the party came together again in 1900, as the organ of the re-united party. Thomas Sexton MP – the Irish party's foremost financial expert – became chairman of the company in 1893. This proved an unhappy arrangement – at least from the Irish party's perspective – because in 1896 Sexton, disillusioned with the continuing divisions within the party, unexpectedly retired from parliament. Afterwards he seemed to regret his loss of influence and compensated for it by using the *Freeman* to try to impose his will on his erstwhile colleagues. He was increasingly out of sympathy with them, and this was reflected in the *Freeman*. When John Dillon complained about the paper's attitude *circa* 1899, Sexton's reply was that 'the people had lost interest in parliamentary work'.[15] Subsequent events suggest that he was right, and more in touch than the parliamentarians were with public opinion.

Relations worsened with the re-unification of the Irish party in 1900, and in 1903 Sexton and the *Freeman* were in open conflict with the party over the land purchase scheme introduced by the Chief Secretary, George Wyndham. Sexton denounced its financial terms as too generous to the landlords. Unlike Dillon, who had similar misgivings, he was unwilling to moderate his opposition for the sake of party unity or even acknowledge the undoubted benefits of the scheme. After Wyndham's bill passed into law, Dillon joined Sexton and the *Freeman* in challenging the efficacy of seeking further areas of co-operation between the party and the landlords – the so-called policy of 'conciliation'. Their concern was essentially that 'conciliation' would not deliver Home Rule and might even undermine the case for Home Rule. The policy was soon abandoned – its failure attributed by Wyndham, in part at least, to the hostility of the *Freeman*.[16]

Despite his reputed financial expertise, Sexton proved incapable of meeting the challenge to the *Freeman* represented by Murphy's revamped *Irish Independent* after 1905. Because of its tribulations in the 1890s, the *Freeman* lacked funds for investment – and Sexton, afraid of losing control, would not raise new capital. The paper was not, therefore, in a position to take advantage of the growing demand for newspapers in Ireland, as elsewhere, at this time. Total sales of daily newspapers in Ireland grew by a factor of seven between the early 1880s and the 1920s – from 75,000 copies per day in the 1880s to over half a million in the 1920s.[17] However, the *Freeman*'s circulation – at between 30,000 and 35,000 copies per day – remained much the same as it had been under Edmund Dwyer Gray in the 1880s, and was quickly exceeded by the *Independent*.[18] With the consequent loss of advertising, the paper began to incur heavy trading losses and no dividends were paid to its shareholders after 1908.[19]

Sexton hung on as chairman for some time, but early in 1912 the Irish party leaders moved to save the paper and forced his resignation.[20] What finally caused them to act was the fear that, if the *Freeman* failed, the party might be left without press support in Ireland for Asquith's Home Rule Bill. The *Freeman* was subsequently run by a group of party stalwarts and subsidised from party sources.[21] It was no longer commercially viable, and its parlous condition was exacerbated by the destruction of its premises during the 1916 Rising. It was now in a *Pravda*-like relationship with the party, unable to resist interference by them in its affairs – in its reportage, as well as in its editorial policy. It was described *circa* 1916 – in an anonymous memorandum in the Redmond papers – as 'a sort of political bulletin circulating amongst already staunch friends of the Party, and bringing them information and arguments with which they supported the movement and [its] policy'.[22]

The *Freeman*'s decline, and its less-than-wholehearted support for the Irish party during Sexton's chairmanship, were considered key factors in sealing the party's fate. Thus, as early as 1907, John Dillon had written to Redmond that

... the chief weakness of the Party lies in the management of the *Freeman*, and the Freeman is ruining itself as well as injuring the Party by the manner in which it is being managed and edited. It is exceedingly difficult to think of any method of dealing with this problem – and if it is not dealt with effectively, I do not see how the Party is to be maintained and the movement carried on. I do not believe it is possible to maintain the Irish party without some newspaper in Dublin which can be counted on to give it loyal, active and intelligent support.[23]

Ten years later, at a moment of crisis in the financial affairs of the *Freeman*, Dillon expressed the same concern rather more starkly in another letter to Redmond: '[If] the *Freeman* goes . . . with it [goes] the Party and the movement'.[24] His analysis is largely endorsed in the historiography of the Irish party, particularly in the work of F. S. L. Lyons.[25]

Ascribing such political significance to the failings of the *Freeman's Journal* and its possible closure brings into focus the question of just how much power and influence newspapers actually had in this period. There is certainly ample evidence that newspapers, both individually and collectively, were then regarded by politicians and others as of very great importance in creating and moulding public opinion, a concept even more nebulous in those days than now. To bind a newspaper to one's cause was seen as establishing a huge advantage in any political controversy, and politicians and others undoubtedly felt threatened by a hostile press and fearful of the damage it might do. Accordingly, a central theme in the history of the *Freeman*, and its contemporary newspapers, is the relationship between these papers and politicians anxious to secure control over their editorial and reporting output. The tension which characterised that relationship is not unfamiliar to us in the early twenty-first century – but it may seem somewhat extreme. Our sense of the power of newspapers is less acute now. The advent of radio, television and the new electronic media – with their greater immediacy in reporting and commenting upon events – has irrevocably broken the supremacy which newspapers once enjoyed in the field of mass communications.

I want to suggest, however, that the overwhelming influence on public opinion usually attributed to newspapers in the late nineteenth and early twentieth centuries was greatly exaggerated. The history of the *Freeman* demonstrates the limits of that influence. For example, we have seen that, in the late 1870s and early 1880s, the then proprietor, Edmund Dwyer Gray, used the newspaper to oppose Parnell's rise within the Irish party, but was soon whipped into line and forced to accept and support Parnell's leadership. Likewise, the *Freeman* in 1890 at first supported Parnell in the split, but was then constrained to throw in its lot with the anti-Parnellite majority. Also, the *Freeman*'s opposition to Wyndham's Land Act of 1903 failed to stop that measure, or even to undermine the Irish party's support of it. More generally, in the months after the Easter Rising in 1916 the press in Ireland – including the *Freeman* – was united in opposition to the rebels but found itself impotent to stem the tide of public feeling in their favour.

One exception to this pattern is the *Freeman*'s success in destroying the policy of 'conciliation', the attempt in the early 1900s to extend the process of co-operation between the party and the landlords that had brought about Wyndham's Act. In fairness, however, this policy would probably have failed anyhow – because the long-term political aspirations of the two sides were just not reconcilable. There were many subsequent attempts at co-operation between unionists and nationalists – for instance, the Irish Convention of 1917 – and none made much progress. So maybe the *Freeman*'s achievement here is less impressive than it appears at first.

Arthur Griffith wrote in 1902 that the *Freeman's Journal* had 'opposed every national movement until the movement became too strong for it',[26] and that statement – a very fair assessment – reveals the extent of the *Freeman*'s repeated inability to build a consensus for its own political agenda. The newspaper had to respond to the changing mood of the country, not vice versa. That reality was conceded by the *Freeman*'s long-serving editor, John Blake Gallaher – editor from the late 1850s to 1884. When the *Freeman* eventually abandoned its opposition to Parnell in the early 1880s, he is quoted as saying that 'the country is going to the devil, but the *Freeman* is bound to go with the country'.[27] In other words, it had to follow public opinion – or perish. Its influence lay not in leading public opinion and converting its readers to particular causes or points of view, but was confined to defining the terms and the tone of political discourse for the already converted.

It seems to me, therefore, that the power of the press at this time – its clout in the corridors of power – was a function of an exaggerated belief in its capacity to sway public opinion. If this is so, then power was conceded to the press gratuitously, by politicians and others, without much basis in reality. Later generations of politicians would be less obliging. The power of the press was successfully challenged many times in the following years, and long before radio and television reduced its influence. The most famous such challenge – still noteworthy, if only because of a memorable phrase – was in 1931 when Stanley Baldwin spoke about certain British newspaper proprietors seeking 'power without responsibility, the prerogative of the harlot throughout the ages'.[28] I think this *bon mot* should be read not as it usually is – as an irreverent, begrudging affirmation of the strength and importance of newspapers – but, on the contrary, as confirmation that their power was limited and did not necessitate obeisance. Baldwin was signalling that the press could be ignored, even ridiculed, almost with impunity. He said, in effect, that the emperor had no clothes; and, lo and behold, the emperor was less than fully clad.

The power of the press was, however, still unimpaired in the late nine-teenth and early twentieth centuries. Indeed, it probably reached its zenith in Great Britain and Ireland at that time. The press was a crucial factor in political and social life – the words and actions of politicians and others illustrate that. Parnell himself clearly recognised the power of the press. Donal McCartney has pointed out that he was 'very much alive to the impor-tance of the role of the press in getting his speeches accurately reported to the public beyond his immediate audience', and his speeches were rarely longer than would make up a single newspaper column so as to ensure that they were reported in full and not distorted by being abbreviated to fill the space available.[29] Moreover, speaking in August 1891 about the *Freeman*'s imminent defection to the anti-Parnell camp, he said:

> The profession of journalism is a great and powerful one in these days. It is likely to become more influential as the years go by. The readers of newspapers increase from time to time, and the press is becoming ever mightier than the politician . . . In these days politics and journalism run very much together, and a tendency is more and more to combine the two.[30]

Nowhere was this tendency of politics and journalism to run together more evident than in Parnell's own party. Many of his closest associates were, or had been, journalists or otherwise associated with newspapers. Apart from William O'Brien, Thomas Sexton and Edmund Dwyer Gray, they included Justin McCarthy, T. P. O'Connor, J. J. O'Kelly and T. C. Harrington – and, in addition, Tim Healy and his uncles, the brothers A. M. and T. D. Sullivan.[31] Unlike George Lee in our own time, these fellows generally stayed the course: Sexton was the only one who retired prematurely, and he had served for over 15 years in the House of Commons.[32]

The phenomenon of the journalist-turned-politician in the Irish Parliamentary Party highlights the intensely political nature of journalism in Ireland at this time. By the 1880s, freedom of the press from formal govern-ment restraint had been established in Britain and Ireland, both in accepted custom and on a firm legal basis.[33] Nevertheless, neither the *Freeman's Journal* nor its contemporary newspapers enjoyed any significant degree of editorial autonomy or independence of journalistic practice. Tim Pat Coogan, writing in 1966, could reasonably claim that 'more of the country's newspapers [were then] coming to see their role as stimulators of the mind and not as retailers of received prejudices'.[34] In the years when the *Freeman* was published, developments of this kind lay very far into the future. Newspapers were highly partisan organs for particular points of view, usually those of their proprietors, and an editor was required to promote in reportage as well as in the leader columns the views of those who owned or otherwise controlled his

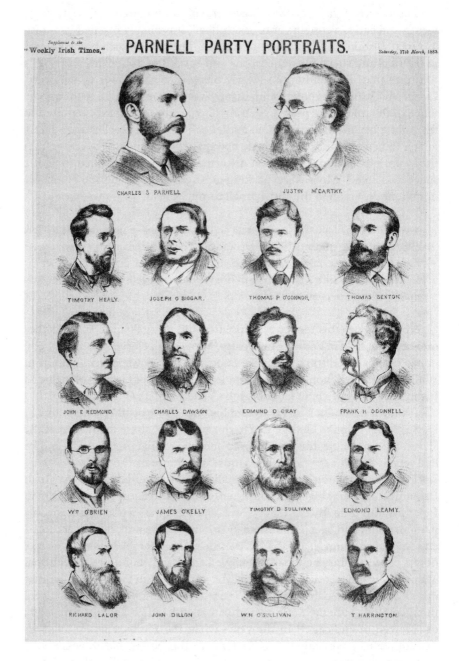

Parnell, without his customary full beard, with seventeen other leading members of the Irish Parliamentary Party – over half of whom had been journalists or otherwise associated with newspapers. Supplement to the *Weekly Irish Times*, 17 Mar. 1883.

paper. To ensure their authority, proprietors often acted as the editor themselves – or retained the editorship in name at least. That was the culture within which journalists worked, and it was not conducive to high standards of journalistic professionalism.

In an important recent essay, Michael Foley identifies some green shoots of professionalism emerging in Irish journalism in the latter half of the nineteenth century – such as 'the use of shorthand to ensure accuracy' and 'a belief in objectivity or impartiality, and the professional skills to deliver it'.[35] Irish journalists also participated in the National Association of Journalists, later renamed the Institute of Journalists, a professional body founded in London in 1884 ; and that body had an Irish president in 1894–5: Thomas Crosbie, editor and proprietor of the *Cork Examiner*. 'Gentlemen amateurs . . . are the curse of a newspaper office' – this sentiment, indicative of a nascent sense of journalistic professionalism, is attributed to the fictional newspaper owner in Matthias McDonnell Bodkin's autobiographical novel *White Magic*, published in 1897 when Bodkin, the former editor of *United Ireland*, was working as chief leader-writer of the *Freeman's Journal*.[36] An acid test of professionalism is, however – as Foley points out – that 'a journalist could work for a newspaper whose editorial position he did not agree with'.[37] By that standard, there were very few *Freeman* journalists, especially in the senior ranks, who would pass muster as true professionals.

Take the case of Edward Byrne, who succeeded John Blake Gallaher as editor of the *Freeman* in 1884. Staunchly pro-Parnell at the time of the split, he left the *Freeman* when the paper abandoned Parnell and became the first editor of the Parnellite *Irish Daily Independent*. Conversely, W. H. Brayden had been a leader-writer on the *Freeman* before the Parnell split, but he dissented from its initial pro-Parnell sympathies and was appointed editor of the anti-Parnell *National Press* in March 1891. Then, when the *Freeman* changed sides and the two newspapers merged, Brayden returned to the *Freeman* as editor. He was still editor in 1916, and, after the Easter Rising, he wanted the *Freeman* to take a much harder line against the rebels than the Irish party leaders would countenance. He was replaced forthwith.[38] His replacement, Patrick Hooper, went on to serve as an independent member of the Senate of the Irish Free State, and was vice-chairman of the Senate when he died in 1931. These were very politically-committed journalists, and in this I believe they were broadly representative of their peers. Rather than upholding professional values such as we might expect journalists today to have, they were actively engaged in the politics of their day, unashamedly partisan – perhaps aspirant politicians, or politicians *manqué*.

A *Freeman* journalist who doesn't quite conform to this model is James M. Tuohy, the London correspondent from 1881 to 1912. His work inevitably brought him into close contact with the Irish party leaders when parliament was in session, and he even acted on occasion as a sort of press officer for the party in London. He was loyal to Parnell at the outset of the split, and was one of the trusted associates who accompanied Parnell to Boulogne at the end of 1890 for the meeting with William O'Brien MP (the founding editor of *United Ireland*) which, it was hoped, would resolve the split. Tuohy, however, remained with the *Freeman* after it switched to the anti-Parnell side and later when it merged with the *National Press* – an apparent affirmation of his professionalism as a journalist, though there is some evidence that it may simply have reflected his growing disillusionment with Parnell.[39] In any case, he also had a very distinguished international journalistic career for he combined his post on the *Freeman* with that of London correspondent and European manager of the *New York World*. He was a close confidant of the *World*'s editor and proprietor, Joseph Pulitzer. When Tuohy died in 1923, the London *Times* hailed him as the 'doyen of American correspondents in Europe'.[40]

The restructuring of the *Independent* by William Martin Murphy in 1905 involved a major advance in professional standards in journalism in Ireland. He appointed as editor of the *Independent* T. R. Harrington, whose prior experience had been on the reporting staff of the newspaper. The usual route into an editorial chair had been through the leader-writing staff – in other words, the commentators, not the reporters, got the job. Harrington determined a new style of reporting for the *Independent*, instructing his staff 'to approach the work with a perfectly open mind . . . and confine themselves as a rule to reporting facts or speeches in a fair and impartial way, following our usual practice of not giving things fully'.[41] Brevity, like objectivity, was not the norm in Irish newspapers at that time. Moreover, he fought for and secured an unprecedented degree of editorial independence. Murphy agreed to remain at a distance from day-to-day editorial matters, and even his spasmodic interventions were rebuffed – though not always successfully – by Harrington. On one occasion, Harrington told Murphy that 'your unpopular political views . . . would, if published in the paper in the form in which you want them, inflict untold injury on it'.[42] Instead, Harrington's approach was to follow public opinion as he perceived it and articulate positions broadly acceptable to his predominantly middle-class, Catholic, nationalist readers – so as not to lose their custom.[43]

This formula generally served the *Independent* well – though not after the 1916 Rising when, in two notorious editorials published on 10 and 12 May, it called for the executions of James Connolly and Seán MacDermott, the only signatories of the Proclamation not already shot.[44] Harrington had acted without the knowledge of Murphy – who repudiated the editorials in private, though never in public (apparently out of loyalty to his editor).[45] The charge of having sought these deaths haunted Murphy until his own death in 1919, and would haunt his newspaper for much longer. Why did Harrington write such bloodthirsty editorials? The probable explanation is that he simply misread the shifting public mood, for he was quoted soon afterwards as saying that 'the crowd cried out for vengeance and when they got it they howled for clemency'.[46]

The *Freeman's Journal* might well have adopted the same uncompromising stance in its editorials after the Rising if W. H. Brayden, the editor who was sacked in 1916, had had his way. The prompt intervention of the Irish party leaders averted that fiasco: political interference in the affairs of a newspaper sometimes has its benefits. However, with the party's defeat in the 1918 general election, the *Freeman* lost its *raison d'être* – and, more importantly, there were no longer party funds to support it. It was in danger of sinking with its political masters. It was saved, for a brief period, by a prominent Dublin businessman, Martin Fitzgerald. He purchased the *Freeman* in October 1919, in partnership with a retired British journalist living in Ireland, Hamilton Edwards. It was for them a business venture, but Fitzgerald had been a Home Ruler and the *Freeman* soon committed itself to a policy of seeking dominion status for Ireland. It was also highly critical of the increasingly repressive nature of British rule in Ireland during the War of Independence. Later, it attacked the new government of Northern Ireland and the anti-Treaty elements in the new Irish Free State.

The *Freeman* strongly supported the Anglo-Irish Treaty of 1921 and the constitutional arrangements that the Treaty put in place. This was hardly surprising given the paper's moderate nationalist sympathies, but there was another aspect to it. Unknown to the public at large, Martin Fitzgerald had played a key part in the process leading up to the Treaty. Once the British government decided to explore settlement possibilities in Ireland, he was able – and willing – to use his standing as a newspaper proprietor to act as an intermediary between Sinn Féin and Dublin Castle. He was in regular contact with both Michael Collins and Alfred ('Andy') Cope, the shadowy Assistant Under Secretary at the Castle who conducted most of the secret British negotiations with the Irish leaders in the period before the Truce of July 1921. Fitzgerald's efforts as a go-between are well attested in contemporary documents.[47] He had, therefore, a personal stake in the Treaty's success.

In time, the *Freeman* became the unofficial organ of the Free State government – a political role similar to that it had had with the Irish party since the early 1880s. In recognition of this role, Fitzgerald was nominated to the first Senate of the Irish Free State in 1922 – and he served in that forum until his death in 1927. Moreover, the *Freeman*'s chief reporter, Seán Lester, was appointed director of publicity in the Free State's Department of External Affairs in 1923 – an apparently seamless transition from journalist to propagandist. Lester went on to have a very distinguished diplomatic career, serving as the League of Nations' High Commissioner in Danzig and the last Secretary-General of the League.[48]

After the last issue of the *Freeman's Journal* appeared on 19 December 1924, *Dublin Opinion* magazine commented: 'The *Freeman* is dead. Bad circulation.'[49] A nice pun, but the reason for the *Freeman*'s demise was much more fundamental. Unlike the *Irish Independent,* it had failed to modernise – and, when Sexton quit in 1912, it was already too late to save it. The *Independent* by then enjoyed an unassailable market advantage. The immediate cause of its collapse was that the partnership of Fitzgerald and Hamilton Edwards ended in grief when Edwards tried unsuccessfully to corner the market in newsprint and then absconded, leaving debts which the enfeebled *Freeman* could not meet. Its assets – including the title – were later bought by the *Independent,* and for decades afterwards the *Independent* carried in its masthead the legend 'Incorporating the *Freeman's Journal*'. Parnell's paper had triumphed in the end – and, by virtue of its triumph and continued survival, the *Independent* must be regarded today as Parnell's most enduring legacy to the people of Ireland.

Notes

1   Delivered at the Parnell Summer School, 11 Aug. 2010. I am grateful to Ian d'Alton, Judith Devlin (UCD), Philip Hamell, Professor John Horgan, Peter Lacy, Mark O'Brien (DCU) and Professor Robert Schmuhl (Notre Dame University, Indiana) for their helpful comments on earlier drafts of this essay. My thanks also to Honora Faul, of the National Library of Ireland, for facilitating my use of the image reproduced on p. 84 above.

2   For a concise account of the history of the *Freeman's Journal,* see Felix M. Larkin, '"A great daily organ": the *Freeman's Journal,* 1763–1924', *History Ireland,* vol. 14, no. 3 (May/June 2006), pp 44–9.

3   Quoted in Emmet Larkin, *The Roman Catholic Church and the Emergence of the Modern Irish Political System, 1874–1878* (Dublin & Washington, D.C., 1996), p. 395.

4   F. S. L. Lyons, *Charles Stewart Parnell* (London, 1977), pp 93–5.

5   See R. Barry O'Brien, *The Life of Charles Stewart Parnell,* (London, 1899), vol. II, p. 291; O'Brien's informant is not named, but is described as 'one of Parnell's Fenian supporters'.

6   The most recent biography of Caroline Chisholm is Carole Walker, *A Saviour of Living Cargoes: The Life and Work of Caroline Chisholm* (Melbourne, 2009 & Walton-on-the-Wolds, 2010).

7   William J. Walsh to Archbishop Tobias Kirby, 22 Feb. 1891, Kirby Papers, Irish College, Rome. Given that Mrs Gray was a devout Roman Catholic and English, her support of Parnell in the first months of the split may be seen as confirmation of Conor Cruise O'Brien's astute observation that 'the Catholicism of the English is not felt to be the same as the religion of the

same name practiced in Ireland' (C. C. O'Brien, *Herod: Reflections on Political Violence* (London, 1978), p. 92).

8　For further information about the three generations of the Gray family associated with the *Freeman's Journal*, see Felix M. Larkin, 'Mrs Jellyby's daughter: Caroline Agnes Gray (1848–1927) and the *Freeman's Journal*' in Felix M. Larkin (ed.), *Librarians, Poets and Scholars: A Festschrift for Dónall Ó Luanaigh* (Dublin, 2007), pp 121–39.

9　Harry Levin (ed.), *The Essential James Joyce* (London, 1963), p. 473.

10　See L. M. Cullen, *Eason & Son: A History* (Dublin, 1989), pp 45, 76–7. I have assumed that the pattern of newspaper sales in Ireland through W. H. Smith – the antecedent of Eason's – was representative of the market generally at this time. I have also assumed that W. H. Smith's share accounted for one third of total sales of newspapers in Ireland (Cullen, *Eason*, p. 355). All estimates of newspaper circulation in Ireland in the nineteenth and early twentieth centuries should be regarded as extremely tentative; figures were generally neither published nor independently verified.

11　William O'Brien, *Recollections* (London, 1905), pp 182–3.

12　John Dillon Papers, Trinity College, Dublin, Ms 6804/126–8.

13　Patrick Maume, 'Commerce, politics and the *Irish Independent*, 1891–1919', unpublished paper read before the 24th Irish Conference of Historians held at University College Cork, 20–22 May 1999; my thanks to Dr Maume for making a copy of this paper available to me. See also Donal McCartney, 'William Martin Murphy: an Irish press baron and the rise of the popular press', in Brian Farrell (ed.), *Communications and Community in Ireland* (Dublin & Cork, 1984), pp 30–8.

14　James Downey, *In My Own Time: Inside Irish Politics and Society* (Dublin, 2009), p. 232.

15　'Extract from a letter of Dillon to [Edward] Blake [MP], 8 Apr. 1904', John Redmond Papers, National Library of Ireland, Dublin, Ms 15,182/6.

16　See J. W. Mackail and Guy Wyndham, *Life and Letters of George Wyndham*, (London, 1925), vol. II, p. 474.

17　Cullen, *Eason*, pp 77, 307 – but see note 10 above. Raymond Williams likewise calculates a sevenfold increase in aggregate daily newspaper circulation in Britain between 1880 and 1920. Williams, *The Long Revolution* (London, 1965, pb edn), p. 198.

18　The circulation figures given here for the *Freeman* refer to 1915 (see John Redmond Papers, National Library of Ireland, Dublin, Ms 15,262/7). By 1915, the *Irish Independent* claimed to have a circulation of 110,000 (*Newspaper Press Directory*, 1915).

19　*Freeman's Journal*, 29 Apr. 1912.

20　For a fuller account of Sexton's chairmanship of the *Freeman's Journal* company, see Felix M. Larkin, 'Two gentlemen of the *Freeman*: Thomas Sexton, W. H. Brayden and the *Freeman's Journal*, 1892–1916', in Ciara Breathnach and Catherine Lawless (eds), *Visual, Material and Print Culture in Nineteenth-Century Ireland* (Dublin, 2010), pp 210–22.

21　For details, see 'Note of moneys advanced for the *Freeman's Journal*, 27 Jan. 1919', in the John Dillon Papers, Trinity College Dublin, Ms 6805/306.

22　John Redmond Papers, National Library of Ireland, Dublin, Ms 15,262/1.

23 John Dillon to John Redmond, 31 July 1907, ibid., Ms 15,182/15.

24 John Dillon to John Redmond, 22 May 1917, ibid., Ms 15,182/24.

25 See, for example, F. S. L. Lyons, *John Dillon: A Biography* (London, 1968), especially pp 244, 389, 440, 455.

26 *United Ireland*, 8 Feb. 1902. For a full analysis of Griffith's attitude towards the *Freeman*, see Felix M. Larkin, 'Arthur Griffith and the *Freeman's Journal*', in Kevin Rafter (ed.), *Irish Journalism before Independence: More a Disease than a Profession* (Manchester, 2011), pp 174–85.

27 Quoted in M. McD. Bodkin, *Recollections of an Irish Judge: Press, Bar and Parliament* (London, 1914), p. 32.

28 This phrase had been suggested by Baldwin's cousin, Rudyard Kipling, and was used in a speech delivered during a by-election campaign in the constituency of St George's, Westminster in March 1931; see Paul Ferris, *The House of Northcliffe* (New York, 1972), pp 293–4.

29 Donal McCartney, 'Parnell and the American connection', in Donal McCartney and Pauric Travers, *The Ivy Leaf: The Parnells Remembered* (Dublin, 2006), pp 38–55, at p. 47.

30 *Freeman's Journal*, 29 Aug. 1891, quoted by Frank Callanan in his introduction to Edward Byrne, *Parnell: A Memoir*, Frank Callanan (ed.), (Dublin, 1991), p. 4.

31 For additional information about journalists in the ranks of the Irish Parliamentary Party, see Felix M. Larkin, 'Double helix: two elites in politics and journalism in Ireland, 1870–1918', in Ciaran O'Neill (ed.), *Irish Elites in the Nineteenth Century* (Dublin, 2013), pp 125–36.

32 George Lee, a journalist with RTÉ, had been a Fine Gael TD for just eight months when he resigned in February 2010.

33 Kevin B. Nowlan, 'The origins of the press in Ireland', in Farrell (ed.), *Communications and Community*, p. 17.

34 Tim Pat Coogan, *Ireland Since the Rising* (London, 1966), p. 174.

35 Michael Foley, 'Colonialism and journalism in Ireland', *Journalism Studies*, vol. 5, no. 3 (2004), pp 373–85, at pp 379, 383.

36 M. McD. Bodkin, *White Magic* (London, 1897), p. 127. *White Magic* is one of three novels associated with the *Freeman*, the others being Fannie Gallaher, *Thy Name is Truth: A Social Novel*, 3 vols (London, 1884) and James Joyce, *Ulysses* (Paris, 1922). Fannie Gallaher was the daughter of John Blake Gallaher, the *Freeman*'s editor from the late 1850s to 1884, and the second chapter in the first volume of her novel – entitled 'Behind the scenes' – is set in the *Freeman*'s offices. The 'Aeolus' episode of *Ulysses* is also set in the *Freeman*'s offices. I am grateful to Professor James H. Murphy, of De Paul University, Chicago, for bringing Gallaher's novel to my attention; see James H. Murphy, *Irish Novelists and the Victorian Age* (Oxford, 2011), pp 174–6. On the *Freeman* and *Ulysses*, see Felix M. Larkin, '"The old woman of Prince's Street": *Ulysses* and the *Freeman's Journal*', *Dublin James Joyce Journal*, no. 4 (2011), pp 14–29.

37 Foley, 'Colonialism and journalism', p. 383.

38 See Larkin, 'Two gentlemen of the *Freeman*', pp 220–1.

39 See J. M. Tuohy, 'Parnell at bay', with an introduction by Frank Callanan, *The Recorder: The Journal of the American Irish Historical Society*, vol. 17, no. 2 (Fall 2004), pp 59–66, at p. 61.

40 *The Times*, 8 Sept. 1923. For further information on Byrne, Brayden, Hooper and Tuohy,

see Felix M. Larkin, 'The dog in the night-time: the *Freeman's Journal*, the Irish Parliamentary Party and the empire, 1875–1919', in Simon J. Potter (ed.), *Newspapers and Empire in Ireland and Britain: Reporting the British Empire, c. 1875–1921* (Dublin, 2004), pp 109–23. Regarding Brayden, see also Larkin, 'Two gentlemen of the *Freeman*'.

41 T. R. Harrington Papers, National Archives of Ireland, Dublin, Ms 1052/3/4.

42 T. R. Harrington to William Martin Murphy, 28 Jun. 1915, quoted in Frank Callanan, *T. M. Healy* (Cork, 1996), pp 485–6.

43 For a more detailed consideration of Harrington's editorship of the *Irish Independent*, see Felix M. Larkin, 'No longer a political side show: T. R. Harrington and the "new" *Irish Independent*, 1905–31', in Mark O'Brien and Kevin Rafter, *Independent Newspapers: A History* (Dublin, 2012), pp 26–38.

44 The *Independent* did not refer to Connolly or MacDermott by name, but called for the execution of the 'ringleaders, instigators and fomenters not yet dealt with' (10 May 1916) and stated unequivocally that 'no special leniency should be extended to some of the worst of the leaders whose cases have not yet been disposed of' (12 May 1916).

45 Thomas Morrissey S.J., *William Martin Murphy* (Dublin, 1997), p. 64. See also Downey, *In My Own Time*, p. 233.

46 Edward Martin Murphy to T. R. Harrington, 29 June 1916, T. R. Harrington Papers, National Archives of Ireland, Ms 1052/5/2.

47 See, for example, Michael Hopkinson (ed.), *The Last Days of Dublin Castle: The Mark Sturgis Diaries* (Dublin, 1999), pp 186, 194, 197.

48 See Douglas Gageby, *The Last Secretary-General: Sean Lester and the League of Nations* (Dublin, 1999).

49 *Dublin Opinion*, vol. 3, no. 35 (Jan. 1925), p. 390.

CHAPTER 6

Mr Parnell's Rottweiler

United Ireland 1881–91

Myles Dungan

The second half of the nineteenth century saw a previously unparalleled communications revolution. Between 1851 and 1881 the number of news-papers published in Ireland alone virtually doubled. Literacy rates went from 47 per cent of the population to 75 per cent. In 1855 stamp duty had been removed from newspapers making the mass-circulation, one-penny paper a reality; and the growth of the railways had permitted the more efficient pene-tration of national newspapers throughout the country.[1] Although this was not strictly necessary as there was a parallel upsurge in the local press, which often 'lifted' copy from the national papers and brought it to a rural readership. In the period 1880–92 thirty-one new provincial newspapers began publi-cation. Two-thirds were overtly or militantly nationalist in their politics. Reading rooms sponsored by the Land League, Irish National League and the likes of the Catholic Young Men's Association ensured that nationalist papers were widely circulated and read. During the heyday of Parnellite politics in the 1880s a highly partisan, often crude, politically motivated nationalist popular press placed its powers of persuasion and propaganda at the disposal of the forces of agrarian reform and separatism.

It was, perhaps, fortunate for Charles Stewart Parnell, a relatively unin-spiring public speaker,[2] that he had no particular need to connect with his audience as directly and viscerally as had, for instance, Daniel O'Connell. Not that the 'Liberator' had failed to cultivate the newspapers of the 1840s, but his utilisation of the direct, unmediated approach of the 'mass meeting' was probably a more effective form of political communication at the time of the failed Repeal movement. For Parnell, operating in the era of the penny journal, 'press' largely replaced 'platform'. This was not only a matter of personal preference but an essential prerequisite for a leader who favoured parliamentarianism over populism and whose visits to his Irish support base became relatively infrequent as the 1880s progressed. Parnell saw a co-operative press as the *sine qua non* of a new form of sophisticated political agitation.

It can be argued that Parnell's public and parliamentary speeches, whether so constructed or not, were even more appropriate for a wider reading public than for an immediate listening audience. His flat, terse, utilitarian delivery, almost devoid of rhetorical flourish or allusion, was more suited to a verbatim report in the *Freeman's Journal* than to whipping up a crowd. He also had an uncanny ability to encapsulate his message in one memorable phrase – a Victorian soundbite – telling his audience in the crucial Westport demonstration of 8 June 1879 for example, to 'show the landlords that you intend to hold a firm grip on your homesteads'[3] – soundbite as mantra. His relationship with individual members of the Irish and British press, like James Tuohy and Edward Byrne of the *Freeman's Journal*, or Alfred Robbins of the *Birmingham Daily Post* was closer, by all accounts, than with many of the ordinary members of his own party.[4]

Parnell's rise to prominence had not, in any egregious sense, been facilitated by the Irish Nationalist press. The venerable weekly the *Nation*, had a clear regard for his activism during the obstructionist period of the 1870s; but the *Nation* was, first, last and always, a reflection of the views of the Sullivan brothers, Alexander Martin and Timothy Daniel, who had assumed control of the newspaper in 1858. The *Freeman's Journal* was far less supportive. Owned by the moderate nationalist MP Edmund Dwyer Gray, it was allied to the faction of the Irish Party led by William Shaw, who would be supplanted by Parnell as party leader before the new session of parliament in 1880.[5] When it came to Gladstone's 1881 Land Act, and, in particular, to the arbitrative Land Courts which emerged from that legislation, both the *Nation* and the *Freeman* opposed Parnell's policy of tempered opposition.

So Parnell was a timpanist without a drum. In July, 1881, he set about rectifying this lack of percussion. With the assistance and approval of Patrick Egan, Land League Treasurer and erstwhile Fenian, funds were made available for the establishment of a weekly newspaper designed to be the mouthpiece of the Land League. It would be a radical, agrarian newspaper oriented towards rural Ireland: the support base of the League. Under its editor William O'Brien, a young *Freeman's Journal* reporter, *United Ireland* would become, as he put it himself: 'a weekly insurrection in print',[6] a snarling Rottweiler snapping at the Castle establishment, the Unionist press, and nationalist apostasy with equal vitriol. *United Ireland* was designed to 'keep other nationalist papers in line, to confront enemies within and without the movement, and especially to develop the cult of Parnell's personality.'[7] It was a crude journalistic bludgeon, a newspaper of record for the 'advanced' nationalist movement, an apologist capable of the most artful contortions and a guard-dog protecting Parnell's left flank against the inroads of radical nationalism. With sales that reached six figures, a readership of up to half a million people a week and an ascetic editor who never strayed too far from his agrarian roots, *United Ireland* became the organ of the disenfranchised. While being, in reality, less reflective of genuine Parnellite orthodoxy than the *Freeman's Journal*, it provided a paper shield behind which Parnell could operate with a certain impunity.

The vehicle used, in July 1881, for the purchase of the moribund press belonging to the ill-starred Richard Pigott was the Irish National Newspaper and Publishing Company. Parnell and Egan were principal shareholders; Justin McCarthy, Joseph Biggar and William O'Brien also had small stakes.[8] Almost all the original shareholders later took flight when a series of potentially crippling libel writs threatened their personal financial security. O'Brien was left in possession of the field and shouldering all the financial risk. As his worldly goods consisted of two large suitcases stored in his room in the Imperial Hotel it was judged unlikely that anyone would bother to bankrupt him.[9]

The foundation strategy was to replace one of Pigott's three weekly papers, the *Irishman*, with a new title and kill off another, *Flag of Ireland*, altogether. Part of the deal (which cost the Land League £3000) was that the irritating Pigott, an avowed but quixotic, to say the least, Fenian 'fellow traveller', would not establish a new title of his own and run it in competition with the new Parnellite weekly.[10] In 1889 Parnell told the *Times* Commission that 'We purchased it in order to terminate Mr Richard Piggot's journalistic existence in Ireland.'[11]

In the end it was the *Flag of Ireland* that was replaced by *United Ireland* while the *Irishman* continued in existence under the aegis of Dr George Sigerson and former IRB treasurer, James O'Connor, as a quasi-Fenian newspaper with an ever-dwindling circulation of doctrinaire Republicans. This was done with the approval of O'Brien and the tacit acquiescence of Parnell. When the latter's patience finally ran out with its extremist commentary, the *Irishman* was laid to rest in 1885.[12]

The first issue of *United Ireland*, published on 13 August, 1881, set a tone that would, by and large, be maintained up to and beyond the 1890 Split. On page one there were calls for Land League branch notices to 'reach us by Tuesday . . . so that the columns of *United Ireland* may form a Weekly National Monster Meeting which cannot be dispersed with buckshot.'[13] The front page also carried the characteristic cartoon, often inspired, though not drawn, by O'Brien himself, who was stronger on anger and invective than on sly humour.

Page four launched 'The World's Week's Work' a political gossip column in attack-dog mode – often used to pour scorn on the Irish Executive, Castle officials, policemen (secret or otherwise), 'nominal' Home Rulers who had rejected the Parnellite whip, Unionist newspapers, rival editors and journalists, and even recalcitrant or refractory Parnellites.

On page seven the new weekly carried an example of the sort of commentary that would ensure it rapidly attracted the malign attention of the Law Officers in Dublin Castle. O'Brien had cut and pasted a rant from O'Donovan Rossa, from his mouthpiece the *United Irishman*, itself published well out of harm's way in New York. It was a warning to landlords which went well beyond the seditious:

> . . . henceforward a record will be kept of every landlord who exercises the power of eviction in Ireland, and for every such death sentence executed on a tenant a death sentence will be recorded by the Irish race against the murderer's house, and the Irish race all the world over will give encouragement to the avenging angel.

On the back page there was a report of a man's arm being eaten by a cob horse in Maynooth, a rare enough item unrelated to the 'struggle' and a story very much in keeping with the populist strain inherent in the 'new journalism' just then on the rise. The advertisements are also interesting. They included a People's Trade Directory, akin to a list of 'righteous Gentiles' – nationalist businesses with whom it was 'kosher' for Land League members to trade; there were advertisements for cheap journeys to Canada – ironic given *United Ireland's* consistent stance against assisted emigration; and there was a notice for 'Hair Destroyer – Alex Ross' Depilatory removes hair from the face, neck and arms, 3s 6d a bottle; sent by post, secretly packed.' This was equally ironic as it was how the paper itself would be despatched for many weeks after the suppression of the Land League in October 1881.

In keeping with its promise to stage a 'weekly national Monster Meeting' (the phraseology harking back to the primary medium of O'Connell's Repeal movement) *United Ireland* lined up its targets and commenced firing. It took aim at the Land Courts,[14] spawn of the 1881 Land Act and a losing battle from the start. Not even O'Brien's vitriolic talents could stem the tide of peasant farmers rushing to arbitration in defiance of the stated Parnellite strategy of testing the legislation on a case by case basis. The editorials, however, clearly signified the newspaper as a hostile force and exposed it to the logic of Gladstone's injunction to Forster of October 1880 in which he deprecated nationalist volubility with the memorable phrase, 'what we want is to enforce silence'.[15]

United Ireland was what we might call today an 'equal opportunities offender'. We may take as read the steady stream of condemnation of the activities of Lords Cowper and Spencer, 'Buckshot' Forster and the Liberal administration in Ireland; but the policy of denunciation extended well beyond Cork Hill and the Viceregal Lodge. In the issue of 17 September 1881 it was announced that the editor of the Unionist *Daily Express*, Dr G.V. Patton (who doubled as Irish correspondent for the *Times*), was 'to have a national statue erected to him at O'Connell's feet – convenient to his right boot.'[16] This was part of a pattern of highly personalised attacks on journalists and editors writing for unionist newspapers in particular, a pattern that flew in the face of professional collegiality and proceeded from the often unsafe assumption that working journalists necessarily subscribed to the editorial line taken by the newspapers for which they wrote. This was undoubtedly true in most, but not in all cases.[17]

In the same issue O'Brien could not resist a swipe at his former employers, who had begun to advertise in his journal. He wrote acidly on page four that, 'We see by an advertisement in another column that the *Freeman's Journal* has at last discovered, not only our existence, but our address. We feel quite six columns bigger for its gracious notice.'[18] Such caustic comments serve as a reminder that another of *United Ireland*'s functions was to keep the *Freeman's Journal* in line. The extremism of O'Brien's paper (as well, of course, as the increasing radicalisation of the country's readership) shifted the fulcrum of nationalist commentary, moving the *Freeman* leftwards. Another factor in the *Journal*'s embrace of the political *zeitgeist* was the unspoken threat that if it clung to its innate conservatism O'Brien would publish *United Ireland* on a *daily* basis in competition. A reading of police files in the National Archives of Ireland reveals that such plans were in place in late 1881 but were abandoned in the face of Forster's campaign to close down *United Ireland* after the arrest of Parnell and O'Brien in October of that year.[19]

Equally, O'Brien often demonstrated that he was capable of biting the hand of his current as well as his past employers. *United Ireland* was barely a fortnight old before he was railing against Home Rulers who did not vote on a motion involving the re-arrest of Michael Davitt. Only 19 of 63 supposed Home Rulers bothered to appear for a division on the issue. Simple arithmetic dictates that some of the defaulters were Parnellites. Nonetheless, with typical hyperbole, O'Brien fulminated that, 'Whoever was absent from that list without satisfactory cause committed a high treason against the Irish cause.'[20] *United Ireland* was perfectly prepared to flog lethargic Parnellites and discourage laxity of any kind.

All this, of course, was mere prologue to the vilification of Forster and his lieutenants in *United Ireland* after the Protection of Person and Property (Ireland) Act was invoked to detain the leadership of the Land League without trial in October, 1881. O'Brien himself was arrested and lodged in Kilmainham for publishing 'treasonable and seditious material.' Despite the invocation of the crime of sedition it is reasonable to suggest that his arrest would not have been possible under ordinary statute law. While some of the material he was writing and publishing was undoubtedly seditious (insofar as sedition is a crime whose parameters are defined by government rather than by legislation), it is unlikely that a Dublin jury could have been assembled that would have convicted him.

If Forster assumed that the arrest of O'Brien would silence *United Ireland* he was mistaken. Within hours of his incarceration O'Brien was composing the wording of the 'No Rent' Manifesto[21] and within days it was being carried on the front page of his newspaper.[22] *United Ireland* continued in existence as the motor of the, ultimately unsuccessful, No Rent campaign.

Indeed the campaign against the payment of rent became its *raison d'être* for most of the succeeding six months. During this period the paper was published in Dublin, Liverpool, London and Paris. Some weeks it failed to appear, some weeks there were two separate editions, some weeks it was reduced from eight to four pages; but, like the famous Windmill Theatre of the London Blitz, it never closed.[23] Its journalists, typesetters and printers were jailed under the Coercion Act or forced to flee the country to avoid that fate. The ground for most of the arrests was 'for instruction against payment of rent.'[24] Of course the net effect of these actions was to confer a warrior-like credibility on *United Ireland* and its editor, and hugely raise the newspaper's profile.

Responsibility for its survival fell, at various different times, on the shoulders of Patrick Egan in Paris, sundry former and current Fenians, the Ladies' Land League and others. O'Brien continued to preside over its editorial content from his prison cell, relying on the same underground methods that facilitated the passage of passionate messages between Parnell and Katharine O'Shea.

When it was clear that *United Ireland* was a journalistic hydra whose publication was not susceptible to the sword, Dublin Castle adopted a different approach. From December, 1881 there was, in effect, a blanket order to seize copies of the newspaper after they appeared.[25] And therein lay a further difficulty. There was no legislative provision for the seizure of a newspaper in advance of publication. In order for a copy of a paper to be judged seditious it first had to appear in print and be monitored by the proper authorities. This, of course, allowed a resourceful publisher to distribute copies before a member of the Dublin Metropolitan Police was enabled to purchase one for himself, take it to the Law Officers in Dublin Castle, have it adjudged to be seditious and have the seizure order confirmed.

It was an unwieldy and unsatisfactory process. Not even the fact that the resourceful head of 'G' Division, Superintendent John Mallon, managed to infiltrate the paper's office in Abbey Street in Dublin by means of an unidentified informant,[26] was of much assistance. There was nothing 'G' Division could do until the paper actually appeared in a newsagent's shop.

Ultimately pragmatism won out and the Liberal administration chose to ignore, circumvent and simply break its own laws and seize copies of the newspaper in advance of distribution – in some cases before they even reached Ireland. Thousands of copies were seized in Dover and Folkestone in the early months of 1882 prompting, for example, the Ladies' Land League to adopt all sorts of ruses to disguise the newspapers (as dried fish, woollen goods, consignments of flour or, in one instance, a shipment of copies of the *Times* itself). One way or another copies of *United Ireland* passed from hand to hand for most of the period during which Parnell and his lieutenants were in Kilmainham and 'Captain Moonlight' had control of events in rural Ireland.

What most incensed the Castle about the reportage of *United Ireland* was not the florid, declamatory and subversive editorials, but a regular feature which began to appear in early November, 1881. It is clear that Dublin Castle took particular exception to a weekly column which was entitled 'Incidents of the Campaign.'[27] The language of the title suggests a state of war between the Land League and the government – the language of the column itself tended to verge on the inflammatory without quite tipping over into outright incitement to violence. Most of the stories were cautionary tales of one kind or another, of people who were being boycotted, who had suffered for not co-operating with the Land League, who had been assaulted or even killed. The cumulative impact of the coverage of what the Castle referred to as 'outrage' would, in the eyes of the Law Officers at least, have had an intimidatory effect on the reader and would have discouraged tenant farmers from, for example, taking land from which another farmer had been evicted.

O'Brien subsequently attempted to distance himself from the column, which was carried in the newspaper while he was in Kilmainham. An example with which he was confronted during his evidence to the *Times* Commission was a piece entitled 'Bathing a Bailiff.' The language of the actual report was factual and relatively neutral, but it dealt with the tarring of a bailiff who was then thrown into a canal. O'Brien was forced to accept, 'that is an exceedingly objectionable thing to publish under that particular heading, but it is a paragraph cut out of some daily newspaper as an ordinary item of news. It was probably in precisely the same words in the London *Times*.'[28]

Much has been made of the convenience for Parnell of his arrest and incarceration in Kilmainham in October, 1881. As he wrote to Katharine O'Shea at the time – 'Politically it is a fortunate thing for me that I have been arrested, as the movement is breaking fast, and all will be quiet in a few months, when I shall be released.'[29] The political martyrdom afforded him by Forster's yearning for coercive powers allowed him to preside vicariously over the demise of a movement that had become something of an obstacle to his plans anyway.

However, not so much has been written about the role played by *United Ireland* in the deification of the, supposedly, cruelly incarcerated chieftain. While Parnell played handball and chess in Kilmainham and smuggled letters out to his 'Queenie' in Eltham, O'Brien set about the creation of the myth of the self-sacrificial, and later omnipotent, leader. The *United Ireland* editor would subsequently assure the *Times* Commission in 1889 that his imprisonment had rendered him *hors de combat* in the propaganda war that followed his own arrest.[30] He was, of course being utterly disingenuous. In O'Brien's own memoirs he wrote that he worked even more assiduously at his journalism while in Kilmainham than he had in the previous twelve weeks of freedom.[31]

Such was the political capital gained by Parnell, much of it purchased for him by the relentless mythologizing of O'Brien from his prison cell, that the Irish Party leader was well protected from attacks emanating from his republican flank after the debilitation of the perceived concessions of the 'Kilmainham Treaty'. O'Brien's unremitting proselytism – involving the expenditure of some of his *own* political capital – as well as Parnell's opposition to the fearsome 'Crimes Act' (the Prevention of Crime (Ireland) Act 1882), introduced after the Phoenix Park murders, restored some of the faith of 'advanced' nationalism in the credentials of the Irish Party leader.

Take, for example, the humiliating debate of 15 May 1882. Forster, who had recently resigned, forced Parnell to read to the House of Commons the full text of a letter to Captain O'Shea, inaccurately dated 28 April, which constituted the entire paper trail and synopsised the compact between Parnell and the Liberals. In a probable sop to O'Shea, Parnell had promised future Irish Party co-operation with the Liberals,[32] – the *démarche* memorably described by Gladstone as a *hors-d'oeuvre* his government had no right to expect.

Like Parnell and Gladstone, in the pages of *United Ireland* O'Brien resolutely denied the existence of the so-called 'Kilmainham Treaty' – he was, of course, technically if not morally correct. O'Brien chose to deal with the debate, and the blatant embarrassment of Parnell, by relegating it to page seven of his newspaper where it vied for attention with the ads for depilatory creams and steamboat tickets. The headline could hardly have been more misleading – 'Mr Forster's malignity raises a question that recoils on him – The real story of what led to Forster's dismissal'.[33] In retrospect, O'Brien's phraseology in the first edition of his newspaper becomes more significant – his hopes for the journal, as expressed on the opening page, that it would become a 'Weekly National Monster meeting'. Presumably this was predicated on his intention to be provocative and his ambition to attract a large readership. He may not have been conscious of an inherent irony. The monster meetings of the Repeal era of the 1840s were not known for the quality of their dialogue, they were the occasions of tendentious harangues, delivered, without mediation, by the leadership to the faithful. In that sense at least, by the effective end of the Land War in May 1882, O'Brien could afford to be pleased with his handiwork.

Even more extreme gymnastic contortions on the part of O'Brien over the logic of the Kilmainham Treaty were, however, largely unnecessary on account of the campaign that followed the introduction of the Crimes Act. This piece of legislation took up where the Protection of Person and Property (Ireland) Act of the previous year left off. Unlike the 1881 legislation, it also included a clause relating to the press. Instead of defending his leader against allegations of having surrendered to Gladstone, O'Brien was enabled by the introduction of the new Act to highlight Parnell's vigorous opposition to the imposition of an even harsher coercion regime on Ireland.

Curiously, the Crimes Act, which one might legitimately have expected to have been deployed by the government as a battering ram against the nationalist press, turned out to be much more limited in its scope when it came to punishing the Irish fourth estate. As originally mooted, Clause 10 of the bill (it would eventually become Section 13) included provision for a surety or security bond of £200.[34]

If a newspaper which had already given offence to the Lord Lieutenant was to cause further perturbation to his Lordship, the surety, in addition to the entire print run of that particular issue of the paper, would be subject to forfeiture. This stipulation, in effect a recognisance or guarantee of future good behaviour, was a variation of the concept of 'caution money' often exacted by continental governments from their newspapers. The provision was ultimately excised before the Committee stage.[35] The likelihood is that it was inserted as a makeweight that could be jettisoned in the course of the sort of internal negotiation that surrounds the passage of most legislation.

The final thrust of Section 13 – which included a standard provision against incitement – was largely designed to remove any ambiguity about the power of the executive to order the seizure of newspapers.[36] The Castle had faced compensation claims from newsagents[37] and *United Ireland* itself on foot of the seizures under the 1881 Coercion Act. It had even been suggested that it might be necessary to introduce an Act of Parliament retrospectively indemnifying members of the executive against such claims.[38]

However, despite arguing in the debate over the Crimes Act that: 'if the case of an Irish newspaper were brought before an Irish jury, there would be no chance of a verdict being obtained against the paper.' – the words of Home Secretary William Harcourt[39] – it was to the courts, albeit a Crimes Act Special Commission court, that the administration took recourse in their next joust with *United Ireland*.

In the twelve months after the first capital cases were taken under the Crimes Act, a number of high profile executions took place despite doubt being cast on the safety of the verdicts reached in certain instances. The executions of Francis Hynes in Clare, Poff and Barrett in Kerry and, notoriously, Myles Joyce, one of the accused in the infamous Maamtrasna murder case, all went ahead despite public concern about the cases made against them by the Crown. *United Ireland* was strident in its commentary against the safety of these verdicts. This campaign led on 23 December, 1882 to the publication of an editorial by O'Brien entitled 'Accusing Spirits'. In this O'Brien pointed to the questionable nature of some of the capital verdicts, arrived at by alleged jury packing and the procurement of informers by Crown prosecutors:

> Upon their trials the ordinary detective machinery – vigilance, resource, the ingenuity to discover scraps of evidence, the intelligence to piece them together – counted for little. Packed juries and bribed witnesses were the all-sufficient implements of justice.[40]

The reaction of the Castle was swift. On the official publication day of the newspaper an order was issued for the seizure of all copies of *United Ireland* under Section 13 of the Crimes Act on the basis that it contained, 'matter inciting to the commission of acts of violence and intimidation.'[41] O'Brien was also to be tried under the longstanding statute legislation against seditious publication.

There is no indication among the Chief Secretary's papers as to why the administration chose to prosecute O'Brien based on this particular editorial. It was one of many diatribes against so-called 'jury packing' and the use of informers and approvers in capital cases. O'Brien's comments were neither exceptional nor especially extreme. In addition, the article was reproduced in full, without any punitive action, in the unionist Dublin *Daily Express*. Not that there was much risk of the readers of the *Express* being provoked by the article into a breach of the peace, unless such a breach were to be aimed against O'Brien or his newspaper. In all probability the decision had as much to do with O'Brien's selection as nationalist candidate in the Mallow by-election of February 1883 (which he duly won) as it did with the specific content of the editorial.[42]

As Daniel O'Connell had discovered during the court case in 1844 that led to his own incarceration, it was notoriously difficult to defend against a charge of conspiracy. A charge of seditious libel was equally problematic. In cases of seditious libel, 'truth' was not a justification or defence – such cases were actually governed by the axiom 'the greater the truth the greater the libel'. Inherent in this apparent paradox was the idea that seditious libel constituted a breach of the peace. Therefore the more accurate the comments the more incendiary they were, and the more likely they were to cause such a breach.[43]

O'Brien was not unconscious of the irony that, as part of the state's retribution for his allegations of 'packing', he himself might face just such a partisan jury. His case was scheduled to come before the Crimes Act Commission court in Dublin – before some of the judges, like Justice Lawson, whose impartiality he had questioned. The Special Juries assembled for Commission courts came from a small group of high net-worth individuals, which obviously included a disproportionate number of unionists. It was possible, and not uncommon, to summon a forty-eight man panel and from that group for the Crown to assemble an exclusively Protestant jury.

O'Brien was defended by A. M. Sullivan, former MP and former *Nation* editor and proprietor. Leading for the Crown was Peter O'Brien, a future Irish Lord Chief Justice, but then an accomplished barrister known as 'Peter the Packer,' based on his alleged expertise in dictating the composition of juries. Sullivan's objective was to set aside the entire notion of truth aggravating the libel in sedition trials – an extremely tall order. He argued his case before a court of 'summary jurisdiction'[44] and before the Queen's Bench – and lost.[45] The case then came before the Commission court on 5 February 1883 with nothing essentially at issue other than to establish that O'Brien was the editor of *United Ireland*. Ten jurors were asked to 'stand aside' by the Crown – tantamount to, though not technically, a challenge. The suspicion, not unnaturally, was that the Crown viewed them as potentially favourable to O'Brien's cause. Sullivan may well have sealed the verdict in his address to the jury – the only form of defence allowed to O'Brien – when he reminded them that they were required to be judges not only of fact, i.e. that O'Brien *was* the editor of *United Ireland*, but of law as well. This permitted the twelve men in the jury box, if they chose to do so, to hold that the editorial did not actually contain 'matter inciting to the commission of acts of violence and intimidation.'[46]

The jury, thus advised, took fifty minutes to decide that it was utterly and unbreakably deadlocked. The foreman of the jury informed Justice Harrison, the presiding judge – a man acknowledged even by O'Brien to have been absolutely impartial – that 'there is not the least chance of our agreeing.' O'Brien was told that he would be re-tried and he would be given ten days notice of when new proceedings were to be taken against him.[47] No such proceedings ever followed.

So the Liberal administration had been frustrated in its suppression of *United Ireland* despite its suspension of *habeas corpus* in the case of the entire editorial, administrative and printing staff, its use of specially designed coercion legislation, and its invocation of the laws of seditious libel. Its last throw of the dice was 'the continuation of war by other means.' The final attempt by the Liberal administration to rid itself of this irritating gadfly, by vicarious civil action, almost achieved a resounding success.

THE 'CASTLE SCANDALS'

On 25 August 1883 Tim Healy, in a fit of pique with the *Freeman's Journal*, managed to libel James Ellis French, Director of Detectives with the Royal Irish Constabulary (their equivalent to Dublin Metropolitan Police Superintendent John Mallon of 'G' Division). The particular piece, inserted without O'Brien's knowledge, suggested that French was homosexual.[48] Somewhat surprisingly, given the seriousness of such an allegation in the 1880s, years before the Oscar Wilde trial, no writ followed until late October.[49]

It is highly likely that the only reason French sued, even at that point (because Healy's allegation was true), was that he was forced to do so by his superiors to avoid losing his job and pension. This is certainly what was alleged by O'Brien.[50] French sought £5000 in damages. *United Ireland* accepted the challenge, refused to retract and implied that it would prove its allegations in court. But O'Brien was actually bluffing. He could produce no evidence to justify the allegation. Healy's piece had been based on gossip, handed on to him by an irate RIC Inspector aware that French had propositioned a number of young RIC recruits. But the Inspector absolutely refused to testify. Sensibly O'Brien engaged the services of a London detective, Meiklejohn. His methods lacked subtlety but he produced the desired results.[51] Not only was Meiklejohn able to stand up the allegation and procure witnesses who *would* testify – he also uncovered evidence that another prominent Castle functionary Gustavus Cornwall, who ran the Irish postal service as Secretary of the General Post Office, was also a well-known homosexual.

Armed with its 'justification' *United Ireland* went on the offensive. It libelled Cornwall in an article on 24 May.[52] The GPO Secretary was far quicker to sue than French and a far more formidable opponent, though *United Ireland* claimed that he too was forced to take an action under duress.[53]

The campaign against French and Cornwall was contrived to encompass the Chief Secretary George Otto Trevelyan and the Lord Lieutenant Lord Spencer. Both were regularly and roundly vilified for retaining the services of men guilty of 'abominations' (the words 'homosexual' or 'sodomy' were never actually used by *United Ireland*).[54] This vicious and sustained campaign was one of the elements in the decision of Trevelyan to resign as Chief Secretary. Spencer was made of sterner stuff.

The kind of editorial error that is all too common meant *United Ireland* also managed to libel another of its favourite targets, Crown Prosecutor George Bolton, in the same fashion. Bolton had been largely responsible for securing the dubious Maamtrasna conviction of Myles Joyce. Bad sub-editing suggested that Bolton too was homosexual – he was a convicted fraud but a heterosexual – so he too sued.[55] On this occasion there was no suggestion that he was coerced into doing so by his employers.

In total *United Ireland* stood to lose up to £70,000 in damages and an untold amount in costs – such a sum would have crippled or closed the journal. There also remained the possibility that the Castle might take a criminal libel case against the newspaper – but the Executive, understandably cautious after the unhappy 'Accusing Spirits' experience, preferred to operate by proxy.

The Castle 'plan' – if such it was, and there is no paper trail to support this thesis advanced by O'Brien and Healy – backfired when, in early July 1884, *United Ireland* produced the three men in court who swore to having had sexual relationships with Cornwall.[56] He was later arrested and tried – as was French. French got two years, whilst Cornwall managed to escape a conviction. Only Bolton (who cleverly sued in Belfast rather than Dublin thus virtually guaranteeing himself an amenable jury) was successful in his suit – and such was his already damaged reputation (he had been found guilty of defrauding his late wife) that the entirely unionist jury only awarded him damages of £3,000[57] – damages O'Brien always insisted he never paid.

All of the above served to enhance the reputation of *United Ireland* and propel it towards weekly circulation figures of 100,000[58] – by way of comparison the *Freeman's Journal* at that time had daily circulation figures of between 30–40,000. *United Ireland*'s relentlessly confrontational rhetoric anticipated the campaigning and radical spirit of the so-called 'new journalism' beginning to emerge in the 1880s, a journalism that would be defined by the likes of W. T. Stead in the pages of the *Pall Mall Gazette* and T. P. O'Connor in the *Star*. 'New journalism' was about the slaying of the dragons of privilege and hypocrisy in a style that appealed to a mass circulation audience. While O'Brien's rather ostentatious prose could make no credible claims on the latter count he can certainly be said to have been the precursor of a new style of investigative and engaged journalism.

UNITED IRELAND UNDER THE SALISBURY ADMINISTRATION, 1887–91

The confluence of a prolonged agricultural depression, the consequent tensions introduced by the Plan of Campaign, and the assumption by Arthur J. Balfour of the role of Chief Secretary in March, 1887, led to the introduction by the Tory government of a stringent new coercion act, the Criminal Law and Procedure (Ireland) Act 1887. The legislation, unlike its Liberal 1882 counterpart, had no dedicated Press clause, however it was designed in a way that no such section was required. In essence, once the Lord Lieutenant had 'proclaimed' a barony, county or district all Irish National League branches in that area were banned, as was any reporting of their activities, on pain of imprisonment. Furthermore, judgment on these newly created crimes devolved upon courts convened by two Resident Magistrates rather than on trial by jury.[59]

The first prosecutions taken under the 1887 Crimes Act suggested that the Tories were perfectly willing to emulate the Gladstone government in a series of lengthy engagements with O'Brien through the courts, using their own special legislation for the purpose. As it happened, despite a weekly front page defiance of the new Crimes Act by *United Ireland* in carrying reports of suppressed branches of the Irish National League, such serial confrontation did not take place. Within weeks of the final passage of the Act both *United Ireland* and the more moderate *Nation* had broken the law by publishing accounts of National League branch meetings in Ramsgrange in Co. Wexford, one of the first districts to be formally proclaimed by the Lord Lieutenant, Lord Londonderry.[60] Consequently, on 6 October, 1887 both editors, O'Brien and T. D. Sullivan, were summoned to appear before the Police Magistrate, C. J. O'Donel – a man well-familiar with the *United Ireland* editor from the 'Accusing Spirits' case in December, 1882.

The contrast between the two hearings could not have been starker. Sullivan, then Lord Mayor of Dublin, arrived, accompanied by nationalist members of the Corporation, wearing his mayoral robes. O'Brien simply failed to appear altogether. Tim Healy appeared for Sullivan, Edward Carson for the Crown. O'Donel, a fair-minded judge not greatly beloved of Dublin Castle, dismissed the charges on the technical grounds of the Crown's failure to produce evidence as to the nature of the proceedings at the proclaimed meeting. He held that the state had failed to prove satisfactorily, outside of the newspaper account itself, that the gathering was indeed one organised under the auspices of the Irish National League.[61] The Crown had failed to offer external corroboration, relying exclusively on the 'confession' of the defendant contained in the article. Were the verdict to stand, the Criminal Law and Procedure (Ireland) Act, 1887 would have failed its first significant test.

The Crown appealed the judgment. O'Donel, at the request of Carson, agreed to state a case to a higher court. Healy, wary of the Queen's Bench where resided the likes of Mr Justice Lawson, asked that the appeal be directed to the Exchequer court. O'Brien's case, in his absence, was adjourned. Mr Justice Andrews of the Exchequer court heard submissions from Healy and Carson. Christopher Palles, the Lord Chief Baron of the Exchequer, as spikily independent of the Castle as was O'Donel himself, ruled, however, that

> the evidence of the written statements of the respondents here amounting to the affirmation in fact that the meeting held was a meeting of the Irish National League was sufficient evidence of that fact . . . and that the case must go back to be reconsidered and determined by him.[62]

On 2 December Sullivan's case was reheard by O'Donel and in the light of the Exchequer Court decision he was jailed for two months[63] – an outcome that, logically, should have followed in the case of O'Brien. That it did not had nothing to do with any lack of will on the part of the government but was owing to the fact that O'Brien, by that time, was already serving the first of a number of jail terms (this one in Tullamore prison) arising out of his Plan of Campaign activities.[64]

Between 1887 and 1891 more than a dozen provincial newspaper editors were prosecuted and jailed for offences similar to those committed by *United Ireland*.[65] In many instances *United Ireland* carried exactly the same reports for which local newspaper editors were imprisoned. Newsvendors were prosecuted and jailed for selling copies of the paper containing reports of proscribed branches in their districts.[66] Yet O'Brien, who always made himself amenable as editor, although most of the editorial work during that period fell to barrister and journalist Matthias McDonnell Bodkin, was never prosecuted despite his paper's weekly defiance of the law. In his memoir, *Recollections of an Irish Judge*, Bodkin wrote that '*United Ireland* in my time had not only immunity from libel actions, but, stranger still, it had immunity from coercion prosecutions.'[67] He did not speculate on why this was the case.

The most likely answer is that the newspaper was actually protected by the frequency of O'Brien's prison terms between 1887 and 1891. His involvement in the Plan of Campaign led to numerous arrests and periods of incarceration for offences against the Crimes Act. Essentially, O'Brien was being imprisoned for transgressions on public platforms than for those being made on the front page of his newspaper. As Bodkin pointed out, O'Brien refused to allow his deputy to accept responsibility, as editor or publisher, for anything that appeared in *United Ireland*.[68] Hence the futility of holding O'Brien accountable for actionable material appearing when he was already under lock and key.

In the only instance of a *United Ireland* prosecution under the Crimes Act – that of October 1887 – the Under Secretary, West Ridgeway, writing to Balfour, while keen to pursue the likes of the *Kerry Sentinel*, recommended the dropping of charges against O'Brien. He did so on the basis that, 'We are winning, and can afford to be generous if we can do so without injury to the public interests . . . [and] . . . It is most undesirable to bring O'Brien out of jail just now.'[69] In the years that followed it would scarcely be more desirable to have O'Brien in court defending freedom of the press when he could simply be kept out of circulation in Tullamore, Cork or Galway gaols.

Only on occasions when *United Ireland* raised the bar in terms of commentary was this tacit immunity threatened. For example, in April 1888 West Ridgeway drew Balfour's attention to the publication of intimidating notices in the paper. However, no action was taken.[70] Later that year the Under Secretary wrote to his Chief about an offending item in *United Ireland* of 29 September 1888 entitled 'Devils citing scripture'. 'No quarter I think should be shown to the Editor.' he insisted, demanding that, 'the Law Officers be instructed emphatically that the first opportunity is taken of prosecuting O'Brien for articles such as this.' However, West Ridgeway then himself highlighted a difficulty in cases such as this that had been a feature of both the Tory and Liberal administrations: 'I say "emphatically" because there is decidedly an inclination in the Law Room to leave O'Brien alone and I do not think that it is based entirely on legal grounds. It would be a great coup to run him in on such a charge.'[71]

West Ridgeway (who described O'Brien in the same letter as 'the meanest and most malignant reptile crawling' was denied his coup and the Law Office prevailed; as it did on numerous occasions in the decade 1881–91 when it appeared a prosecution against *United Ireland* was warranted or imminent. Such pusillanimity is understandable given the previous history of legal actions against the newspaper. Successive Law Officers, given the frequency of O'Brien's incarcerations on a variety of charges, simply decided to leave well enough alone when it came to *United Ireland*.

UNITED IRELAND AFTER THE SPLIT

After Parnell's success in regaining control of *United Ireland* from its acting editor, Bodkin, at the end of 1890, in a forceful coup involving the virtual storming of the paper's offices,[72] editorial priorities changed radically. Under O'Brien the paper had only a passing acquaintance with moderation. With Parnell and his acolytes now in direct control the newspaper became a byword in partisanship. In 1891 *United Ireland*, to all intents and purposes, ceased to resemble a newspaper and became a factional Parnellite propaganda sheet. The preponderance of the 159 editorials in that year were philippics aimed at 'the Seceders', the McCarthyite faction (34 per cent); the antagonistic Roman Catholic Church (16 per cent); and other nationalist newspapers – mostly the *Journal* after its switch of allegiance in August 1891 and Tim Healy's *National Press* – (10 per cent). Much of the remainder (25 per cent) related to commentary on the three crucial by-elections and praise poems for Parnell himself, and his principal lieutenants John Redmond and Timothy Harrington.

As the year went on the level of invective was ratcheted upwards. A reading of the frequently venomous commentary in the post-Split *United Ireland* clearly indicated that reconciliation was not in the air in the wake of the three Parnellite electoral defeats and, particularly, after the death of Parnell himself. Editorials that year also reflected some of the alliances Parnell was trying to forge in order to shore up his critical political situation. There was, for example, a new-found admiration for all things Fenian. This included favourable coverage of the return to Ireland of James Stephens[73] and strident condemnation of the death in prison of the leading IRB member, P. W. Nally.[74] There was also evidence of an attempted *rapprochement* with Unionism[75] and with Labour.[76] It is clear from the contents of the newspaper during this period that Parnell was exercising a more direct personal influence on the editorial line than he had been during O'Brien's hegemony. He was certainly spending more time in Ireland than he had during O'Brien's stewardship of his newspaper.[77] A reflection of this re-ordering of priorities came in an editorial immediately prior to Parnell's death. In the issue of 3 October 1891 in an editorial headed 'What of these, Masters?' doubt was cast on the prioritisation of agrarian reform by the Irish political hierarchy during the 1880s.

'Is the Irish farmer Ireland?' asked a newspaper with a long-standing record of favouring the interests of the farmer over the labourer, industrial development and labour itself:

> Is there no man in this island worthy of the consideration of her politicians but he who rents the soil? For sixteen years we have fought for this man, agitated for him, gone to jail for him, and turned the English House of Commons topsy-turvy for him. Is there no other man?

United Ireland, clearly a recent convert to class politics, proceeded to answer its own question:

> Ah, fellow countryman, politics or no politics, let us be just. Let us, especially, be just to our own poor countrymen. The brave fisher folk gazing wistfully at the shoals of mackerel so near, and yet so far beyond their reach; the poor patient Irish labourer in his hovel, the poor Irish labourer who has stood so nobly for Irish Nationality, notwithstanding all his poverty; these, we do respectfully submit, are as pathetic figures in our National life as any rack-rented farmer. Are they to be left to their fate?[78]

This new line was undoubtedly a function of Parnell's ebbing support in rural Ireland where the clergy had a far greater influence than in the cities. After the death of Parnell, *United Ireland* failed to sustain, editorially at least, such an invigorating level of enthusiasm for the 'brave fisher folk' or the 'poor Irish labourer.'

In its final issue of 1891 *United Ireland* welcomed the arrival of a new Parnellite newspaper, the *Irish Daily Independent*, opining that, 'in every important particular which constitutes a National organ this the *Independent* is all that could be desired.'[79] There was not, of course, the slightest chance that the *Irish Daily Independent* would live up to its name, in the short term at least. Neither was there even the vaguest hint of any sense of irony emanating from the *United Ireland* editorial pen. In just over a decade the newspaper had gone from being an 'insurrection in print' to defining insularity in print. The paper itself struggled on for a few more years (to 1893) as a partisan battering ram before succumbing to its own irrelevance.

Despite certain obvious caveats *United Ireland* had, largely, been at the disposal of the wider nationalist movement in the 1880s. From the moment at the end of 1890, when Parnell displayed more interest in the newspaper than he had done since the establishment of the Irish National Newspaper Company in 1881, it degenerated into a tool of empty factionalism. In his memoir *Evening Memories* O'Brien makes no reference whatever to the decline of his project. The journal that had weathered the best efforts of two coercion regimes to close it down, had, metaphorically, ended up by smashing its own presses.

Jürgen Habermas in his influential work, *The Structural Transformation of the Public Sphere*, writes about the movement towards a mass circulation press in the late nineteenth century and attests that it 'paid for the maximisation of its sales with the depoliticisation of its content.'[80] By the 1880s, daily newspapers in Britain were becoming more like their Sunday equivalents which had long since adopted a 'domestic' over a 'public' model. Sunday publications like *Lloyd's Weekly* and *Reynolds Weekly Newspaper* (a radical weekly), with their emphasis on court cases and sensation had been rewarded with circulation figures far in excess of the dailies. A move towards emulation of the Sunday newspaper template by many of the dailies, including some of the established titles like the *Pall Mall Gazette*, led to a situation where, according to media critic Alan Lee, ' . . . the cheap and the tawdry, the trivial and the sensational, kept out of the market place the valuable, the authentic, and the serious.'[81]

United Ireland came into being at the start of a decade that witnessed an acceleration of this process of mass market populism. Yet *United Ireland*, while not really challenging the thesis of Habermas, is a notable exception. It was a mass circulation newspaper that was highly politicised. In fact its politicisation was, arguably, the sole basis for its existence. It was more akin to newspapers like Cobbett's *Political Register* and Feargus O'Connor's *Northern Star*. The *Political Register* had led the radical charge for parliamentary reform in the early part of the nineteenth century; the *Northern Star* had sought to advance that agenda during the mid-century Chartist agitation. The received wisdom from media theorists like Raymond Williams, is that such radical or even politicised journals should not have thrived in the 1880s.[82]

Of course the case of *United Ireland* does not negate the notion that by the early 1880s the press had largely abandoned its political, civic and social roles. But why did *United Ireland* buck the prevailing journalistic trend away from political engagement and debate and towards the more sensationalist, recreational mode Clearly because Ireland was an exceptional 'market'. While it experienced all the factors contributing to the rapid expansion of the press in the latter half of the nineteenth century – higher literacy, the abolition of 'taxes on knowledge' and a good rail distribution network – it had some unique characteristics of its own.

There was, for example, the lack of a well-developed 'domestic' mode in Ireland. The new templates being adopted by English newspapers in their own rapid commercialisation – an increased focus on sport and entertainment and the relative avoidance of high political debate – did not have quite the same resonance in Ireland. Despite the foundation in 1884 of a populist organisation like the Gaelic Athletic Association, Ireland was not yet as well developed a 'recreational' society as England. Ireland of the 1880s was rather more like the England of the upheavals of the Chartist period, where O'Connor's *Northern Star* and John Cleave's *Weekly Police Gazette* (which anticipated 'new journalism' by half a century by combining crime reporting with support for radical causes) had joint circulations similar to that of *United Ireland* at its height. In a highly politicised and activist society there was clearly a market for a highly political and activist newspaper. By the 1880s the radical equivalents of the *Political Register* and the *Northern Star*, unable to attract funding from advertisers, had retreated into a high-priced specialist ghetto often characterised by tedious didacticism. Raymond Williams refers to it as the 'pauper press'.[83]

Ireland was also accustomed to campaigning journalism as an adjunct to mass movement politics. During the Repeal campaign of the 1840s, three of those tried for conspiracy during the State Trials of 1844 were the newspaper editors John Gray (*Freeman's Journal*), Charles Gavan Duffy (*Nation*) and Richard Barrett (*Pilot*). The weekly purchase of *United Ireland*, which often fetched sums well in excess of its cover price in the wake of the many attempts to seize its print run, was more than just an attempt on the part of the purchaser to access information. It was a participatory gesture, akin to the payment of the Catholic Rent during the Emancipation campaign of the 1820s. Even the cover price was the same.

Furthermore, if one accepts the premise of Charles Townshend's thesis viz. that much Irish political agitation and violence was based on a fundamental philosophical dissent and was a function of 'the upholding of a different system of law or of social control,'[84] then *United Ireland* can be seen as the *Dublin Gazette* of such a parallel polity.

There is another possible explanation for the countervailing phenomenon that was *United Ireland*. It was launched just as the sensationalist or 'yellow' press was asserting itself forcefully in the marketplace. However, as Habermas himself contends, 'In the end the news generally assumes some sort of guise and is made to resemble a narrative . . .'[85] This was also a characteristic of O'Brien's stewardship of *United Ireland*. He personalised, sensationalised, lionised (Parnell, Sexton, Healy) and demonised (Forster, Spencer, the 'Nominals', Frank Hugh O'Donnell). He thus created a meta-narrative: conflictual, simplistic, and adversarial; designed to be consumed by a highly motivated readership.

Ultimately however, O'Brien, despite his political loyalty – not to mention his personal closeness – to his leader, was more distraction than defender; more of a red herring than a Rottweiler. He enjoyed more latitude than did most of Parnell's other lieutenants. There is little evidence of the party leader exercising an overtly censorious influence over O'Brien, other than in his increasingly urgent attempts to get his editor to close down the quasi-Fenian stable member *The Irishman* as a *rapprochement* with the Liberals became more likely. The evidence is just as compelling that Parnell, for his own purposes, actually egged O'Brien on in some of his more intemperate campaigns. For example, O'Brien's excoriation of Joseph Chamberlain and Charles Dilke prior to their proposed tour of Ireland in 1885, appears to have been secretly supported or even prompted, by Parnell, who wished to distance himself from a radical faction seeking to undermine Gladstone.

Parnell allowed O'Brien his head because *United Ireland* served his ends well. It was a useful noticeboard, unequalled in its ability *pour épater le Château*, and in its mythologizing of Parnell helpfully presented him as the radical leader of a quasi-revolutionary movement. He was anything but. He simply required the services of a skilful propagandist who was prepared, often in *Pravda*-like fashion, to justify the ways of God (Parnell) to man (advanced Irish nationalists). The newspaper that more accurately reflected Parnell's own philosophy was the *Freeman's Journal*, but intimidated, as it was commercially and politically, into 'deviation phobia'. The *Journal* may have been owned by the Gray family but, after the first appearance of *United Ireland* in 1881 – aggravated by the arrest of Edmund Dwyer Gray for contempt of court the following year in the wake of the Hynes case[86] – its politics was the politics of Parnellism.

United Ireland was, without doubt, Parnell's Rottweiler, but this particular canine was a convenient and intimidating decoy with attention-grabbing, permanently-bared fangs. The real Cerberus, the true guardian of the Parnellite political philosophy was the *Freeman's Journal*, the ageing hound, rather like his beloved Grouse, trotting after the aristocratic grandee and former High Sheriff of the County of Wicklow.

Notes

1   Marie-Louise Legg, *Newspapers and Nationalism: The Irish Provincial Press, 1850–1892* (Dublin, 1999), ch. 9 'The militant nation, 1880–92'; and Stephen Koss, *The Rise and Fall of the Political Press in Britain*, vol. 1 (London, 1980), prologue.

2   James Loughlin, 'Constructing the political spectacle: Parnell, the press and national leadership, 1879–86', in D. George Boyce and Alan O'Day, *Parnell in Perspective* (London, 1991) p. 223; and Alan O'Day, 'Parnell: orator and speaker' in ibid., p. 202.

3   Myles Dungan, *The Captain and the King: William O'Shea, Parnell and late Victorian Ireland* (Dublin, 2009), p. 29.

4   Edward Byrne, *Parnell a Memoir*, Frank Callanan (ed.), (Dublin, 1991), p. 2; and Alfred Robbins, *Parnell: The Last Five Years* (London, 1926), p. 23.

5   See above, ch. 5, Felix M. Larkin, 'Parnell, Politics and the Press in Ireland, 1875–1924'.

6   William O'Brien, *Evening Memories*, (Dublin, 1920), p. 14.

7   Loughlin, 'Constructing the political spectacle', p. 233.

8   *Hansard*, 3rd series, vol. 266, col. 802 (16 Feb. 1882).

9   William O'Brien, *Recollections* (London, 1905), p. 308fn. O'Brien wrote 'As prosecutions and actions for libel thickened, Parnell and the others wisely withdrew from their nominal Directorship. The entire responsibility was thenceforward my own.'

10   James O'Connor, *Recollections of Richard Pigott* (Dublin, 1889), p. 14.

11   Special Commission proceedings, (London, 1890), vol. 7, p. 165, 60318.

12   Ibid., vol. 8, p. 89, 70737, (21 May 1889). O'Brien told the Commission: 'I would not be a party to depriving the extreme nationalists of what they might regard as their organ.' He claimed that his hope was to see the *Irishman* die a natural death as its dwindling circulation continued to fall. O'Brien admitted to paying scant attention to its content even though he had editorial responsibility for its output.

13   *United Ireland*, 13 Aug. 1881.

14   Ibid., 19 and 26 Nov. 1881.

15   British Library, Add. Ms 44157 ff. 184–185, Gladstone to Forster, 25 Oct. 1880.

16   *United Ireland*, 17 Sept. 1881.

17   Andrew Dunlop, *Fifty Years of Irish Journalism*, (Dublin, 1911), p. 46; and Michael Foley 'Colonialism and Journalism in Ireland' in *Journalism Studies*, vol. 5, no. 3, 2004, p. 381.

18   *United Ireland*, 17 Sept. 1881.

19 Mallon to Talbot, 8 November, 1881, National Archives of Ireland (hereafter NAI), CSORP 38894/1881, Police and Crime Division Reports, III, Compensation Cases, Crimes Act, 1882–3, Carton 6.

20 *United Ireland*, 27 Aug. 1881.

21 O'Brien, *Recollections*, p. 362.

22 *United Ireland*, 22 Oct. 1881.

23 John Denvir, *The Life Story of an Old Rebel*, (Dublin, 1910), ch. xvii; and O'Brien, *Recollections*, ch. xvi.

24 John Naish memo, 25 Nov. 1881, NAI, CSORP 1881-42170, Police and Crime Division Reports, III, Compensation Cases, Crimes Act, 1882–3, Carton 6.

25 Ibid., 15 Dec. 1881, NAI, CSORP 1881-45113, Police and Crime Division Reports, III, Compensation Cases, Crimes Act, 1882–3, Carton 6.

26 Mallon to Talbot, 14 Dec. 1881, NAI, CSORP 1881-45113, Police and Crime Division Reports, III, Compensation Cases, Crimes Act, 1882–3, Carton 6.

27 *Hansard*, 3rd series, vol. 276, col. 627 (22 Feb. 1883). W. E. Forster singled out the column in an attack on Parnell in the Commons, alleging that it supported his charge of the latter's tacit approval of crime.

28 Special Commission proceedings, vol.8, p. 154, 71460-1 (22 May 1889).

29 Katharine O'Shea, *Charles Stewart Parnell: His Love Story and Political Life* (London, 1973), p. 117.

30 Special Commission proceedings, vol.8, p. 104, 70827, (21 May 1889).

31 O'Brien, *Recollections*, p. 378.

32 *Hansard*, 3rd series, vol. 269, cols 672-4 (15 May 1882).

33 *United Ireland*, 20 May 1882.

34 *Freeman's Journal*, 16 May 1882.

35 *Hansard*, 3rd series, vol. 269, col. 1714 (18 May 1882).

36 *Public General Statutes passed in the forty-fifth and forty-sixth years of the reign of Her Majesty Queen Victoria*, (London, 1882), p. 60.

37 NAI, CSORP 1882-149, 17 Dec. 1881, claim of R. Burke for copies of *United Ireland* seized; Ibid., 1882-21783, 8 Apr. 1882, claim of W. B. Massey for copies of *United Ireland* seized.

38 NAI, CSORP, 1881-36081, 21 Oct. 1881, John Madden to Forster.

39 *Hansard*, 3rd series, vol. 270, col. 1690 (19 June 1882).

40 *United Ireland*, 23 Dec. 1882.

41 Order for the Forfeiture of Newspapers Under Section 13, 23 Dec. 1882, NAI, CSORP, Police and Crime Division Reports, III, Compensation Cases, Crimes Act, 1882–3, Carton 6 1882-47393.

42 O'Brien, *Evening Memories*, p. 16.

43 Hugh Fraser, *Principles and Practice of the Law of Libel and Slander with Suggestions on the Conduct of a Civil Action* (London, 1897), pp 185–6.

44 *United Ireland*, 6 Jan. 1883.

45 *Daily Express (Dublin)*, 16 Jan.1883.

46 *Freeman's Journal*, 10 Feb. 1883.

47 *Daily Express (Dublin)*. 12 Feb. 1883.

48 *United Ireland*, 25 Aug. 1883.

49 Ibid., 20 Oct. 1883.

50 Ibid., 1 Dec. 1883.

51 *Hansard*, 3rd series, vol. 289, col. 695 (17 June 1884).

52 *United Ireland*, 10 May, 1884.

53 Ibid., 24 May, 1884.

54 Ibid.

55 O'Brien, *Evening Memories*, pp 24–5.

56 *Freeman's Journal*, 8 July, 1884.

57 *United Ireland*, 9 Aug. 1884.

58 Evidence of William O'Brien to the Special Commission on Parnellism and Crime, Book 8, 72018, p200, 1890 – supported by Accounts for the Irish National Newspaper & Publishing Company, William O'Brien Papers, University College, Cork AA, f. 81.

59 *Public General Statutes passed in the fiftieth and fifty-first years of the reign of Her Majesty Queen Victoria*, (London, 1887), pp 49–59.

60 *United Ireland*, 1 Oct. 1887; and *Nation*, 1 Oct. 1887.

61 *Freeman's Journal*, 7 Oct. 1887.

62 Ibid., 11 Nov. 1887.

63 Ibid., 3 Dec. 1887.

64 National Archives, London, CO 903/1, p. 5. Memo – 'as this gentleman was convicted of another offence at this time at Mitchelstown, the press prosecution was never proceeded with.'

65 Most notably Edward Harrington of the *Kerry Sentinel* (*Kerry Sentinel*, 9 Dec. 1887) and John Hooper of the Cork Herald (*Cork Herald*, 20 Dec. 1887).

66 For example, the case of Denis McNamara of Ennis – jailed for seven days. *United Ireland*, 26 Nov. 1887.

67 Matthias McDonnell Bodkin, *Recollections of an Irish Judge: Press, Bar and Parliament* (Dublin, 1915), pp 150–1.

68 Ibid., p. 154.

69 British Library, Add. Ms 49808, ff. 14–17, Joseph West Ridgeway to Arthur Balfour, 10 Nov. 1887.

70 Ibid., ff. 101–102, Joseph West Ridgeway to Arthur Balfour, 10 Apr, 1888.

71 Ibid., ff. 234–235, Joseph West Ridgeway to Arthur Balfour, 29 Sept. 1888.

72 Bodkin, *Recollections*, ch. xvii.

73 *United Ireland*, 3 Oct. 1891, 'Welcome'.

74 Ibid., 14 and 21 Nov. 1891. It should, however, be noted that the death of Nally would have attracted similar treatment in O'Brien's *United Ireland*.

75 Ibid., 28 Mar. 1891, 'Irish Protestants and the crisis'; and 16 May, 1991, 'Two Letters'.

76 Ibid., 9 May, 1891, 'Labour Day in Dublin'.

77 Ironically, up to the end of 1890 O'Brien's name still appeared on the bottom right hand corner of page eight as the named proprietor, just as it had done since 13 Aug. 1881.

78 *United Ireland*, 3 Oct. 1891.

79 Ibid., 26 Dec. 1891.

80 Jürgen Habermas, *The Structural Transformation of the Public Sphere* (Cambridge, Mass. 1992), p. 169.

81 Alan J. Lee, *The Origins of the Popular Press in England: 1855–1914* (London, 1976), p. 28.

82 Raymond Williams, *The Long Revolution* (London, 2001), p. 210.

83 Ibid., p. 210.

84 Charles Townshend, *Political Violence in Ireland: Government and Resistance since 1848* (Oxford, 1983), p. 5.

85 Habermas, *Structural Transformation*, p. 170.

86 Myles Dungan, *The Captain and the King*, pp 146–55.

CHAPTER 7

Defending the Cause

Parnell and the Drink Interest

Fionnuala Waldron

On the death of Parnell, the Dublin Licensed Grocers' and Vintners' Protection Association (LGVPA) passed the following resolution:

> That we, the Committee of the Dublin Licensed Grocers' and Vintners' Protection Association, desire to place on record our sense of the loss sustained by the country in the sad and untimely death of Charles Stewart Parnell; we feel that in him the trade which we represent has lost a friend who on many important occasions rendered the most signal services to the cause which we are engaged in defending; and we beg to tender to his widow and the other members of his family our sincere sympathy in their bereavement.[1]

In the months following the O'Shea divorce case, Dublin publicans were conspicuous in their support of Parnell, leading to the contemporary characterisation of the Parnellite victories in the 1892 election as 'a triumph of publicanism'.[2] While there was some division within their ranks, that support was sustained in the following years and publicans formed the backbone of Parnellism in the city at local and municipal level throughout the 1890s. The LGVPA itself, however, maintained an outwardly neutral stance. Keen to preserve its collective unity and wary of losing political support from either side in its ongoing parliamentary battle against temperance-inspired legislation, the vintners' association adhered to a non-partisan approach during the split and its aftermath. Given the internecine war that engulfed nationalist Ireland as a consequence of the Parnell Split and divided loyalties amongst the publicans themselves, maintaining associational unity was no mean feat; indicating both the strength of trade identity amongst Dublin vintners and the primacy of trade interest. The success of the Association in negotiating that difficult terrain was, in part, due to its ability to conflate trade interest with Home Rule; an ability that was greatly enhanced by Parnell's 'signal services to the cause'.

While the Association's dismay at the death of Parnell was genuine, Parnell's relationship with the drinks trade began badly. In 1876 as newly-elected MP for Meath, Parnell voted for a resolution in favour of the closing of public houses in Ireland on Sundays, and in 1878 supported the Sunday Closing (Ireland) Bill – a position that helps explain the hostile reception he received from Cork publicans when he visited that city as an election candidate in 1880.[3] Yet, in the years between his 1876 vote and his death, Parnell came to be perceived by publicans as a defender of their interests. Examining that evolution can reveal something of the nature of trade interest and identity, and of Parnell's capacity to steer a course through the competing needs of disparate groups in pursuit of an ultimate goal. Parnell's relationship with the drinks trade is necessarily set against the temperance campaigns of the nineteenth century which sought to make Ireland sober, and the consequent rise of vintners as an organised interest group, particularly in Dublin. For Parnell, faced with the task of forging and maintaining a united, disciplined and focused parliamentary party out of the diverse and loosely organised Home Rule movement, the role of vintners as organisational men at local level meant that he could ill afford to ignore them. Over the course of the nineteenth century the licensed trade became skilled at political lobbying, and adept at using the discourse and practice of nationalism to defend its interests. Parnell, for his part, in seeking to maintain some balance between the competing constituencies of temperance and liquor, was both adroit and vigilant.

Parnell's personal relationship with alcohol, such as we know it, was not without its tensions. While his brother, John Howard Parnell, records that at dinner he invariably drank claret, his preferred drink in later life according to Katharine O'Shea was 'a still Moselle' which he drank on the advice of his doctor, Sir Henry Thompson.[4] Parnell's younger days had been marked by less cautious tastes however. By the time he cast his vote in favour of Sunday closing, he had already experienced the negative consequences of alcohol in his personal life. His sister Emily's marriage to Arthur Dickinson in 1864 was marred by her husband's developing alcoholism, which kept them dependent on a succession of small annuities and allowances and on the charity of her family.[5] Parnell's social life as a young man reflected Arthur's influence, leading, in Roy Foster's words, to 'a certain amount of roistering', and most famously, in 1869, to a *mêlée* in the Glendalough Hotel which resulted in the appearance of Parnell and Dickinson before the Rathdrum Petty Sessions.[6] To be fair to Dickinson, this was not the first time Parnell had ended up in court due to an excess of alcohol. In May of the same year, Parnell had been sent down from Cambridge as a result of a court case which found him guilty of a drunken assault on a local small businessman whose only offence appears to have been, depending on whether you accept the account of the defendant or the victim, either that of displaying an impertinent curiosity as to Parnell's condition or of making a foolhardy attempt to assist an intoxicated student whose afternoon of champagne, sherry and biscuits with his friends had left him the worse for wear.[7] In any case, it is unlikely that Parnell's personal and family experiences with alcohol had any real influence on his decision to support the 1876 resolution and the subsequent legislation in 1878. It is more likely that he was influenced by the temperance campaigns that dominated public discourse around drink throughout the nineteenth century and which provided the impetus for the 1876 resolution.

The late 1820s had seen the appearance of the first large-scale temperance societies in Ireland, located predominantly in Dublin and Belfast.[8] Motivated largely by concerns about the physical and social effects of excessive drinking, the temperance movement of the early nineteenth century focused primarily on the notion of 'reformation', and on the personal redemption of individual drinkers, irrespective of whether they were spirit-drinking Catholic peasants, beer-swilling urban artisans or port-imbibing members of the landed gentry. In the 1830s a fault line developed within the movement between those who believed in teetotalism and those who supported the idea of moderate drinking. It was a tension that was to remain evident – particularly within the Catholic Church – until the end of the century, helping to consolidate the largely sectarian character of the movement itself. Increasingly under clerical control, Catholic temperance became distinctly devotional in form, posing little or no threat to the interests of the drinks trade. Despite Fr Mathew's crusade in the 1840s, which had succeeded in bringing the temperance issue together for the first time with the twin forces of Catholicism and nationalism, temperance, as Diarmaid Ferriter observes, 'was not historically seen as a particularly Catholic virtue.'[9] In fact the temperance movement itself remained essentially Protestant in character. While teetotalism had won out over moderationism by the end of the 1830s, prohibitionism itself also gave way (at least in the short-term) to the more meliorative aim of reforming the licensing regulations through restrictive legislation. This legislative approach represented the dominant strain in temperance campaigning in the latter half of the century.

The temperance movement which emerged across Britain and Ireland in mid-century, was concerned chiefly with the public context of drink and the regulation of the public spaces in which it was sold.[10] This switch in focus from personal redemption to legislative reform was accompanied by the development of increasingly professional and effective campaign organisations, headed by full-time advocates such as T. W. Russell.[11] In 1866, the

Irish Sunday Closing Association was formed in Dublin under Russell's leadership. Three years later, he helped found the Irish Permissive Bill Association to campaign for a local veto (or permissive bill) that would grant communities a voice in deciding on the need for licences in their local area. Both associations merged in 1878 to form the Irish Association for the Prevention of Intemperance. The campaign for Sunday closing, in particular, took fire during the 1870s, dominating political discourse for long periods during this decade.

While the campaign for restrictive legislation had a characteristically religious dimension, Parnell's support for the 1878 bill seemed to have a more practical motivation. Certainly, his brief – and lukewarm – interjection in support of the bill during the House of Commons debate, anchored that support firmly in his desire to represent the wishes of his Meath constituency rather than in any personal commitment to the idea of temperance, acknow-ledging that 'He had always himself felt considerable doubts as to the principles of the Bill'.[12] Parnell's identity as an employer of labour and his interest in industry make it unlikely that he was unaware of the class-based discourse that surrounded the issue.[13] The campaign to abolish Donnybrook Fair, for example, which finally succeeded in 1868, was part of a wider, sustained attempt to control the social life of Dublin's working-class in the name of religion, class, industry and respectability.[14] Given the working-class character of public houses and other retail outlets such as beer-houses and spirit dealers, campaigns to restrict the opening hours and the availability of licences can also be seen as forming part of a wider process of moderni-sation and industrialisation seeking to impose a time discipline on workers accustomed to a more task-based approach. In this unfamiliar environment, time became a currency which was 'not passed but spent' and workers were subjected to what E. P. Thompson has called the 'propaganda of time-thrift'.[15] This focus on a uniform and disciplined approach to time reconceptualised drunkenness as an 'anti-social vice' rather than an individual lapse into excess.[16] Customs such as arriving late to work, drinking on the job, or allow-ing the task to determine when one would finish work did not sit well with the factory-based practices of an industrialised economy. The practice of 'Saint Monday', for example, which resulted in workers taking Monday off work, is a case in point. When Nicholas C. Whyte, MD, coroner to the city of Dublin, in his evidence before the Select Committee on Sunday Closing Acts in London in 1888, complained of the difficulty of getting a workman on Monday, he was articulating a well-worn temperance argument:

> My experience is that the men are prone to drink on Saturdays and Sundays; the consequence is that 'Saint Monday,' as it is called, is very well kept by that class of

people, and that continues till Tuesday. In fact I wanted a coat to come over here, and I could not get it because I gave my order rather late and the tailor said he could not execute the order on the Monday or the Tuesday.[17]

It is likely, then, that in voting to support Sunday closing, Parnell was thinking more in terms of the need for a sober worker than a temperate landlord.

Parnell was not alone amongst Home Rule MPs in his support for temperance legislation. When Richard Smyth, Liberal MP for Derry, introduced his resolution in favour of Sunday closing in 1876, it drew the support of 29 Home Rule MPs; while nine Home Rulers, primarily representatives of cities and towns with important drinks industries, opposed it.[18] In the wider political environment, the temperance politics of the period led to a growing identification of parties with one side or the other. While that identification was never absolute, the Liberal party, prey to its nonconformist conscience, became increasingly associated with temperance while the Conservatives came to be seen as the staunch supporters of the drink interest.

When the Sunday closing bill passed in 1878, however, it included two important Government amendments: the exemption of Dublin, along with Cork, Waterford, Limerick and Belfast from the terms of the bill; and the imposition of a three-year time limit. The concerted campaigning of the Dublin-based LGVPA and, to a lesser extent, that of the vintners' associations in Belfast and Cork had had some limited success. The LGVPA recognised that these concessions were won largely because of the support it received from its allies in the English trade who feared that restrictive legislation passed for Ireland would serve as a precedent for the rest of the United Kingdom. This was a fear the Dublin vintners were eager to stoke. Referring some years later to the 1870s campaign, Michael Dwyer, secretary of the LGVPA recalled his persuasion of the English trade:

> Ireland was simply an outwork of the citadel, and that once Ireland was disposed of, the turn of England would come. Their enemies had taken Ireland; they were taking Wales, trying to make Cornwall, and . . . they were looking hungrily towards Yorkshire.[19]

The bill itself had a rough passage. Its sponsors were reluctant to accept proposed amendments, prompting Parnell to threaten to walk out of the House if they continued to refuse to compromise.[20] In an ironic twist, opponents of Sunday closing, such as the Home Rule MPs, Philip Callan, W. H. O'Sullivan and Major Purcell O'Gorman, in alliance with Conservative MPs and facilitated by a reluctant government, used the tactics of obstruction in an attempt to talk the bill out.[21] While the bill was finally passed in August 1878, the exemptions and the three-year limit ensured that the campaign for

Sunday closing remained an ongoing political issue. When the Sunday Closing Act was finally made permanent in 1906 it represented the culmination of over thirty years of campaigning. In any case, Sunday closing alone was unlikely to satisfy the temperance lobby, which continued to agitate for early Saturday closing and for the right of local communities to determine the number of licences in their areas. Parnell's formal ascent to the leadership of the Irish Parliamentary Party in the aftermath of the 1880 election, however, heralded the end of his brief flirtation with temperance; there were other voices he was obliged to heed and other interests to which he needed to attend.

With the number of public houses in Ireland growing from approximately 15,000 in 1850 to almost 20,000 by 1911, it is perhaps unsurprising that the brewing and distilling industries were among the few successful, indigenous manufacturing industries in Ireland of that period; although not all areas of the industry were equally successful.[22] Certainly, during the eighteenth century and for much of the nineteenth, the Irish preference for whiskey over beer was marked. The consumption of spirits, which had increased massively during the eighteenth century, peaked in 1838 with a consumption level of over 12 million gallons. By the 1860s, however, this had fallen to around 4.4 million gallons. Mary Daly identifies three main reasons for this fall in consumption: the influence of Father Mathew's temperance campaign; the lessening in demand due to the fall in population resulting from the Famine; and consumers' response to Gladstone's swingeing increases in spirit duty in his budgets of the 1850s.[23] Between 1857 and 1910, the consumption of spirits fell from 1.1 gallons to 0.63 gallons per capita.[24] Irish brewing on the other hand, entered a sustained period of expansion from the mid-nineteenth century. Changing tastes, improvements in brewing methods and increased urbanisation ensured a growing market for beer.

In general, the output of the brewing industry in Ireland trebled between the 1850s and 1914. Most of this growth was attributable to Guinness, which had become the largest brewing company in the world by 1914.[25] While the expansion of Guinness in the earlier part of the century has been attributed to its growing market in Britain, in the post-Famine period it was mainly driven by an increasing share of the developing urban market in Ireland and improved access to markets outside Dublin. It is probable also, that the collapse of many small breweries between 1838 to 1852 created a void which Guinness in particular was in a position to exploit.[26] For Dublin, brewing was seen as one of the city's success stories – in 1864 there were eight breweries in the city. Guinness' main competitor in Dublin was D'Arcy's Anchor Brewery on Usher Street, which was established in 1740. In 1886, when Alfred Barnard wrote his influential *Noted Breweries of Great Britain and Ireland*, D'Arcy's brewery was second in consequence to Guinness, with capacity to produce 250,000 barrels of beer per year.[27] However, given that by 1881, Guinness was already producing one million barrels of beer annually, the gap between Guinness and its nearest competitor in Dublin was prohibitively large.[28] Domestically, the Cork brewers offered the strongest resistance to Guinness, helped largely by their retention of the tied house system which gave them a guaranteed market. Nonetheless, by the turn of the twentieth century, the combined output of James J. Murphy & Co. and Beamish & Crawford, Cork's two leading breweries, was barely one-eighth that of Guinness and focused almost entirely in Munster.[29]

In the Dublin economy, the liquor industry provided one of the few examples of industrial success in the latter half of the nineteenth century. But it had its limitations. Most of the 3,000 workers employed in the brewing industry were labourers; Guinness, as the dominant brewer, pursued a policy of self-sufficiency with regards to its needs, creating few forward or backward linkages, which would have encouraged and supported the development of ancillary industries.[30] Moreover, Dublin distillers, who collectively employed upwards of 1,000 workers, stubbornly clung to the traditional pot-still whiskey long after it had been replaced in popular taste by less distinctive blended varieties, thus limiting their market.[31] Nonetheless, in a city characterised by a shift in occupations from manufacturing to general labouring and service between 1841 and 1911, the liquor industry remained a significant employer.[32] Therefore, in the particular context of the Irish economy, liquor manufacturing was an industry that no nationalist leader in Ireland of the period could ignore.

Neither could he ignore the claims of Irish publicans alarmed by the successful passage of the Irish Sunday Closing Act (1878). While the earlier temperance campaigns did not demonise drink sellers[33], the legislative campaign begun in the 1850s and 1860s deliberately targeted them. Trade resistance to temperance-inspired legislation was spear-headed by Dublin vintners, whose trade association gave them the kind of collective presence necessary to organise 'pressure from without' – campaigning to influence public opinion, lobbying parliament and government officials, and developing arguments to counter those of temperance.[34] Collectively, Dublin publicans had a vigorous sense of themselves as 'the trade'. Fostered by their early organisation and by the necessity to combine against restrictive legislation, their trade identity included a sense of belonging to a wider grouping which encompassed suburban and provincial vintners, manufacturers and wholesalers – though rarely the hapless spirit grocers and beer sellers who were seen as fomenting the kind of criticism that gave the temperance campaigners some credence. Dublin vintners also saw themselves as part of a wider collective that went beyond the national borders of the Irish trade. Over the course of the 1870s, 1880s and 1890s the Dublin association consciously developed relations with trade organisations in Britain, particularly those representing the English retail trade.[35]

Commenting on a meeting of vintners in November 1889, the *Irish Sportsman* posited the following characteristics of members of the licensed trade: 'Foremost in every charitable work, generous in subscribing to every deserving object, they are elected to every representative position which it is possible for a citizen to fill'.[36] Almost a decade later, in his evidence before the 1898 Royal Commission, Timothy Harrington MP proclaimed that 'there could not be a more respectable body of men than the publicans who have the trade in Dublin. They stand at the very head of the commercial men of Dublin'.[37] The idea that Dublin publicans, collectively and individually, were men of substance, of status and of moral rectitude was a common theme in contemporary sources sympathetic to the liquor trade. Moreover, inspired in part by the need to defend their interests against the onslaught of temperance-inspired rhetoric, it was strongly present in the discourse of vintners themselves. Nonetheless, as with all archetypes, the idea of the city vintner as a substantial man of commerce does not have a general applicability. Individual vintners could be male or female; licensees of small hovels or proprietors of prosperous establishments; owners of multiple licensed houses or of single, more modest premises; property speculators *par excellence* or simple publicans, dispensing pints of porter and drams of Dublin whiskey to a local trade.[38] What they all shared, however, was a collective interest in the economic and legislative context in which their businesses operated.

While there is some disagreement on the year in which the Dublin Licensed Grocers' and Vintners' Protection Association was founded, the *Whiskey Trade Review* dates the organisation of Dublin vintners from 1810.[39] As an association, it was conceived of as having a dual role, i.e. that of a benevolent society that protected its members from destitution, and that of a defence society that looked after the interests of the trade. It is likely that in the first half of the century, it was seen 'more as a benevolent than as a protective body'.[40] The Dublin association underwent a number of name changes over the course of the century, reflecting, to some extent, the varying levels of threat to trade interests and the balance of concern with its benevolent role. Thus, in the 1830s it was known as the Fair Trading Vintners' Society and Asylum, encapsulating its twin purpose of defending the economic and legislative environment which the vintners collectively inhabited, as well as providing for the individual vintner and his or her family some protection against indigence. By 1862 it had become the Licensed Grocers' and Vintners' Society with meeting rooms at 13 Cork Hill.[41] By 1865 it was being referred to as the Licensed Grocers' and Vintners' Trade Protection and Benevolent Society, again giving due emphasis to its collective and individual roles. By the early 1870s both roles had been subsumed under the idea of protection and the association adopted the title that was to remain in use until the 1950s: the Dublin Licensed Grocers' and Vintners' Protection Association (LGVPA). By this stage, its offices and meeting rooms had moved to Commercial Buildings in Dame Street.

It is difficult to assess the level of membership of the Association, as no membership lists exist for the period. In his testimony before the Select Committee on the Sale of Intoxicating Liquors on Sunday (Ireland) Bill in 1877, the then secretary of the LGVPA, Michael O'Dwyer, reluctantly agreed that the membership was somewhere between three and four hundred.[42] The Association had a potential membership of over 700 and, given the sustained threat to the trade over the 1880s and 1890s, it would be reasonable to expect some increase in that membership over the period. The *Whiskey Trade Review* gave its membership as 700 in 1891, a figure that is certainly inflated.[43] On the other hand, the membership figure of 100, used by the Association as a basis for the payment of affiliation fees to the British vintner societies, seems an underestimation. The best indication of member-ship for the period – the number of ballots sent out to paid-up members for the annual committee elections – suggest that the membership remained at the mid 300s for the remainder of the century. Despite the unprecedented level of organisation and campaigning in the preceding two decades, there had been little or no increase in membership.[44]

The politicisation of Dublin publicans as a collective was primarily driven by the need to provide a sustained response to the legislative campaign of the temperance movement in the second half of the century. From the initiation of the parliamentary campaigns for Sunday closing and for local control of licen-sing in the 1860s and 1870s, the issue of trade defence increasingly dominated the agenda of the LGVPA. Far from marking the culmination of the temp-erance campaign, the enactment of the Sunday Closing (Ireland) Bill in 1878 heralded in almost four decades of intensive temperance activity in parliament. Almost every parliamentary session included some focus on temperance, bringing with it the need for new campaign initiatives and political lobbying – petitions were organised to counteract the pro-temperance petitions of the Irish Association for the Prevention of Intemperance; memorials were pre-sented to government representatives; and large trade and/or public meetings were organised in support of its position. The most powerful tool used by the LGVPA, however, was that of political lobbying. From the 1870s onwards the Dublin vintners were rarely without a presence at Westminster, closely monitoring the progress of bills and the parliamentary attendance of their supporters, and liaising with the British trade to ensure the support of British Tories. While the economic importance of the liquor industry provided a material base for the Association's capacity to exert political influence, its effectiveness was greatly enhanced by the extent to which publicans as individuals were embedded in nationalist politics of the period.

Predominantly nationalist and Catholic, Irish publicans in general have been identified as active in a succession of nationalist movements from the end of the eighteenth century. Dublin vintners were prominent at the grassroots level of the United Irishmen; were strong political and financial supporters of Daniel O'Connell; and active in the organisation of Ribbon societies and Fenianism.[45] As the nineteenth century progressed, the involvement of publicans on a national basis was quite substantial. During the Land War, for example, publicans had a disproportionate representation amongst those arrested under the Coercion Act of 1881.[46] Given the nature of their business, it is not surprising that they should find themselves at the centre of political action, particularly at local level. In his seminal study of drink and temperance in early Victorian England, *Drink and the Victorians*, Brian Harrison describes the public house as 'one of the few buildings, apart from the church, which all could enter'.[47] As a focus of camaraderie, sustenance, enjoyment and social intercourse, the public house presented a promising environment for political intrigue and subversive activity. Also, a high level of enfranchisement in the trade gave them considerable influence as an electorate at both municipal and parliamentary level, while the role of drink in the canvassing of votes made public houses central locations during election campaigns.[48] The potential for public houses to provide cover for revolutionary politics was recognised in legislation – the 1833 Licensing (Ireland) Act brought in measures designed, in part, to tackle the role of the public house as a site of subversion. Under the Act, vintners were required to obtain a certificate of good character from the chief constable or from two parish overseers.[49] From mid-century, however, publicans were increasingly anxious to project a view of themselves as respectable and law-abiding, and the dominant view of the Dublin vintner of the Parnell period is closer to that of the burgher than the revolutionary.[50] The Dublin publican of the last quarter of the nineteenth century was a substantial figure – a friend of the Church, and no longer an object of suspicion by the police. Moreover, he was influential in local politics; and amongst the occupations most likely to be represented on Dublin Corporation and the North and South Dublin Union Boards.[51]

City publicans, then, were well poised to become the organisational men of the Irish National League on its foundation in 1882. Much of the influence exerted by Dublin vintners on the Home Rule movement was indirect. As active members of the National League they attended meetings and conventions, and canvassed and organised the registration of voters.[52] As members of Dublin Corporation, their influence and organisation at ward level provided a ready resource to the League. Individually and collectively, vintners contributed financially to the survival of the Irish Party at this time. That their contribution was substantial is indicated by the frequency with which their generosity is mentioned by the party in its dealings with the Dublin LGVPA.[53] While the dominant mode may have been in the form of National League subscriptions, vintners were major contributors to the Parnell tribute and there is evidence of informal funding through testimonials and contributions to election expenses.[54] Furthermore, the many deputations to Westminster were not without some benefit to the targeted MPs. The advice given to one such deputation by a committee member in 1889, to 'exercise a reasonable generosity in their social intercourse with MPs and officials' suggests a practice of hospitality that was customary rather than unique.[55]

For most of the time, Parnell was able to keep the management of the publicans at one remove, relying on the trade's supporters within the Irish Parliamentary Party to see that their needs were met.[56] Certainly, in John O'Connor, ex-Fenian and MP for Tipperary South (1885–92), the vintners found their most consistent champion during this period. 'Long John' O'Connor was himself a publican and had been an ally of P. N. Fitzgerald in the Cork IRB, and county secretary of the Land League in Cork in 1880.[57] While others such as Peter McDonald, MP for Sligo North (1885–91) and Daniel Crilly, Mayo North MP (1885–1900), were active in their support, it was to O'Connor that the LGVPA turned for advice and influence.[58] O'Connor's services were called upon to safeguard the interests of the vintners on a continual basis throughout the late 1880s. The relationship between O'Connor and the LGVPA remained strong until the Parnell Split, when his role was, to a large extent, taken over by Parnellite MP for Louth North, Joseph P. Nolan.[59]

While opinion within the Irish Parliamentary Party remained divided on the issue of temperance, the majority of the party adopted a position of positive 'neutrality' on the issue. This was manifest in the high rate of absenteeism and abstention when divisions were called on temperance legislation. For example, in a vote on a local veto bill brought forward in 1890 by temperance campaigner T. W. Russell, MP for Tyrone South, 11 voted for the bill, eight voted against and the majority – including Parnell – either abstained or were conveniently absent. Parnell had indicated to the LGVPA that he would oppose Russell's bill without voting, a position that allowed him to satisfy the vintners while maintaining a position that had the public appearance of neutrality. The logic of his position, derived from a commitment given to the vintners in 1886, proved to be a seminal development in the defence of the Irish liquor trade.

When the LGVPA deputation had proceeded to London in April 1886 to lobby the Irish Party to push for the exclusion of Ireland from the Intoxicating Liquors (Sale to Children) Bill, it came away with what was deemed by the vintners to be an even greater victory in the form of 'a public declaration from Mr Parnell that the Irish Liquor Question was one to be dealt with by a native legislature'.[60] This represents a critical moment in the relationship between the vintners and Parnell. While they had frequently made the argument that temperance legislation was detrimental to home manufacture, Parnell's declaration allowed vintners to publicly align their interest with the national cause in a way that had not previously been possible.[61] Moreover, it allowed Parnell to sidestep the issue of temperance, and keep an important group onside without openly arguing against restrictive legislation. And furthermore, it provided an ideological cloak behind which those Irish nationalist MPs who were sympathetic to temperance but fearful of alienating a powerful lobby group, could hide. For its part, the LGVPA used the declaration as its starting point in all subsequent dealings with Parnell, calling on the leader and members of the Irish Party to honour the declaration in successive campaigns against restrictive legislation. Thus, in response to lobbying by LGVPA on the Saturday Closing Bill put before the House in April 1888, Parnell recalled the pledge given in 1886 and said that he would keep his word. In the reported words of Henry Campbell, Parnell's secretary, 'the Sunday Closers may go down on their knees but no Bill hostile to the vintners will pass this Session'.[62]

Publicans were particularly adept at making their presence felt at election time when politicians were seen to be vulnerable to trade interest. In 1865 for example, Dublin vintners abandoned their traditional Liberal allegiance to support the Conservative brewer Benjamin Lee Guinness because it was seen to be in the trade interest.[63] By the 1880 general election the LGVPA had already developed a particular approach to elections that followed a predictable formula: having proclaimed its political neutrality, it asserted its interest in getting elected those who supported the trade. Despite their reputation as nationalists, it could not be assumed that national feeling would inevitably win out over the needs of the trade. Questions were submitted to parliamentary candidates of all parties to ascertain their stance on issues pertaining to the liquor trade and their responses were published. Throughout the period, pro-temperance MPs such as J. G. Biggar, A. M. Sullivan and Maurice Healy, found their constituencies targeted by visiting deputations of Dublin publicans intent on encouraging opposition to their candidature amongst the local trade. The possibility that publicans would run their own candidates was periodically voiced – particularly on occasions when the Party was seen to be less supportive than expected.[64]

It was essential to the parliamentary strategy of the vintners that the candidates selected by the Party to represent Dublin were sympathetic to the trade. While concerted efforts were made to apply a whip for conventions, the LGVPA also conducted direct lobbying to ensure the selection of favourable candidates. Given the limited power of conventions to select candidates, it is not surprising that the vintners were not prepared to rely solely on their involvement as individuals or as Corporation members for a favourable result.[65] In advance of the 1885 elections, for example, the LGVPA engaged in this two-pronged approach to ensure that candidates acceptable to the trade were selected for the Dublin divisions. The secretary of the LGVPA was instructed to visit the prominent members of the trade in the city wards to ensure a full representation at the Dublin convention.[66] A deputation was sent to Timothy Harrington, secretary of the National League, to ask him to make representations to the Irish Party at the next meeting to guard against the return of anyone hostile to the trade.[67] Harrington's response to the deputation is significant:

> [He] had found the Licensed Trade of Dublin ever ready to assist him and his party by their time and pecuniary support and that a great measure of the Party's success in Dublin was due to the exertions and support of the Trade. Under these circumstances he was quite prepared to promise the Licensed Grocers' and Vintners' Association as the body representative of the Dublin Trade that no member hostile to Trade Interests would, with the assent of the Irish Parliamentary Party, be returned for Dublin. Moreover he was willing to receive suggestions from the Committee as to who the candidate of their choice w[oul]d be.[68]

Harrington, who was himself returned for Dublin city in 1885, went on to assure the vintners of his own support for the trade and his intention to defend them 'from unjust assailants' in Parliament.[69] The LGVPA was so reassured by Harrington's response that it decided to take no further part as an association in the forthcoming election. It had every reason to feel reassured: Harrington had given the LGVPA a guarantee that its interests would be protected and had gone so far as to offer the Association some say in the selection of candidates

Harrington was again called on by the LGVPA to ensure the interests of the trade were kept in mind in the lead-up to the St Stephen's Green division by-election in 1888 (caused by the death of Edmund Dwyer Gray).[70] On this occasion, Harrington's assurances that no candidate hostile to the trade would be put forward were not considered satisfactory and he was requested to lay the views of the Association before Parnell himself. The choice of Gladstonian Liberal, Thomas Alexander Dickson, to fight the division as a Home Rule candidate could have been problematic for the LGVPA, given the general identification of the Liberals with temperance. At the beginning of May, however, Peter McDonald indicated to them that Dickson had 'pledged' himself to act with Parnell in opposing restrictive legislation.[71] Moreover, at a meeting with the assistant secretary of the LGVPA, Henry

Lalor, Dickson committed himself to follow Parnell's lead on issues relating to the licensed trade, stating 'I object to any social legislation being forced on Ireland by English votes. You will understand what I mean when I say social'.[72] On the following day, the LGVPA committee meeting was attended by Timothy Harrington who brought with him the following telegram from Parnell:

> Kindly inform Licensed Vintners who had telegraphed me that Dickson will not support any measure directed against their interests that he adopts my attitude that no such question should be touched by Imperial Parliament but should be reserved for the consideration of an Irish Parliament. Parnell.[73]

The extent to which Parnell was prepared to take on board the views of the vintners is again suggested by another telegram on the selection of candidates sent by Parnell to Davitt. While the telegram is undated it seems to relate to the same by-election. Having refused to consent to W. S. Blunt as a candidate, Parnell goes on to suggest, rightly, that Alfred Webb would be distasteful to the publicans and suggests that the advice of Thomas Sexton MP, then Lord Mayor of Dublin, be sought.[74]

Despite his apparent support for the vintners, however, it is doubtful if Parnell's personal attitude towards temperance legislation had changed dramatically in the interim between his vote in support of Sunday closing in 1876 and his commitment to the vintners ten years later. Indeed, in his most extensive statement on temperance, which he made as part of the 1888 debate on Sunday closing and early Saturday closing, Parnell continued to express some sympathy with the issue of temperance:

> I am still most desirous that there should be greater temperance, greater abstinence from drinking. I believe it is a very great evil. I am, with perhaps, a single exception, the largest employer of labour among the Irish Members of all Parties, and it has been brought constantly to my notice that the question of intemperance is undoubtedly a very great impediment to the progress of the industries of Ireland, and to the success of manufacturing and other operations, as well as to the welfare and well-being of the people.[75]

Parnell used the Home Rule argument to great effect: issues relating to the control of the liquor trade were better dealt with by an Irish legislature, and, ideally, at the level of local government. In any case, temperance-inspired legislation coming from Westminster would inevitably fail in Ireland where it would be viewed as coercive and would be administered unfairly.[76] Parnell's commitment to temperance, such as it was, was driven by economic and social concerns rather than moral or religious ones and he rejected the characterization of the Irish as less temperate than the English or the Scots.[77] Parnell also recognised that temperance had the potential to cause deep divisions within the party. He was alive to the damage that could be done to the unity of the party by members speaking on opposite sides of the debate, and characterised as 'a scandal' debates in which 'Irish members flew at each other's throats'.[78]

However, Parnell was also acutely aware of the harm too strident an advocacy of the vintners' cause could inflict on the Liberal alliance, and it would be wrong to infer a complete lack of sympathy on Parnell's part with the temperance agenda. Towards the end of his contribution to the 1888 debate, Parnell laid claim to the nomenclature of 'a temperance man' and to the belief that one of the 'great works in the future must be to make the Irish people more sober than they are'; a project whose best chance of success among the people of Ireland lay in spreading temperance 'by voluntary action among themselves and by their own Representatives'.[79] To what extent this statement reflected a real, if deferred, commitment to the idea of a sober Ireland rather than a sop to acknowledge the sensibilities of his Liberal allies and his pro-temperance supporters is a moot point. Indeed, Paul Bew notes that Parnell's concern with 'the much-vaunted unity of the Parnellite bloc' may have had a personal cost in terms of self-censorship.[80] In any event, Parnell's opposition to temperance-inspired legislation at Westminster cannot be taken as an indicator of what might have happened if Home Rule had been achieved. While his suggestion during the debate that 'Irishmen acting at home, discussing this question amongst themselves'[81] would go beyond the level of reform put forward in the bill may have owed more to polemics than policy. Nevertheless, it was taken by vintners as a warning that an Irish parliament might propose far 'more drastic' measures for the regulation of the drinks trade than any proposed at Westminster.[82]

The approach adopted was not without its ironies for the vintners. By declaring that Westminster had no right to legislate for Ireland in relation to licensing, it cut off any possibility of promoting constructive legislation on their behalf. Confined by this strategy to a purely defensive role, and unable to utilise their supporters in parliament to instigate legislation that might redress some of their grievances, the vintners had to some extent manoeuvred themselves into a legislative cul-de-sac. Nowhere did this become more obvious than in relation to the issue of compensation. From the perspective of the vintners, members of the trade who suffered financially as a result of restrictive legislation, and, in particular, legislation such as the local veto bills, deserved compensation. When, as part of the budget in 1890, the Conservative government introduced a Local Taxation Bill which offered publicans the possibility of compensation, the LGVPA found itself unable to reconcile its interests with those of the Irish Party.

This was not the first time this issue had arisen in a form that was potentially divisive. In 1888 the president of the local government board, C. T. Ritchie, proposed a Local Government (England and Wales) Bill which vested the power to administer licences in county councils rather than in magistrates. These councils would also have the power to get rid of surplus licences and to offer compensation to licence holders equivalent to the difference between the value of their licensed and unlicensed property. This compensation was to be funded by an increase in licence duty of 20 per cent.[83] Although the Bill was confined to England and Wales and was ultimately withdrawn by the Salisbury government, it was seen by the LGVPA as a possible breakthrough on the issue of compensation.[84] Gladstone, however, was opposed in principle to the idea of compensation for licence holders. This was felt by the trade to be particularly galling considering his support of compensation in relation to slave-ownership and his defence of compensation for tenants who improved their holdings in the debate on the Irish Land Bill in 1870.[85] The freedom of the vintners to capitalise on these inconsistencies, however, was hindered by their desire not to alienate the Irish Party. As noted by the secretary of the LGVPA, Michael McCarthy, in his advice to the committee,

> he thought it unwise to challenge any present remarks of Mr Gladstone's on the compensation question seeming it might involve us in unpleasantness with the Parnellites who were inclined as a body to be friendly.[86]

It is likely that the inability of the LGVPA to pursue with full vigour the campaign against Gladstone's views on compensation in relation to the Local Government Bill stretched its tolerance of the Liberal alliance to its limit. By the time the Local Taxation Bill of 1890 was proposed by George Goschen, Chancellor of the Exchequer in the Salisbury government, the patience of the Dublin vintners had worn thin. Goschen's proposal again gave county councils the power to compensate licence holders for the forfeiture of their licences, but in this case the compensation was to be met from increased taxes, some of which were also to be committed to education.[87] The wider trade in Dublin was divided on the issue, with manufacturers such as John Jameson and James Talbot Power opposing the increase in duties, while publicans were prepared to accept the increases in the interest of achieving their long term goal. A compromise resolution was agreed that protested against the proposed increase in taxes, while 'recognising the justice of the principle of compensation adopted by the Government' and, at a meeting of the LGVPA on 13 May, the Association called on the party to support the Local Taxation Bill.[88]

Within a matter of days, the campaign in support of Goschen's proposal had begun in earnest. At the same time, the LGVPA was also conducting a campaign to defeat the perennial Intoxicating Liquors (Ireland) Bill that again sought to extend Sunday closing to the exempted cities and to bring in early Saturday closing. An interview with Tim Harrington, however, brought the LGVPA face to face with the crux of the problem: Harrington, though reported to be 'personally altogether in our favour', held that the Irish Parliamentary Party could not withdraw its support from Gladstone in his opposition to the Local Taxation Bill; neither could it remain neutral.[89] Nonetheless, Harrington promised to do everything in his power to defeat the Intoxicating Liquors (Ireland) Bill and, if necessary, to put down an amendment exempting the city of Dublin from the proposed changes. Furthermore, he recommended that the LGVPA should send a deputation to Parnell asking him to either support the amendment or remain neutral. As a result of the meeting, P. J. Lennox, who became secretary of the LGVPA in 1889, was instructed to 'wait on Mr Harrington with a draft of the amendment concerning the exemption of Dublin'.[90]

At a general meeting of the licensed trade on 6 June, the following resolution in relation to the Local Taxation Bill was proposed by Philip Little, an active member of the Association:

> That we, the members of the retail licensed trade of Dublin, strongly approve of the Local Taxation (Customs and Excise) Duties Bill; we consider the provision applying portion of the fund to the benefit of the National teachers of Ireland worthy of approval, and the clauses dealing with the purchase of public houses deserving of the support of all real friends of temperance. On these grounds we respectfully request the Irish Parliamentary Party to modify their opposition to the measure.[91]

In his speech, Little argued that a bill which promised extra remuneration to national teachers, 'a class to whom in a very large degree the moral training of the future manhood and womanhood of the country was entrusted' should be approved of by everyone. Characterising teachers as 'scandalously underpaid', he argued that the Irish Parliamentary Party 'would be doing a service to the public at large by supporting a bill which had among others of its objects such a deserving one as that'. Little then moved on to the real purpose of the proposal. His arguments reveal some of the contradictions inherent in the vintners' own agenda and the limits of trade solidarity:

By the provision of the bill power was to be given to the local authorities to extinguish licences in any locality where licensed premises were thought to be too numerous on payment of a fair and equitable sum to the holders of the licences to be extinguished. The result of this would be that the lower class of publichouses would be gradually done away with, and the morals and temperate habits of the people would be safeguarded by the respectable publichouses to which they have recourse.

The Local Taxation (Custom and Excise) Bill, would therefore, not only justly compensate vintners for the loss of their licences, it would serve to consolidate the retail trade, closing down the smaller, poorer premises and further increase the value and trade of the more prosperous ones. Moreover, not only would this be good for the Association's members, it would be good for public morals and temperance. Little went on to make his argument for the support of the Irish Parliamentary Party:

The time had come when they must protect their interests and their means of livelihood. Some years ago, when he was chairman of the association, a letter was written to him by one who held high place in the councils of the Unionist party, and in that letter the writer stated that if the trade would support the Unionist candidate for the St Stephen's green Division of the city of Dublin in opposition to Mr Dickson they might always rely on having a sterling champion of trade interests in the House of Commons. He (Mr Little) never mentioned anything about that letter to anybody, but he went down the following evening to Mr Dickson's committee rooms in Earlsfort terrace, and openly advocated the candidature of the Home Rule candidate, and he thought it now exceptionally hard for the party for whom the licensed vintners had done so much, and sacrificed so much should oppose, as a party, a measure which proposed to mete out nothing but bare justice to the vintners of Dublin and of Ireland.

Little's speech illustrates clearly the nature of the relationship between the vintners and the Irish Party. His words held an implicit threat, underlining subtly that the support of the vintners for the party was conditional on that party looking after their interests in Parliament; while they were loyal and hardworking supporters of the Irish Parliamentary Party, their allegiance should not be taken for granted. Others were looking for their support and were prepared to champion their cause in Parliament. It was not inconceivable that the vintners, seeing their livelihoods threatened and unable to rely on the party to which they had given so much, would reconsider their allegiance in the light of the failure of the Irish Parliamentary Party to protect their interests.

That the party had been remiss in this respect was brought home by a second resolution which called on the Irish Party and, in particular, the Dublin members, to vote against the Intoxicating Liquors (Ireland) Bill introduced into the House by Thomas Lea, Liberal Unionist member for Londonderry North. Speaking for the resolution, James McDonnell outlined the extent to which the Party had let them down in relation to Lea's bill. 'It was monstrous' he argued, 'that on the occasion of the second reading of the bill only 29 out of a party of 86 were present, and those who were absent included the four members for Dublin'. The meeting concluded with a motion that

> ... a deputation, including representatives from Dublin, Belfast, and Cork, should convey the foregoing resolutions to Mr Parnell, and put before him the views of the trade on the various licensing proposals at present before Parliament.

While it is questionable whether the allegiance of the LGVPA (and Dublin vintners in general) to the Irish Parliamentary Party was ever in any real danger, there is no doubt that relations and tempers were strained at this point. From the LGVPA perspective, it was bad enough that it had to suffer the divisions within the party on temperance issues in general, but the high level of absenteeism of Irish members when temperance legislation was on the floor of the House, and the failure of the Dublin members to look after their interests, was even harder to stomach. The support of the Irish Parliamentary Party was something that 'gratitude as well as justice' required.[92] Certainly, the level of disenchantment evident at the general meeting stands in contrast to the far more compliant attitude adopted by the Cork licensed vintners at their meeting on the same day, where a resolution 'approving the principle that compensation ought to be made for any restriction of the trade, but that they placed themselves and their interests entirely in the hands of Mr Parnell and the Irish Parliamentary party' with regard to Lea's bill, was adopted.[93] The durability of the ties between the vintners and the party was the subject of speculation at the time in government circles. In a letter to the Under Secretary, David Harrel, the Dublin Metropolitan Police commissioner, expressed his opinion that the prospect of a split was unlikely and that the licensed trade in Dublin were taking far more interest in the Intoxicating Liquors (Ireland) Bill than in the compensation issue. In Harrel's estimation, the allegiance of the vintners to the Party would not be severed.[94]

According to Harrel, the 'important and influential deputation' that met with Parnell in the House of Commons on 11 June 1890 was received 'most courteously'. If Parnell was courteous in his reception of the vintners, they left him in no doubt about their sense of anger at the injustice being visited on them by the party, some of whose members 'never lost an opportunity of injuring and opposing the interests of the Irish Liquor Trade'. Threatening to 'nominate their own men' at the next election, they singled out Maurice Healy for particular opprobrium.[95] In Harrel's account of the meeting, Parnell, though conciliatory in tone, refused to modify his policy of allowing a free vote on temperance legislation and offered little solace on the Local Taxation Bill beyond a vague commitment to ensure that the vintners' interests would be looked after at committee stage.[96] The LGVPA's own account of the meeting, however, was more positive and included the following more specific commitments from Parnell:

1 To see in what way the opposition of himself and his party to the Local Taxation (Customs and Excise) Duties Bill could be modified.

2 To ensure that whatever measure of compensation to publicans was passed for England should also be passed for Ireland.

3 To use his influence to prevent the Intoxicating Liquors (Ireland) Bill from passing into law.

4 To endeavour to bring it to pass that, should that Bill pass into law, the hours for closing should not be earlier than 10 on Saturday and 6 on Sunday in the five exempted cities.[97]

While Parnell was not prepared to jeopardize either his relations with the Liberals or the unity of his party in order to mollify the vintners, he did go some way towards meeting their demands: promising parity with the vintners of England in relation to compensation; a broadening of the idea of compensation to include loss of revenue caused by a restriction of licensing hours; and a commitment to limit the damage of the Intoxicating Liquors (Ireland) Bill by pursuing a compromise position. His refusal to apply a whip on the issue did mean though, that the LGVPA was again thrown back on the mercy of individual supporters within the party to safeguard its interests. Harrington's promised amendment to the Intoxicating Liquors Bill failed to materialise, and, despite the efforts of the vintners to prevent the bill reaching the floor of the house, the Intoxicating Liquors (Ireland) Bill only escaped discussion by five minutes.[98] Notwithstanding the active support of a group of Irish members, the tacit neutrality of a substantial majority of the Irish Party and the explicit commitment of the leader to a policy that consigned temperance to a Home Rule legislature, the vintners had come closer to defeat than at any time since 1878. Meanwhile, temperance pressure on Liberal Unionists forced the government to abandon Goschen's proposal.[99]

In the longer term, the Liberal alliance presented a real threat to the interests of the vintners and, when forced to choose, Parnell prioritised the maintenance of the alliance over the need to satisfy the LGVPA. Within months however, from Parnell's perspective, that alliance was damaged irreparably. For the vintners, the fracturing of the nationalist consensus in the wake of the O'Shea divorce case created a complex and uncertain terrain in which the relations of the previous decade could no longer be taken for granted. When the vice president of the Cork society argued that 'the trade had now a golden opportunity which should not be lost' to exploit the crisis for its own ends, the response of the Dublin Association was to restate its non-political nature and its intention to take no collective action; adding, however, that 'its members in their individual capacity and as members of public bodies etc. had given expression to their views'.[100] In seeking to avoid political confrontation within their own organisation in 'a family falling-out', the Dublin vintners had found, perhaps, the best formula for preserving a unified association; a formula that allowed them to continue their skilled and delicate balancing of trade and nation.[101]

Parnell was to make one last intervention in the battle between the vintners and the temperance movement when he opposed the second reading of the Intoxicating Liquors (Ireland) Bill in 1891. Freed from the constraints of the Liberal alliance, and conscious of the need to keep the vintners onside, this was his most forthright endorsement of the publicans' case. Characterising the bill as 'a patronising attempt on the part of the majority of the English Members in the House of Commons to make the Irish people sober', he goes on to question the exceptional nature of the proposed legislation and argued strongly that licensing should be dealt with by a Home Rule parliament and that the proposed bill was little more than coercion:

> The Irish people will naturally say, 'Make yourselves sober first.' Why should this experiment be made upon the body of the Irish people? Perhaps on the principle of *Fiat experimentum in corpore vili*. Anything is good enough for Ireland, no matter how doubtful its character. No doubt that is the view of the great majority of the Liberal Party in the House, but a measure conceived under such auspices is fore-doomed to failure. The Irish people will naturally say this is a part of the insolent system to which we have been accustomed for so many years on the part of the English nation; and we decline to believe in our excessive drunkenness in comparison with our kind English friends.[102]

Within six months Parnell's death ensured that his position as 'a friend of the trade' would undergo no further revision. While his support of the vintners' interests was both pragmatic and conditional, he had nonetheless provided a consistent and powerful buffer against the onslaught of temperance legislation from the mid-1880s, and, while he had refused to apply a whip on anti-temperance votes, his support for the vintners had ensured that the pro-temperance lobby within the party remained a minority voice.[103]

The capacity of the vintners to attract such consistent support derived, in large part, from their involvement as individuals in nationalist politics. It was the ability of the LGVPA to create and maintain an over-arching trade identity, however, that allowed the vintners to translate that individual commitment into collective power. They were fortunate, also, that their period of greatest threat coincided with a time when Irish politics was undergoing a radical transformation.[104] While the LGVPA had engaged in political lobbying in the 1870s, the foundation of the National League had provided urban vintners with significant 'pathways to influence' which enabled them to influence decision-making at the highest level; and to create a discourse that allowed them to link their economic destiny with that of the Home Rule cause.[105] Parnell's most valuable gift to the vintners remained his 1886 declaration that legislation on the liquor question was the prerogative of a Home Rule parliament. It was an assertion to which the vintners returned again and again when seeking parliamentary support for the remainder of the century, providing nationalist MPs such as John Redmond, whose allegiance before the split had been to temperance, with the perfect justification for giving it.[106]

Notes

1   Minutes of the LGVPA, 13 Oct. 1891.

2   After the 1892 election, William Martin Murphy was reported to have said that the Parnellite victories in Dublin were 'as much a triumph of publicanism as Parnellism'. *Freeman's Journal*, 14 July 1892. For the LGVPA's rejoinder see *Irish Daily Independent*, 20 July 1892.

3   Select Committee Report on Sunday Closing Acts (Ireland) 1888, p. 423.

4   John Howard Parnell, *Charles Stewart Parnell: A Memoir* (London, 1916), p.180; Katharine O'Shea, *The Uncrowned King of Ireland* (Stroud, 2005 edn), p. 215.

5   R. F. Foster, *Charles Stewart Parnell: The Man and his Family* (Sussex, 1976), pp 96–7.

6   Ibid., pp 120–1.

7   Ibid., pp 320–1.

8   Elizabeth Malcolm, *'Ireland Sober, Ireland Free': Drink and Temperance in Nineteenth-century Ireland* (Dublin, 1986), p. 56. Malcolm offers the single most authoritative account of the temperance movement in Ireland in the nineteenth century.

9   Diarmaid Ferriter, *A Nation of Extremes: The Pioneers in Twentieth-century Ireland* (Dublin, 1999), p. 10. For a detailed consideration of the ideology underpinning the Catholic Church's approach to temperance see Paul A. Townend, *Father Mathew: Temperance and Irish Identity* (Dublin, 2002). For an examination of the Fr Mathew Crusade, see also Colm Kerrigan, *Father Mathew and the Irish Temperance Movement 1838–1849* (Cork, 1992); H. F. Kearney, 'Fr Mathew: Apostle of modernisation', in A. Cosgrove and D. McCartney (eds), *Studies in Irish History* (Dublin, 1979); John F. Quinn, *Father Mathew's Crusade: Temperance in Nineteenth-century Ireland and Irish America* (Boston, 2002).

10 James Kneale, 'The Place of Drink: Temperance and the Public, 1856–1914', in *Social and Cultural Geography*, vol. 2, no. 1 (2001), pp 44–5. The renewal of the temperance movement in Ireland mirrored the rise in militant Sabbatarianism in Britain during the same period. 1853 saw the formation of the United Kingdom Alliance for the Suppression of the Traffic in all Intoxicating Liquors (UKA), which became the dominant temperance voice in the UK for the remainder of the century.

11 Born in Scotland in 1841, Russell moved to Dungannon, Co. Tyrone in 1860 where he worked in a soap factory. He became involved in temperance work in 1863 when he was elected secretary of the local temperance society. Having impressed temperance organisers with his energy, he was appointed a permanent agent of the Irish Temperance League in Dublin in 1864. He continued to lead the temperance interest until his election as member for Tyrone South in 1886. It was a common charge against the temperance campaigners that they were 'Scotch interlopers'. *Freeman's Journal*, 9 Apr. 1883. For a biographical note on Russell, see James Loughlin, 'Russell, Sir Thomas Wallace', in James McGuire and James Quinn (eds), *Dictionary of Irish Biography*. (Cambridge, 2009) and http://dib.cambridge.org/

12 *Hansard*, 3rd series, vol. 237, col. 1696 (14 Feb. 1878). See, also, ibid., vol. 240, col. 109 (16 May 1878).

13 See for example, Parnell's speech at Inchicore in June 1891, *Evening Telegraph*, 8 June 1891. See also, *Hansard*, 3rd series, vol. 352, cols 632–5 (15 Apr. 1891). Parnell's interest in industrialisation has been commented on at length in Liam Kennedy, 'The economic thought of the nation's lost leader: Charles Stewart Parnell' in D. George Boyce and Alan O'Day (eds), *Parnell in Perspective* (London, 1991), pp 171–200. See, also, Frank Callanan, *The Parnell Split 1890-91* (Cork, 1992), pp 290–3.

14 Fergus A. D'Arcy, 'The Decline and Fall of Donnybrook Fair: Moral Reform and Social Control in Nineteenth Century Dublin' in *Saothar*, no. 13 (1988), p. 13.

15 E. P. Thompson, 'Time, Work Discipline and Industrial Capitalism' in *Past & Present*, no. 38 (1967), pp 61, 90.

16 Lilian L. Shiman, *Crusade against Drink in Victorian England* (New York, 1988). p. 2.

17 Select Committee Report on Sunday Closing, 1888, p. 356. See also Select Committee Report on the Sale of Intoxicating Liquors on Sunday (Ireland) Bill, 1877, p. 145. Saint Monday was probably rooted in the workshop practices of the pre- and early industrial periods. Research into the custom of Saint Monday in the Birmingham area by Douglas A. Reid suggests that, by the mid-1800s, traditional Monday activities of bar-games and entertainment focused on the ale-house had evolved to include such worthy and beneficial pursuits as railway excursions, exhibitions and lectures, cricket and walking. While the exigencies of steam-generated power eroded the practice of St Monday, Reid argues that it was the campaign for the Saturday half-holiday which began in mid-century that sounded the death knell of traditional working-class leisure patterns in this regard. Because of the loss of Saint Monday, few workers achieved an increase in leisure hours through the standardisation of the Saturday half-day. Saint Monday survived in the Birmingham area into the late nineteenth century in small workshops and in some industries where skilled workers maintained their traditional right

to a leisurely Monday, confident in the indispensable nature of their skills. Douglas A. Reid, 'The Decline of Saint Monday 1766–1876', in *Past and Present*, no. 71 (1976).

18 Malcolm names the following nationalist MPs as strong supporters of temperance legislation, speaking in favour of restrictive legislation and in some cases sponsoring bills: A. M. Sullivan, John A. Blake, John Redmond, Arthur O'Connor and J. G. Biggar, Maurice Healy, Jeremiah Jordan, Pierce Mahony and Alexander Blaine. Malcolm, *Ireland Sober*, pp 91, 263.

19 Report of Great Aggregate Meeting, Freemasons' Hall, May 1882, Licensed Victuallers' National Defence League *Annual Reports 1876–1886* (London Metropolitan Archives, National Licensed Victuallers' Association papers, ACC 3122/403). According to Malcolm, with regard to the 1870s, 'the drink trade was forced to rely heavily on its English counterpart and the sympathy of many English Tory MPs. This was politically embarrassing for a group with nationalist leanings, and ultimately it proved ineffective'. Malcolm, *Ireland Sober*, p. 250. However, while this conclusion has some merit in relation to the campaign against the 1878 bill, it cannot be sustained in the longer term. Over the following three decades, Dublin vintners continued to develop their relations with the British trade, with very little evidence of embarrassment and with some effect. See F. Waldron, 'A Triumph of Publicanism: Dublin Licensed Vintners in the late Nineteenth Century' (PhD thesis, UCD, 2007, pp 136–84.

20 *Hansard*, 3rd series, vol. 237, col. 1696 (14 Feb. 1878).

21 Commenting on the long and arduous debate, Gladstone noted in his diaries that the bill had been met 'by an obstruction really scandalous', 1 Apr. 1878 in H. C. G. Matthew (ed.), *The Gladstone Diaries Volume IX: January 1875–December 1880* (Oxford, 1886), p. 303.

22 Lee identifies the liquor industry as 'Virtually the only major expanding market dominated by Irish businessmen' between 1850 and 1914. Joseph Lee, *The Modernisation of Irish Society 1848–1918* (Dublin, 1973), p. 14.

23 Excise duty increased from 6s 2d to 8s per gallon. Mary E. Daly, *Dublin, the Deposed Capital: A Social and Economic History 1860–1914* (Cork, 1984), p. 27.

24 Cormac Ó Gráda, *Ireland: A New Economic History 1780–1939* (Oxford, 1994), p. 298.

25 Ibid., p. 304. For a comprehensive history of Guinness see Patrick Lynch and John Vaizey, *Guinness's Brewery in the Irish Economy 1759–1876* (Cambridge, 1960); also Stanley Raymond Dennison and Oliver MacDonagh, *Guinness 1886–1939: From Incorporation to the Second World War* (Cork, 1998).

26 Joseph Lee, 'Money and Beer in Ireland', *Economic History Review*, vol. 19, no. 1 (1966), p. 186.

27 Alfred Barnard, *Noted Breweries of Great Britain and Ireland*, (London, 1886). The Anchor Brewery was taken over by the D'Arcy family in 1818 for the substantial sum of £35,000. Like the Guinness family, the D'Arcy family extended its interests into the political sphere. John D'Arcy became Lord Mayor of Dublin in 1852, while his son, Matthew, was deputy lieutenant and magistrate for the counties of Dublin and Wexford, which he represented in Parliament from 1868–74. In 1889 James F. D'Arcy succeeded his father to both the deputy lieutenancy of Dublin and to the management of the brewery. Lynch and Vaizey, *Guinness's Brewery*, pp 91–2.

28 Daly, *Dublin*, p. 24.

29 Ó Gráda, *Ireland*, p. 304. See also Diarmuid Ó Drisceoil and Donal Ó Drisceoil, *The Murphy's Story: The History of the Lady's Well Brewery, Cork* (Cork, 1997).

30 Daly, *Dublin*, p. 5.

31 Ó Gráda argues that distilling was never a significant job-provider in Ireland with the overall workforce rising from 1,416 in 1870 to 2,423 in 1907. Ó Gráda, *Ireland*, p. 297.

32 Daly, *Dublin*, pp 2–6.

33 Indeed, as Shiman points out, many English temperance societies included wine merchants and brewers amongst their patrons. Shiman, *Crusade against Drink*, p. 11.

34 Cause-based interest groups such as the temperance movement and economic interest groups such as the LGVPA can be seen as part of the broader associational culture that contributed to the modernisation and democratisation of European states in the nineteenth century. For a consideration of the modernising influence of interest groups see Graham Wootton, *Pressure Groups in Britain 1720–1970: An Essay in Interpretation with Original Documents* (London, 1975).

35 And see also n. 19 above.

36 *Irish Sportsman*, 9 Nov. 1889.

37 Royal Commission on Liquor Licensing Laws, vol. vii (Ireland) (House of Commons, 1898), p. 174.

38 Based on the valuations provided in the *Official Register of Licensed Vintners* for 1895 compiled by M. J. F. McCarthy, the median valuation for Dublin city premises in 1895 was £36. Dublin premises were skewed substantially towards the lower end of the scale, with 25 per cent valued at £25 or lower and 75 per cent at £50 or lower. Women accounted for 14 per cent of licensees and were predominantly clustered in the lower end of the valuation scale and in the food and lodging sector. See Waldron, 'A Triumph of Publicanism', pp 71–81 for a more detailed analysis. Dublin premises were deemed to be undervalued during this period and the revaluation of property provided for by the Dublin Corporation Act 1900 led to an increase of almost 50 per cent in the combined valuations of licensed premises, as opposed to the general increase of 17.5 per cent for the city as a whole. See Daly, *Dublin*, p. 238.

39 *Whiskey Trade Review*, 5 Nov. 1891. There is some uncertainty in relation to the exact date. There is agreement, however, that licensed vintners in Dublin were organised from circa 1815. Extant records of minutes date from March 1831. The Licensed Vintners Association's website cites 1817 as the founding year of the association. See website www.lva.ie

40 *Whiskey Trade Review*, 5 Nov. 1891.

41 Minutes of the LGVPA, 1 May 1862.

42 Select Committee Report on Sale of Intoxicating Liquors, 1877, p. 112.

43 *Whiskey Trade Review*, 5 Nov. 1891.

44 See, for example, minutes of the LGVPA, 11 Dec. 1891 and 21 Nov. 1895.

45 Malcolm, *Ireland Sober*, p. 53; Shin-ichi Takagami, 'The Fenian rising in Dublin, March 1867', *Irish Historical Studies*, vol. xxix, no. 115 (May 1995).

46 Samuel Clark, *Social Origins of the Irish Land War* (Princeton, 1979), p. 268. Garvin estimates that of the eighty-one IRB activists under police surveillance between 1880 and 1902, one fifth were shopkeepers who were mostly publicans. Moreover, 30 per cent of the leaders

identified by Garvin were resident in Dublin. Tom Garvin, 'The Anatomy of a Nationalist Revolution: Ireland, 1858–1928', in *Comparative Studies in Society and History*, vol. 28, no. 3 (1986), pp 479, 480. Furthermore, in 1884, the majority of IRB leaders in Carlow, King's County and Queen's County were publicans. Owen McGee, *The IRB: The Irish Republican Brotherhood from the Land League to Sinn Féin* (Dublin, 2005), p. 130.

47 Brian Harrison, *Drink and the Victorians: The Temperance Question in England, 1815–1872* (London, 1971), p. 55.

48 K. Theodore Hoppen, *Elections, Politics and Society in Ireland, 1832–1885*, (Oxford, 1984), p. 433. In his testimony before the Select Committee on Sunday Closing Acts (Ireland) in 1888, Maurice Healy characterized the municipal franchise in Ireland as 'a publican franchise' i.e. 'It is a franchise which is up to the level of the average public-houses, which excludes persons who are below that level'. Select Committee 1888, p. 418. Maurice Healy, brother of Tim Healy, was MP for Cork city 1885–1900 and a temperance supporter. The buying of drink for prospective voters, known as 'treating', was not confined to Ireland. Commenting on the role which temperance played in losing support for the Liberals in England, T. P. O'Connor noted that the drink trade 'is in daily communication with the corruptible elements in all the constituencies. If they stand together and use that influence it must tell . . . you know in Lancashire they have an expression about 'a long pull'. With 'a long pull' a barman can give you a full pint and a good deal more for your money; with a short pull he can give you half froth.' *Freeman's Journal*, 22 July 1892.

49 Furthermore, publicans were forbidden to allow illegal societies or meetings on their premises, with particular reference to societies that required members to swear an oath or go through a rite of admission. Moreover, flags or emblems of such societies could not be displayed. Edward B. McGuire, *Irish Whiskey: A History of Distilling, the Spirit Trade and Excise Controls in Ireland* (Dublin, 1973), p. 283.

50 This evolution is reflected in changing attitudes towards public houses evident in police records. While in 1883 police searches of public houses in Dublin frequently resulted in finds of weapons, by 1892, despite a feared revival of Fenianism in Dublin, Superintendent John Mallon was confident that public houses were not involved. Rather, he pointed to the 'so called social labour clubs which are in reality big shebeens'. Report by DMP to Chief Secretary G. O. Trevelyan, March 1883 (Chief Secretary's Office Registered Papers 1883/6705); John Mallon 26 July 1892 (Dublin Metropolitan Police Files 1892 3/714 Box 12 Report 2370). Nonetheless, throughout the 1880s and early 1890s, a small number of publicans appear with great regularity in police files. See for example, 'Fenian doings in Dublin City 16 May to 7 June 1887' (Dublin Metropolitan Police Files, 3/794/3-2); 'A list of dangerous Fenians within the Dublin Met Police District', 23 Sept. 1886 and 5 Jan. 1888 (Dublin Metropolitan Police Files, 3/794/3-2). See Waldron, 'A Triumph of Publicanism', pp 244–9.

51 Select Committee on Sunday Closing, 1888, p. 432; Royal Commission on Liquor Licensing, 1898, p. 305; Daly, *Dublin*, p. 204. For a detailed analysis see Waldron, 'A Triumph of Publicanism', pp 249–53.

52 Indeed, involvement in the National Registration Association was seen by the LGVPA to be an important aspect of the work of the trade. See for example, Minutes of the LGVPA, 10 July, 11 July 1883 and 6 May 1884.

53 See, for example, Minutes of the LGVPA, 10 Nov. 1885.

54 See, for example, Minutes of the LGVPA, 31 Aug. 1888 and 19 Feb. 1889. See also Malcolm, *Ireland Sober*, p. 265.

55 Minutes of the LGVPA, 25 Feb. 1889.

56 Alan O'Day argues that between 1883 and 1885, the Irish Parliamentary Party was reshaped from a party premised loosely around the issue of self-government to a 'party of social integration' which championed a programme of reform and attended to constituency needs and issues in a way hitherto unknown in Irish politics. Moreover, this reformist incarnation allowed the Irish Party to distance itself even further from the revolutionary undertones of the Land League and incorporate the interests of the Catholic bourgeoisie. Alan O'Day, *Irish Home Rule 1867–1921* (Manchester, 1998), pp 85–6. Tending to the economic interests of publicans could be seen as part of that incorporation.

57 McGee, *The IRB*, p. 77. For a biographical note on John O'Connor see Georgina Clinton and Owen McGee, 'O'Connor, John', in James McGuire and James Quinn (eds), *Dictionary of Irish Biography* (Cambridge, 2009) and www.dib.cambridge.org

58 Peter McDonald had a direct interest in the liquor industry. He was partner in the firm Cantwell and McDonald, wine merchants of Dublin and High Sheriff of Dublin in 1886. Crilly was a journalist at A. M. Sullivan's the *Nation* newspaper from 1880. *Thom's Street Directory* 1888.

59 For O'Connor, the failure of the LGVPA to support his election campaign in Kilkenny during the 1892 election must have been a bitter disappointment. While it caused some hand wringing within the Association, the need for the Association to maintain its neutral stance won out over loyalty for services rendered. See Minutes of the LGVPA 24, 27, 28, 29 June and 5 July 1892.

60 Minutes of the LGVPA, 11 May 1886. The Sale to Children Bill sought to outlaw the sale of alcohol to children under the age of 13. In the debate on the second reading of the bill in the House of Commons, Parnell had argued that 'the question of temperance and of the control of the liquor trade, is one which, of all others, could most suitably and properly be left to an Irish Legislature to deal with.' He also maintained, wrongly, that he had never voted on temperance, preferring to steer clear of the issue. *Hansard*, 3rd series, vol. 304, col. 694 (2 Apr. 1886). See also Malcolm, *Ireland Sober*, pp 263–4.

61 Even in the weeks leading up to the declaration, the vintners' use of the Home Rule argument was by association. Thus, in arguing against William Johnston, Independent Conservative MP for Belfast South in March 1886, the chairman of the association, Patrick Kenny, argued that as Johnston's views on Home Rule and on the land question were not taken by the government as representative of Irish opinion, 'therefore, logically they could not tamper with the Irish liquor question at the gentleman's request or in accordance with his views if they aimed at governing the country according to Irish ideas'. *Freeman's Journal*, 17 Mar. 1886.

62 Minutes of the LGVPA, 23 Apr. 1888.

63 In the 1865 election, the traditional Liberal allegiance of the Dublin publicans was challenged by the threat of a pro-temperance Conservative candidate, John Vance. Fearful that Vance would secure the second seat after the Liberal candidate, Jonathan Pim, the LGVPA advised against a 'plump for Pim' policy in favour of support for the candidacy of Conservative brewer, Benjamin Lee Guinness. *Freeman's Journal*, 12 Oct. 1865. In the event, Guinness headed the poll, leading

Pim by 660 votes with Vance trailing by a further 580 votes; it would seem that the vintners who advocated against a 'plump for Pim' policy made the right call on this occasion. Brian M. Walker (ed.), *Parliamentary Election Results in Ireland 1801–1922* (Dublin, 1978), p. 102.

64 See, for example, Minutes of the LGVPA, 16 and 25 Mar. 1880. See, also, Minutes of the LGVPA, 4, 9, 10 and 11 July 1895 outlining the activities of the trade during the 1895 election and its success in preventing the selection of the pro-temperance anti-Parnellite incumbent, Charles Diamond, in favour of Daniel McAleese. McAleese, who received a contribution of £100 from the LGVPA towards his election expenses, went on to win the seat. The Association vigorously responded to subsequent rumours that a safe seat would be found for Diamond, and, while the extent to which the opposition of the vintners influenced the anti-Parnellites can only be guessed at, the object of the campaign was successfully achieved. See Minutes of the LGVPA, 17, 18, 19 and 23 July, and 6 and 29 Aug. 1895.

65 The power of local conventions to influence the choice of candidates decreased even more in the aftermath of the Galway convention of 1886. However, even before this débâcle, the 'inner circle' exerted considerable control over the selection of candidates. See Conor Cruise O'Brien, *Parnell and his Party 1880–1890* (Oxford, 1957), p. 260. Maura Cronin also notes tensions in Cork and Limerick between 'localism and centralisation' in choosing of candidates which were resolved by the appearance of consensus at National League conventions. 'But though ostensibly free debate took place on the merits of potential candidates, the tendency was to select the individual most obviously backed by Parnell, the decision being reached by public consensus with little room for dissenting voices.' Maura Cronin, 'Parnellism and Workers: The Experience of Cork and Limerick', in Fintan Lane and Donal Ó Drisceoil (eds), *Politics and the Irish Working Class, 1830–1945* (New York, 2005), p. 145. See, also, Lee, *Modernisation of Irish Society*, p. 108.

66 Minutes of the LGVPA, 27 Oct. and 3 Nov. 1885.

67 Ibid., 9 Nov. 1885.

68 Ibid., 10 Nov. 1885.

69 Ibid.

70 Ibid., 3 Apr. 1888.

71 Ibid., 3 May 1888.

72 Ibid., 4 May 1888.

73 Ibid., 5 May 1888.

74 Telegram, Parnell to Davitt, undated, Davitt papers, Trinity College, Dublin. I owe this reference to Carla King. Wilfrid Scawen Blunt was an English poet and diplomat who became involved in politics in the 1880s. He was a critic of British Imperialism and championed nationalist causes in India, Egypt and Ireland. For a biographical note see C. J. Woods, 'Blunt, Wilfrid Scawen', in McGuire and Quinn (eds), *Dictionary of Irish Biography and* www.dib.cambridge.org. Alfred Webb's family were radical Quakers and printers. He was involved as a young man in the anti-slavery movement and was a prominent temperance activist. Webb was a prominent nationalist and was MP for West Waterford 1890–5. He became president of the Indian National Congress in 1894. See Marie-Louise Legg (ed.), *Alfred Webb: the Autobiography of a Quaker Nationalist* (Cork, 2000).

75 *Hansard*, 3rd series, vol. 325, cols 1785–8 (9 May 1888).

76 Ibid.

77 Ibid. Opposition to restrictive legislation for Ireland on the basis that it was exceptional legislation was strongly voiced by nationalist politicians who supported the liquor trade. Timothy Harrington, for example, made this argument very strongly when addressing the Royal Commission in 1898, arguing in particular against the slur on the Irish character implicit in it: 'I may say I have seen more drunkenness in Glasgow on one Saturday night than I have seen in half the year in Dublin on Saturday nights . . . I dispute the proposition which seems to be so constantly before the House of Commons and the country that we are a drunken race of people in Ireland'. Royal Commission 1898, p. 167. Nationalist politicians and vintners argued, also, that nationalist publicans were discriminated against in the implementation of existing legislation, a bias that was likely to continue with any new restrictions. See Malcolm, *Ireland Sober*, pp 261–3.

78 Minutes of the LGVPA, 5 May 1888. In his biography of Parnell, Barry O'Brien notes: 'No quarrels was certainly a favourite thought, if not a favourite expression of Parnell. To have any single force which made for Irish nationality in conflict with any force which could be made in the same direction was utterly abhorrent.' R. Barry O'Brien, *The Life of Charles Stewart Parnell, 1846–1891*, vol. 1, (London, 1898), pp 303–4, quoted in Paul Bew, *Enigma: A New Life of Charles Stewart Parnell*, (Dublin, 2011), p. 201.

79 *Hansard*, 3rd series, vol. 325, cols 1785–8 (9 May 1888).

80 Bew, *Enigma*, p. 201.

81 *Hansard*, 3rd series, vol. 325, cols 1785–8 (9 May 1888).

82 Minutes of the LGVPA, 10 May 1888.

83 David W. Gutzke, *Protecting the Pub: Brewers and Publicans against Temperance* (New Hampshire, 1989), p. 100.

84 Ibid., p.101. See also Minutes of the LGVPA, 4 May 1888.

85 'Annual Report 1896', *Licensed Vintners' National Defence League Annual Reports 1893–96* (National Licensed Victuallers' Association papers, ACC 3122/406, London Metropolitan Archives); 1877 Pamphlet, *Pamphlets and Reports, various authors 1868–1881* (National Licensed Victuallers' Association papers, ACC 3122/454, London Metropolitan Archives).

86 Minutes of the LGVPA, 18 May 1888.

87 Gutzke, *Protecting the Pub*, p. 104. Áine Hyland and Kenneth Milne (eds), *Irish Educational Documents: A Selection of Extracts from Documents Relating to the History of Irish Education from the Earliest Times to 1922*, (Dublin, 1987), pp 210–11.

88 Minutes of the LGVPA, 24 Apr. and 13 May 1890.

89 Ibid., 3 June 1890.

90 Ibid.

91 *Freeman's Journal*, 7 June 1890. All further references to this meeting and its discussions are from this same source.

92 Ibid.

93 Ibid.

94 Harrel to Under Secretary, 10 June 1890 (Chief Secretary's Office Registered Papers, Ms 1890/9138).

95 Ibid.

96 Ibid.

97 Minutes of the LGVPA, 13 June 1890. At the following meeting of the committee, Philip Doran added to the list of promises given by Parnell; should the Intoxicating Liquors (Ireland) Bill passing into law in advance of a local government bill for Ireland, Parnell would seek that the £40,000 identified for compensation purposes in the Local Taxation (Customs and Excise) Duties Bill would be used to compensate vintners for losses that would accrue from the curtailment of their hours of sale. Minutes of the LGVPA, 17 June 1890.

98 Ibid., 4 July 1890.

99 Gutzke, *Protecting the Pub*, p. 105.

100 Minutes of the LGVPA, 9 Dec. 1890. For an analysis of the contribution of Dublin vintners to the politics of the split and an analysis of their role in the 1892 election, see Waldron, 'A Triumph of Publicanism', pp 291–335.

101 Ibid., 12 Dec. 1890.

102 *Hansard*, 3rd series, vol. 352, cols. 632–5 (15 Apr. 1891). *Fiat experimentum in corpore vili* translates as: Let the experiment be made on the body of no value. See also Malcolm, *Ireland Sober*, p. 271. While, as noted earlier, this was a well-rehearsed nationalist argument against temperance legislation, the bitter undertones of Parnell's speech undoubtedly reflect his sense of betrayal by his Liberal allies in their response to the divorce crisis; it may have been fuelled, also, by a more personal bias. Paul Bew notes Parnell's dislike of what he saw as English hypocrisy, which was evident before he entered politics. Paul Bew, *Enigma*, p. 11.

103 Elizabeth Malcolm describes Parnell as 'not greatly interested in the issue of temperance for its own sake'. His pragmatic approach saw temperance as 'a matter to be exploited or ignored, depending on the political advantages to be gained'. Malcolm, *Ireland Sober*, p. 265.

104 Alan O'Day describes the years between 1879 and 1884 as 'unprecedented for defining national identity and mobilising the Irish masses' and for 'the development of political discourse'. O'Day, *Irish Home Rule*, p. 59.

105 Interest groups such as the LGVPA can use their resources to activate 'pathways to influence', seeking, for example, direct access to decision makers; influencing selection of decision makers; using voice strategies to shape public opinion; and employing structural coercion power. Andreas Dür and Dirk de Bièvre, 'The question of interest group influence' in *Journal of Public Policy*, vol. xxvii, no. 1 (2007), p. 8.

106 Minutes of the LGVPA, 30 Apr. and 9 May 1895. See also E. Sheppard, 'The Irish Parliamentary Party and the Irish Licensed Trade and the Politics of the 1909 Budget' (MA thesis, NUI, 1983).

CHAPTER 8

The Parnells and Paris[1]

Pat Power

CHARLES TUDOR STEWART (1818–74)

The association of the Parnell family with the city of Paris began when Charles Tudor Stewart, brother of Delia Tudor Stewart, settled in the city sometime after 1854. Charles Tudor Stewart was born in Boston *c.*1818, and was the younger brother and only living sibling of Delia (who was born in 1816). Their father was the celebrated American naval hero Commodore Charles Stewart (1778–1869), one time commander of the famed battle ship *USS Constitution* (and now berthed as a national monument in Boston Harbour). Due to the fame of the ship, and the longevity of the Commodore (he survived almost a full century), both received the sobriquet '*Old Ironsides*'. Commodore Stewart married Delia Jarvis Tudor of Boston (1787–1860) in 1813.[2]

Six years after the birth of Charles Tudor an irrevocable rift occurred in the marriage between the Commodore and his wife and they parted company, never speaking to one another again. Three years of bitterness then began over the custody of the Tudor Stewart children. Claims and counter claims were made as to the financial recklessness and disloyalty of Delia to her husband; and the counter-allegation of the profligacy of the Commodore (he had taken to living with a lady outside of the marriage). After a long and quarrelsome period a settlement was reached: Delia Jarvis Tudor received a modest allowance and the custody of her daughter Delia; while Charles was sent to live with his father permanently, but with Delia allowed limited access. Despite the family disruption Charles Tudor Stewart and his sister had great affection for one another, probably seeing each other as orphans of the parental storm.

Despite his thrifty ways the Commodore did not stint on his son's education and Charles Tudor attended a prestigious boarding school in Baltimore, Maryland before attending law and engineering schools where he graduated in both disciplines. His primary career was engineering, and he is recorded as working on the burgeoning railway systems then getting organised in the eastern United States. As a Tudor of Boston he would also have had the ethos of financial canniness from some (though not all) of his Tudor relatives who had amassed considerable wealth in the industrial and commercial expansion of that city. Young Charles Tudor also had a penchant for politics, and as often as time allowed, attended the United States Congress in Washington taking a deep interest in the business of the House. Much to the distress of his future brother-in-law, John Henry Parnell of Avondale, Charles Tudor Stewart showed no interest in the sporting world of fur and feather having 'no taste for sport of any kind'.[3]

Delia Tudor Stewart married John Parnell in New York on 31 May 1835 after what only could be described as a whirlwind courtship – they knew each other for only a couple of heavily-chaperoned weeks. Delia's father and her brother, Charles, saw the young, married couple off as they embarked for their new life together at Avondale. The loss of 'this almost twin sister'[4] affected the 17-year-old Charles Tudor but he was happy in the opinion that John Parnell would be an ideal husband to her and a life of contented happiness lay before her. As things turned out, however, it was a view seen through rose-tinted spectacles.

Charles Tudor Stewart's early years after he left full time education are sketchy. He appeared to have inherited the financial acumen of the Tudors and realised a lot of money while still relatively young. Whether he also pursued a legal career as well as engineering is possible as he acquired valuable portfolios of railway shares and bonds which formed the basis of his future wealth. In 1837 John and Delia returned to the United States for a family visit – John Parnell suffering intolerable boredom, and Charles Tudor tried to speed-rectify the deficiencies in Delia's poor education by encouraging her to take to the books. Three more years followed in Ireland for Delia who pined for her American relatives, especially her mother. Though pregnant again with her fifth child in six years, the Parnells made a second turbulent Atlantic crossing between the births of Emily in 1841 and John Howard in 1842. Charles Tudor Stewart was in high hopes that his sister might have a son (the previous child being baby Emily) and that he would be named after him. As things worked out Delia had the son, but her choice of name was overruled and the child was named John Howard after his aristocratic Wicklow family relatives: Howard of Shelton Abbey, Earls of Wicklow. Obviously disappointed, Delia was obliged to inform Charles Tudor of the outcome, but both hoped things might be rectified in the future. Children continued to arrive, Sophie in 1845, and then in the following year another son. This time brother Charles Tudor Stewart was not disappointed, the child being christened Charles Stewart. Was there any inkling to mother, father or uncle, as water was poured over the baby's head, that he would ensure that the name of Charles Stewart would be forever enshrined in Irish history?

NO 122 CHAMPS-ÉLYSÉES

The exact year in which Charles Tudor Stewart settled in Paris is not known, but he was certainly there by his early twenties. Entries in the diary of Mrs Alice Clarke of Rathdrum, who knew Delia Parnell well from her first arrival at Avondale, cites two separate visits to Paris by Delia and her husband: one in 1851 and another in 1852; during one of which she suffered a bad fall and had to remain on while John Henry returned home.[5] While there is no specific mention of Charles Tudor in Mrs Clarke's references, such frequent visits to Paris suggest he was already there. Correspondence between Delia and Charles show that he was definitely resident in Paris by 1853, he having journeyed from there to London where Delia had arranged to visit him. The settlement of the young engineer in France was due to the friendship between the Stewart family and the family of Prince Lucian Murat, a cousin of Louis-Napoléon Bonaparte, future Emperor of France in the Second Empire. The principal members of the Bonaparte families were expelled from France after the battle of Waterloo. Lucian Murat's uncle, Prince Joseph-Napoleon Bonaparte, elder brother of the great French leader, settled in Bordentown, New Jersey on a property adjoining Commodore Stewart's estate '*Ironsides*'. Contemporaries in age, Charles Tudor and Prince Lucian became well acquainted. It was through this contact that Charles Tudor later secured lucrative and long-term timber contracts supplying the French Navy with American timber after Lucian Murat's return to France in 1848. Secure in the friendship of Prince Lucian (who had become a pivotal figure in the French government) Charles Tudor prospered in Paris and acquired a palatial apartment on the first floor of the six storied building at No 122 Avenue des Champs-Élysées, that wonderful street laid out between the Arc de Triomphe and the Obelisk of the Place de la Concorde. This superb townhouse flat was, fortunately, large enough to accommodate all the Parnells on their frequent visits. Although the incursion of children must have at times stretched the patience of the lifelong bachelor – Uncle Charles – there are few hints that he wasn't anything but amused at their presence and he genuinely welcomed the company of his sister on her frequent residences. Here, Delia, like the proverbial mother hen, preened her older daughters, Delia and Sophie, and looked out for possible husbands while mixing with the American expatriate community in Paris.

Her efforts met with partial success when the eldest of the Parnell children Delia (1837–82) married an American, James Livingston Thompson. It was, however, not a happy union. Thompson was allegedly a jealous and possessive husband, keeping Delia partially confined in their apartment on the fashionable Boulevard St-Michel.[6] Such were the depths of her misery that Delia made an attempt on her own life by ingesting a poison. Only the quick intervention of her younger sister, Anna, who was lodging in the apartment at the time, saved her. Despite the loveless marriage, however, they had one child Henry (born 1861) – whose funeral Charles Stewart Parnell was granted temporary release from Kilmainham Gaol to attend during the height of the Land War in 1882.[7]

It is difficult to ascertain exactly how many times Delia visited Paris between her arrival in Avondale in 1835 and her husband's death in 1859, but they were frequent – and quite remarkable considering the number of children to be brought along with her. So much time was spent in Paris that the elder Parnell daughters – the Misses Delia, Emily and Sophia – were partially schooled there up to their teens through the generous bounty of Uncle Charles. It was while Delia was again in Paris with seven of her eight children (the exception being the young Charles Stewart, then aged 13, who did not travel because of an illness), that her husband John Henry died suddenly on 3 July 1859. In consequence only Charles Stewart Parnell attended his father's funeral. The following year Delia's and Charles' beloved mother died suddenly when on a visit to the rented Parnell house in Dun Laoghaire. Her demise further strengthened the bond between brother and sister.

Following her husband's untimely death, Delia was forced to leave Avondale due to financial constraints and probate problems. Over the next eight years she took rented accommodation in Dublin at a number of addresses. One of the few solaces of her widowhood was that she could now, subject to her limited finances, visit her brother as frequently as she wished. And this she did often, with her younger daughters – Misses Anna, Fanny and Theodosia – in tow. Over time all became fluent French speakers, writers and readers. This nomadic existence between Ireland and France was rudely interrupted by the American Civil War. Charles Tudor felt incumbent to return to the United States and watch over his business interests. Whether he had an actual military career during the Civil War is not clear but Jane McL. Côté in her well-researched book, *Fanny and Anna Parnell: Ireland's Patriot Sisters*, states that he returned to Paris in 1866 styling himself 'Colonel'. Côté was unable to throw any light as to which army, if any, he served in, and adds that the rank of 'colonel' was sometimes used as an honorary title by the Confederate States.[8]

From 1868 to 1874 Delia, and daughters Fanny, Anna and Theodosia, were more or less in permanent residence at No 122. Delia quickly became part of the lively American colony in Paris, joining those who were drawn to the city by its glamour and cosmopolitan ways, and the fact that the Emperor of the Second Empire (Louis-Napoléon, now Napoleon III, cousin to the family friend Prince Lucian) was well disposed to Americans – especially wealthy, successful ones. Americans in Paris, however, tended to be conservative. Their lifestyle, revolving mainly around social mobility and money, failed to impress Fanny and Anna Parnell, particularly once they reached maturity. But for Delia, Paris was heaven. Out of deference to their mother the very eligible, if slightly impoverished, Parnell girls, Fanny and Anna, attended the *soirées* and balls arranged by the friends of Charles Tudor Stewart; and he in turn acted as host when Delia gave her own *soirées* at No 122. In 1870, when she reached her eighteenth year, Anna had had enough of Paris and left for London to study art. Fanny and Theodosia remained on.

Charles Stewart Parnell and his brothers, John Howard and Henry Tudor, ploughed their own particular furrows during these years. Although no strangers to Paris as children, by the time Delia was in a position to settle there permanently, all the male children had more or less flown the family's nomadic nest. Charles Stewart, now over 21, was embroiled in semi-bankrupt Avondale. John Henry was in the United States struggling to establish his peach farm in Alabama; whilst young Henry Tudor was still at university (at Trinity College, Cambridge). One sojourn in Paris made by Charles Stewart Parnell was to have profound consequences for him. Politics still lay in the future, and there is little evidence that at this stage of his life he nurtured any intentions in the political field. What brought him to visit his uncle Charles in Paris may have been the quest for advice, and perhaps finance – he had just inherited a run down and decrepit Avondale. In the course of his stay at No 122 it is possible that Charles Tudor, a bit of a 'man about town', advised his nephew to try the marriage market as a means of raising cash now that he had come into 'his own'.[9] Whatever the purpose of his stay, the young Parnell entered into the Paris social scene and met a well brought-up – and wealthy – Miss Woods of Newport, Rhode Island. They seemed to get along well together and romance blossomed, or at least Charles Stewart thought so. This romance and its aftermath are discussed in greater detail below.[10]

In 1869, advanced in years and greatly honoured by his countrymen, Rear Admiral Charles Stewart died aged 94 in Bordentown, New Jersey, leaving all his property jointly to Delia and Charles Tudor. This marked another watershed in Delia's life, for she now had the means (and the property) to do what she had probably yearned for since her marriage – to return permanently to the United States. However, before this could be fully arranged momentous events were to befall her adopted city.

Delia's association with Paris had coincided with the years of the Second Empire of Louis Napoleon III (1852–70), when the classical Paris of today was largely created.[11] He had entrusted his loyal Prefect of the Seine, Georges Haussmann, with the task of modernising the capital city. Delia on her numerous visits would have witnessed Haussmann's transformation of the city. By 1868, the efficient Prefect of Police reported that there were 5,987 Americans resident in the city. Whether the Parnells had any exposure to the thriving art colony in Paris is not clear, but Anna may well have been encouraged by the artistic inspiration of the city in her desire to become a professional artist.

In July 1870 the Parisian world of the Second Empire crashed in ruins with the outbreak of the Franco-Prussian War and the subsequent Siege of Paris with its bloody aftermath, the Paris Commune. The previous year, as the clouds of conflict had gathered Dr Thomas Evans, the Emperor's dentist, and the most influential American private citizen in Paris, had, within a few months, organised a very efficient medical relief volunteer service known as the American Ambulance. Borrowing from their experiences in the American Civil War, many of the American ladies of Paris set aside their social calendars and freely gave time, money and effort in preparing for the coming war, unaware of the sensational turns it would quickly take. Shortly before the Prussian army besieged the city, Dr Evans, a rapacious man but a great humanitarian nevertheless, organised a full field hospital located on a secluded plot of one and a half acres off Avenue d'Imperatrice (now Avenue Foch) close to the American Residency.[12] It was equipped with the latest hospital tents from America, along with a mobile surgery, medicines, and clothing – all paid for with funds raised by the American community and donations from the United States.[13] Delia and Fanny Parnell were praised by Evans for their diligence and work in preparing the Ambulance, attending the hospital and ministering there until late in the war. Evans later recorded:

An attempt was made to organise a Ladies' Branch Committee as a cooperative and subordinate association. But many of the ladies who intended taking part in it were forced to leave town, and the 'Branch' as a distinct organisation ceased to exist. Nevertheless a good many ladies used to meet daily for the purpose of giving their aid to the cause in the rooms of the Committee in the Rue de la Paix, where they made ready a liberal supply of linen, lint, bandages, clothing & c, for the forty or fifty beds of the ambulance which the committee proposed to establish. Conspicuous for zeal and perseverance in this group of lady workers were Mrs and Miss Parnell, and Mrs Koch, and Miss Benson, among its American members, and Miss Bewick among its English ones. All laboured diligently and effectually and rendered valuable service in preparing the instruments of benevolent work upon which the Committee was anxiously desirous to enter.[14]

In her short, but patriotic, life Fanny Parnell was to draw later on these experiences of the American Ambulance when organising the Ladies' Land League. In September 1870 the net was closing around Paris, and Prussian troops occupied the forts protecting the city. Just before the siege proper began, Delia and Fanny, in little more than what they could carry, left the city on foot in company with other Americans. Whether uncle Charles or Delia Thompson were among the refugees is not clear. Mother and daughter eventually found refuge in London.[15]

Thanks to the exertions of the American Consul in Paris most of the property belonging to Americans was spared looting and destruction. Thus in 1872 the Parnells returned, and Charles Tudor Stewart found his spacious, ground floor apartment and its furnishings still intact. Paris life resumed. But this was a different Paris. War-damaged, demoralised, betrayed by an incompetent Emperor, and the final terrible shame of conquest by a hated foreign enemy – the Prussians had marched in victory the full length of the Champs-Élysées and under the great Arch – this great city was now filled with ruin and suspicion. Charles Tudor Stewart's affairs reflected the shaken city. His financial standing was dented due to the loss of valuable timber contracts with the French Navy; and his high-political and social circle was shattered as the Bonaparte family of the Second Empire (along with their immediate entourage) were again sent into exile. Delia who may now have thought the world a cruel place was about to find it crueller. With the death of the Parnell's kindly, paternal granduncle, Sir Ralph Howard, in County Wicklow modest bequests were made to the Parnell daughters and to Delia – enabling those who wished to do so to live on in Paris with some means. It was short-lived however. In September 1873 the American stocks and bonds market crashed and thousands of investors were ruined. Charles Tudor Stewart was among those hard hit. Though not reduced to beggary, he was badly shaken financially.

Côté speculates in her biography of the Parnell sisters that it might have been his sliding financial affairs that took Charles Tudor to Rome in March 1874.[16] There was no succour in that city: whilst there he contracted typhus. He survived long enough for Delia to hasten to his bedside, before expiring in the Hotel Ruspoli, Rome, aged 56. Abruptly Delia's Paris base ceased. Although Charles left her the bulk of his estate, the financial crash of 1873 had reduced his generous bequests of stocks, shares and bonds to Delia and the Parnell nieces to very modest sums. The lease on the prestigious address at No 122 was almost immediately terminated. Within two days of his death Fanny and John Howard Parnell had begun winding up his Paris affairs. Soon after, Delia and Fanny left for the United States where new chapters were to open in Fanny Parnell's life in Bordentown, New Jersey, home of her grandfather.

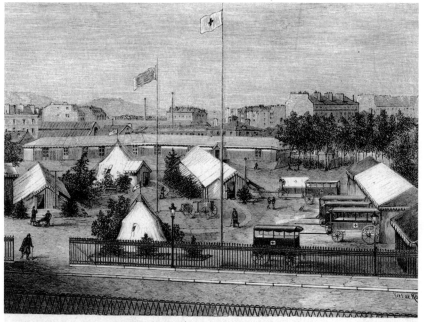

GENERAL APPEARANCE OF THE AMERICAN AMBULANCE.

The American ambulance or field hospital established in Paris during the Franco-Prussian War

PARNELL'S PARIS ROMANCE

In many of the biographical and historical studies of Charles Stewart Parnell, there are passing mentions of a short, but intense, relationship that took place mainly in Paris between a young Parnell and the elusive 'Miss Woods' of Newport, Rhode Island. When mention is made of the affair, it is usually dismissed in a few brief lines. But perhaps there was more to this formative episode in Parnell's life that deserves more attention than it has presently received from historians. John Howard Parnell, in the biography of his brother, makes a few references to the affair; but there appears to be little else written on the subject other than a reiteration of his brief account. In *The Providence Sunday Journal* for 17 September 1939, there appeared an article by John W. Tebbel entitled 'The Rhode Island Romance of Charles Stewart Parnell', and sub-titled 'Kitty O'Shea became his Wife, but He Loved a Newport Girl'.[17] The substance of the article – based on references to the affair in John Howard's memoir and Katharine O'Shea's biography of her lover – couched in the language of romantic fiction, may be synopsised as follows: at a soirée in the home of his uncle Charles Tudor Stewart in April 1870 Parnell then aged 25 was introduced to a 20-year-old Miss Mary Woods, the only child of a wealthy Newport couple. The meeting was possibly arranged by Parnell's uncle to specifically introduce the heiress. Charles Tudor Stewart was socially pragmatic and advised his nephew, now that he had come into his inheritance in Avondale, to look for an eligible and wealthy American heiress whose money would help Parnell to develop his estate. Love, if not already there presumably would follow. The young pair seemingly hit it off immediately and throughout the following two months attended numerous social activities and occasions within the Franco-American community. Both Mary Woods and Parnell were high-strung personalities and though the couple frequently quarrelled they just as soon made up. Mary Woods' parents were well disposed to Parnell and thought highly of him as a companion to their daughter.

In June Parnell had returned to Avondale, and according to the article, began to make the place ready for its second American bride. Meanwhile the Woods family continued their European sojourn by moving to Rome for a flavour of its cultural offerings. In October Parnell returned to Paris where he spent two days with his uncle before proceeding to Rome, rejoining the Woods family in their social round. Mary Woods and her parents were genuinely surprised and touched by Parnell's romantic ardour in following them to Rome, and staying for over two months. Again the couple appeared to enjoy one another's company, until the morbid fear of catching disease in the sometimes-fetid climate of nineteenth century Rome disturbed Parnell so much that he had to leave the city and return to Ireland. The relationship had now blossomed so romantically, and his warm reception by her parents, left Parnell in no doubt – in his mind at least – that his engagement was complete. There is, however, no reliable historical evidence that Parnell ever formally asked Mary, or her parents, for her hand in marriage. On balance, it is hard to believe that Miss Woods could spend so much time in Parnell's company in Paris and Rome without some understanding of his intentions. Whether formally engaged or not, Charles Stewart Parnell was in no doubt they would very soon become man and wife.

Parnell returned to Paris again in April 1872 for a brief visit. The romance was now running a year and showing no signs of dampening. In the same month he was back again in Avondale, but had only returned a few days when a short letter from Paris followed stating, briefly, that Mary and family were returning immediately to Newport, Rhode Island. The exact contents of the letter is not fully known, but it deeply disturbed Parnell in that it bore no mention of their engagement, nor seemingly any sentiment that she wanted to see him again. Parnell, displaying a second manifestation of his 'crisis energy' (his first being the trip to Rome), left immediately for Paris.

He was too late: the Woods family had already shipped to their native Rhode Island. Undaunted by the long journey, he immediately set sail for the United States, where, to the amazement of the pursued, he landed on the doorstep of their home in Rhode Island. Parnell was well received and Mary seemed genuinely pleased to see him again. The social round resumed and a number of engagements were attended by both Parnell and Mary as a 'couple'. But then a final separation took place and Mary broke off the relationship. The article in the *Providence Sunday Journal* claims that Mary finished the affair by saying: 'I could never bring myself to marry you, an obscure Irishman, who has no higher ambition than to run an estate. When I marry, I want a brilliant and famous man, whom I can respect as well as love.' There is no reliable evidence however, to prove or disprove this version of events. The truth of the separation might lie rather in a worry by both Mary Woods, and her parents, about the general tenor of life with the Parnells. Delia Parnell may well have painted a bleak picture of a lonely Avondale for an American lady used to the company of 'upper society'. Knowledge of an attempted suicide by Charles Stewart's sister, Delia Thompson, in Paris might not have helped the marriage prospects either. There might also have been other suitors in the wings more acceptable to Mary's parents. Whatever the cause Parnell was distraught at the rejection. He stayed around Newport for a short time until finally leaving for Alabama where his brother John Howard had settled.

Eight years later Parnell and John Dillon made their famous visit to America to publicise the Irish cause. One of their speaking engagements took them to Providence, Rhode Island. If the reporting of the *Providence Sunday Journal* is correct, Charles Stewart Parnell may well have been accorded the first authentic text message generations before the invention of the mobile phone, for above the entrance to the Music Hall where he was to speak hung a banner emblazoned: *Parnell – in the name of Roger Williams U are welcome 2 our state.*

After his public engagements, Parnell is alleged to have sought out Mary Woods – which he may well have done as he was still very much unattached: Mrs O'Shea having not yet entered the stage. Mary was still unwed and was reportedly delighted to see him. They both attended a ball in Parnell's honour, at which Mary gave him a love note comprising a few lines by Elizabeth Barrett Browning. If she was hoping to rekindle Parnell's interest in her however she was too late, Minerva's owl had flown and Parnell's love life was soon to fly in another direction. It was at the same ball that Mary Woods is reputed to have met her future husband (a successful Boston lawyer) and married soon after. Parnell and Mary never met again. John Howard, with his sister Theodosia, did visit her, and it is from this meeting that the story arose of her deep regrets about not having married Charles Stewart Parnell.

THE PARIS FUNDS

With the founding of the Irish National Land League in 1879, it became necessary to find a safe and secure haven for any funds acquired by the League. The main sources of such funds were collections from Irish-Americans. From their foundation in 1858, the Fenians had become very adept at raising money in the United States and, over the years of their cloak-and-dagger existence, fiscally wise in keeping the funds not only safe from the prying eyes of authority, especially the British, but from sequestration by factions within their own ranks. They quickly discovered that control of funds could be the Achilles heel of the organisation. From advice dispensed by Clan na Gael and old Fenian hands during their American trip in 1880, Charles Stewart Parnell and John Dillon decided that it was prudent to deposit any monies that the Land League received out of the reach of British authorities. This became all the more expedient with the intensification of the Land War throughout the 1880s. The implementation of the 1881 Coercion Act in Ireland made it even more imperative to place the Land League monies in a secure location, hence the setting up of the 'Paris Fund Accounts 1 and 2'. The transfer was placed in the hands of Patrick Egan, one the three treasurers to the Land League. An ex-Fenian and an astute and trustworthy financial adviser to Parnell, Egan was not a banker but a baker by profession, owning a successful bakery in Dublin. For the next few years he was to play a pivotal role in the Paris finances of the Land League and later the Irish National League.[18]

In February 1881, an important strategic meeting of the Land League executive was held in Paris. Holding the meeting in any Dublin, or indeed Irish venue, was deemed too dangerous for the senior members of the League were expecting to be arrested at any moment – a fear not misplaced as things turned out. Parnell's Paris headquarters was predominantly the Hôtel Brighton at No 218 Rue de Rivoli. He stayed here on a number of occasions after the loss of his uncle Charles' apartment. This venue was not only important for the fortunes of the Land League, but had a bearing on the future private life of Parnell.

According to Tim Healy's version of this event, when the Irish MPs, including himself, Joseph Biggar, John Dillon and others, assembled after their long journey to the city, Parnell did not show up.[19] Nor did he appear on the following day when the meeting was scheduled, nor indeed the day after. He was not seen, nor was there any communication, for a week. At their wits' end as to what had happened to their leader, it was decided to open a private letter which arrived at the hotel addressed to Parnell to see if it could throw any light on his whereabouts.[20] While the contents of the letter are disputed, it is generally believed that it was from Katharine O'Shea to Parnell; and that this was the first inclination to any of his close colleagues that Parnell had embarked on a relationship. When he learned the private letter had been opened, that notorious iceberg that was Parnell, chilled all those around him. From this incident perhaps came the eventual rift between himself and some of his colleagues, especially Tim Healy. Despite the atmosphere, the critical meeting took place; business was concluded and a strategy was agreed as to their conduct in the event of coercion and arrest.

Egan remained on in Paris, acting as bursar for the League funds when the leaders were incarcerated in Kilmainham Gaol under the feared Coercion Act. His role as treasurer in Paris was crucial to the success of the Ladies' Land League, which, under Anna Parnell's leadership, carried on the League's activities in that time.[21] From the Paris funds, Egan doled out money to Anna for her causes – though not always sanctioned by Charles Stewart. Imprisoned, he was in no position to stop it. A crunch came when Alex Sullivan, a high-ranking member of the American Clan na Gael arrived in Paris, and with Egan's compliance, withdrew £20,000 from the account to foster 'agitation'. Parnell was furious when he learned of the withdrawal, and on gaining temporary release for a compassionate visit to Paris (the funeral of his nephew Henry mentioned earlier), ordered the Paris funds to be frozen. His presence in the city did not go unmarked by the French secret police. There is a report in the Prefecture of his demeanour as he made the brief visit at what was the height of the Kilmainham crisis.

After the general release of the Land League executive following the 'Kilmainham Treaty' they were once again able to control directly the destinies of the organisation. By now they were anxious to dispense with the Ladies' Land League, seeing in their work a drain on expenses and a faction that was not fully under their control. Parnell killed the Ladies' League by the simple expedient of freezing their access to the Paris money. His sister Anna was especially dismayed at the decision. One of the excuses used to close-off the funds was a subscription of £50 from the Paris money which Anna had sent to help poor, evicted cottiers during the Ushaw Moor Colliery strike in Durham, England.[22] Patrick Egan also paid off the Ladies' Land League accumulated debt of £5,000, after which he resigned as treasurer, nevertheless leaving it in a still very healthy state with a balance of £35,000. He did not step totally away from service to the Land League, or from Parnell. In exposing the Pigott forgeries Egan was to play a vital part.

Over the next few years as Parnell continued his inexorable rise to national prominence, the Paris fund became crucial to the whole existence of the newly named Irish National League. For a quarter of the Irish Home Rule Members of Parliament, the fund from Paris was their only source of income. Twenty-five members, at least, drew two to three hundred pounds a year from it for their salaries, for it must be recalled that MPs at that time were not paid. By 1885 there were two separate funds: account No 1, the 'General Fund', much of which was collected in America at various fundraising events, and from which were dispensed expenses incurred in the fight against landlordism; and the second fund known, to those who were party to it, as the 'Special Fund', from which money went to pay the expenses and salaries of some MPs. This was a key weapon for Parnell in his hold over his colleagues. Controlling wages was a powerful lever in influencing how the poorer members behaved. The basis for the 'Special Fund' was always controversial and, at the fall of Parnell, was to cause much rancour. By 1886 there was an estimated £45,000 in the fund – and at the time of the Split perhaps much more. Certainly Parnell's rigid control over it caused the widest controversy. Throughout the Split, his appeared to be the faction with the least money problems. Some of the Special Fund monies came from donations and fundraising events in America, but a substantial amount originated more controversially. The Parnell Tribute of 1883 provided one substantial lodgement; the Special Commission Defence Fund provided another. Cecil Rhodes, super-rich from his exploitation of resources in South Africa, gave Parnell a gift of £5,000 and a promise of more; and a colleague of Rhodes, one John Morrogh, gave him a further £1,000. John Howard Parnell alleged that he was owed £5,000 from the Paris money as such a sum was raised from yet another mortgage on Avondale. When the split finally came, the Paris funds were central to the bitter row. Some of the MPs were completely dependent on it for their monthly income and Parnell's withholding of payments to those who refused to follow him only heightened the animosity towards him.

Yet despite the intensity of 'The Split', John Dillon and Parnell could still jointly agree to withdraw funds from Paris for some purposes – for example tenant relief, for which £8,000 was sanctioned. But it was control of the Special Fund that raised the temperature, for Parnell had structured the dispensation in such a way that his permission was required to draw money out. It was this fact that provoked Archbishop Croke to look publicly for an audit of the funds, giving Tim Healy the inspiration to publish his infamous 'Stop Thief' article where he openly accused Parnell of stealing the Paris funds.[23] Parnell's association with the controversy did not stop with his untimely death in 1891. A huge row over the Paris funds continued after his death, prompted by an attack on Katharine Parnell by T. M. Healy. After that, the funds were generally used for their original purpose – salaries, expenses, relief of evicted tenants – until they were exhausted.

Hôtel Brighton - Paris *(Facing Tuileries Gardens)*
218, rue de Rivoli

The Hôtel Brighton, No 218 Rue de Rivoli, Charles Stewart Parnell's Paris base. Here the crucial Land League meeting took place in February 1881, setting up the Paris fund; here also some of Parnell's colleagues first learned of his relationship with Mrs O'Shea.

Notes

1   This paper was written originally as part of a series of Parnell Society commemorative events held in Paris in Sept. 2007. It draws in part on the following works: Jane McL. Côté, *Fanny and Anna Parnell: Ireland's Patriot Sisters* (London, 1991), particularly ch. 5, 'La Vie Parisienne'; Alistair Horne, *The Fall of Paris: the Siege and the Commune, 1870–71* (London, 1965); *Providence Sunday Journal*, 17 Sept. 1939; Diary of Eithne Clarke (in private possession).

2   On Admiral Stewart and 'Old Ironsides', see Colin Stewart and Jean Costelloe, '*Old Ironsides': the Story of a Man and a Ship* (Rathdrum, 2001).

3   Côté, *Fanny and Anna Parnell*, p. 36.

4   Ibid., p. 26.

5   Diary of Mrs Alice Clarke, Rathdrum, 1834–57. In possession of Michael Clarke, Bishop's Castle, Shropshire. Alice Clarke was a daughter of William and Mary McMurray of Rathdrum. On her mother's side, she was a descendant of Edward Hayes, Cherrymount, Avoca. In 1829, she married Charles Clarke, a physician from New Ross who was dispensary medical officer for Rathdrum.

6   The ground floor of the house is now a distinctly unfashionable McDonald's fast food outlet.

7   For this incident, see Pauric Travers, 'The Blackbird of Avondale: Parnell at Kilmainham', in Donal McCartney and Pauric Travers, *The Ivy Leaf: The Parnells Remembered* (Dublin, 2006), pp 35–6.

8   Côté, *Fanny and Anna Parnell*, p. 276, n. 1.

9   Ibid., p. 74.

10 The Woods family continued their European tour to Rome and Charles Stewart followed, advised by his worldly uncle to avoid the 'Rome disease' when in that city. Uncle Charles may have had some previous experience of Rome.

11 On Paris and the Second Empire, see Robert Tombs, *The Paris Commune, 1871* (London, 1999), pp 13–40. Walter Benjamin famously described Paris as 'the capital of the nineteenth century'. Ibid., p. 21.

12 Evans had made vast wealth trading property around Paris.

13 On the history of the American ambulance during the siege of Paris, see Thomas W. Evans, *History of the American Ambulance Established in Paris During the Siege of 1870–71, Together with the Details of Its Methods and Its Works* (London, 1873).

14 Ibid. See also Côté, *Fanny and Anna Parnell*, pp 76–9 for a paraphrase of this narrative by Evans.

15 The history of the Paris Commune of 1871 is outside the scope of this essay. The best single account remains Alistair Horne, *The Fall of Paris, the Siege and the Commune 1870–71*.

16 Côté, *Fanny and Anna Parnell*, p. 81.

17 *Providence Sunday Journal*, 17 Sept. 1939.

18 For a short discussion of the political context as well as details of Parnell's meetings with George Clemenceau and Victor Hugo see Frank Callanan, *T. M. Healy*, (Cork, 1996), pp 46–55.

19 T. M. Healy, *Letters and Leaders of my Day* (New York, 1928), vol. I, pp 107–9.

20 For a critical discussion of this episode, see below ch. 9, 'Parnell and Sexual Scandal'.

21 For Anna Parnell and the Ladies' Land League, see above ch. 3, 'Anna Parnell: Challenges to Male Authority and the Telling of National Myth'.

22 R. F. Foster, *Charles Stewart Parnell: the Man and his Family* (Sussex, 1976), p. 275.

23 Callanan, *T. M. Healy*, p. 293; F. S. L. Lyons, *Charles Stewart Parnell*, p. 589, 1977 edn.

CHAPTER 9

Parnell and Sexual Scandal

Donal McCartney

Parnell's name has been connected with three major sex scandals. The best known, the Katharine O'Shea affair, was clearly proven and publicly acknowledged. Whatever about the mitigating circumstances, Parnell's intimate relationship with Mrs O'Shea had gone on for over ten years prior to Captain O'Shea's divorce proceedings against his wife naming Parnell as co-respondent. The undefended, lurid details that emerged from the court hearing destroyed what, according to Davitt, had promised to be the most successful career ever devoted to the cause of Ireland.[1] He was no longer deemed fit by the majority of his former supporters to be leader of a catholic nation – no longer the Uncrowned King, but an emperor without clothes exposed remorselessly to the ridicule of bitter enemies who were once his lieutenants, and to the powerful anathemas of the Irish bishops.

As if the O'Shea scandal had not been enough to destroy his reputation as well as his career, two other sex scandals, hidden from the public during his lifetime, were to be charged against him long after his death. If the O'Shea case was derisively referred to as the Kitty affair, the two that emerged posthumously may be called the 'Daisy' and 'Lizzie' scandals respectively.

THE 'DAISY' SCANDAL

The alleged Daisy scandal was reported for the first time by Parnell's sister, Emily, in her book, *A Patriot's Mistake,* published in 1905 (14 years after her brother's death).[2] She said she would willingly have drawn a cloak of silence over the whole episode except for the baneful influence it exercised on his later life, and the truth of the scriptural mandate: 'Whatsoever a man soweth, that shall he also reap'. In a style that would have done credit to any nineteenth-century tragic romance, Emily told the story of how Charles, as a student at Cambridge, while boating along the river, spotted in a nearby

161

fruit-garden, Daisy – an innocent, 16-year-old, poor fruit-farmer's daughter: with 'blue eyes and golden hair' and 'of remarkable loveliness'.[3] The 19-year-old Charles was entranced. A timely accident to one of his oars and the necessity of borrowing some cord, allowed him make her acquaintance and arrange to meet her secretly on future evenings. In these long evening walks, their friendship 'ripened into a deep and trusting affection on the girl's part, and an equally strong, though less pure and unselfish passion on the boy's part'.[4] 'They were lovers and happy . . . until their paradise was spoiled by an impulse of young passion.'[5] The social gap between them made marriage impossible. Her increasing wretchedness led to her suicide by drowning in the river near the place where they had first met.

It so happened that Charles was walking along the river bank when he saw a small crowd of villagers gathered round 'the slender, dripping form' of a young girl that had just been dragged dead from the water. 'Pushing aside the crowd with a gasp of horror, Charles recognised the body of his little wife, as he had called Daisy.' With 'wild looks and frenzied exclamations, as he knelt beside the body . . . he got some of the onlookers to assist him in conveying the earthly remains of Daisy to the village inn.' 'His first thought was of her old father' and a message was sent to inform him of the tragedy. An inquest was held at which Charles was a witness, where he admitted his friendship with Daisy. When the college authorities learned of Charles' acquaintance with the dead girl, his 'name was formally removed from the books of his university'. A 'torturing remorse . . . was to haunt him for the greater part, if not all of his life.[6]

Such was Emily's story. But what hard evidence had she for it, and for all the minute detail with which she coloured it? Precious little, as it turned out. She claimed that long after the event, she noticed Charles had become the

> frequent victim of violent nervous attacks. In these would appear before him, in the dead of night, standing at the foot of his bed, the dripping white-clad form, with locks like a cataract of golden rain, which he had seen that morning on the river bank.[7]

The cause of these attacks was unknown to any of his family until several years later when Emily and her husband, Captain Dickinson, were staying at Avondale. The Captain, who at Charles' request had shared a bedroom with him, reported to Emily the next morning that his brother-in-law had been moaning and calling out about 'some Daisy' and a vision at the foot of the bed. Emily was shocked because she had always considered Charles 'something of an anchorite.' Now though, she 'remembered chance words and allusions and the sudden termination of his college career' – from which damning evidence she 'discovered with a flash of insight the whole cause of his altered and careworn looks'.[8] No hard evidence then, but a 'flash of insight' – or the sentimental imaginings more appropriate to the contemporary novelette. Only the all-knowing mind and all-seeing eye of the fiction writer could have described the innermost thoughts and feelings of the tragic, young lovers, or provided such an amount of colourful detail for the alleged incident. One almost expects to find the disclaimer often appended to novels: 'The characters in this story are fictional and bear no resemblance to people living or dead.'

Parnell's youngest brother, Henry Tudor, considered the Daisy story as the worst 'I have ever heard about our dead brother'.[9] In correspondence with the authorities at Cambridge, Henry was assured that there was no foundation whatsoever for Emily's allegation that Charles was removed from the university as a result of such an episode. Nor were the authorities aware of any rumours connecting Parnell with any such scandal.[10] Indeed, Barry O'Brien's biography of Parnell, published as early as 1898, had given the actual reason why he was sent down from his college: a drunken brawl involving Parnell, a fellow student and two townsmen, resulting in a court fine for damages against Parnell; and because of his appearance in court, temporarily excluded from Cambridge for the remaining two weeks of term. The case was fully reported in the local newspapers of 22 May 1869, making it clear that the brawl had occurred during Parnell's fourth and final year in Cambridge when he was 23. In other words, he was not, as Emily would have it, a 19-year-old in his second year, removed from the university because of an unwise love affair and the unfortunate suicide of the girl.

Henry Harrison, whose book, *Parnell Vindicated*, published in 1931, went to the trouble of checking with the coroners' courts of the county and borough of Cambridge for details of suicides by drowning during Parnell's years at Cambridge (1865–9). They certified that no girl called Daisy was drowned, nor the subject of any inquest during that time. Nor was there an inquest on any drowned woman during the eleven months preceding Parnell's departure from the university.[11] Dr Ged Martin, in his article on Parnell's time at Cambridge, and based on official college records and local newspapers, concluded that the Daisy story was 'a fabrication'.[12] The verdict pronounced by Harrison and Martin has been accepted by Parnell's most reputable biographers – Foster, Lyons and Kee. Foster believes the Daisy story 'is effectively demolished' by Harrison and Martin; dismissing it as an 'apocryphal tale', commenting that it is 'probably as fantastic as the rest of the chapter, in which Mrs Dickinson allowed her considerable imagination full rein'.[13] Lyons agreed, saying that the story was one of Emily's 'more bizarre fabrications'.[14] More charitably, Robert Kee decided that whatever substance there was to the facts of the story, these facts were 'distorted by the long interval between occurrence and recording, but also by the efforts of some ghost-writer to make the book as vivid as possible in the light of Parnell's final notoriety'.[15] Kee discovered that a local servant girl, Annie Smith, had been found drowned during Parnell's second year in Cambridge. The verdict was that she had committed suicide after accidentally setting fire to the curtains in the local inn where she worked. It is not impossible that Parnell may have known her and been affected by the tragedy. But no undergraduate was reported as a witness at the inquest; and the post-mortem revealed that she was not pregnant, thus precluding that as a possible motive.

The question has to be asked: why would Emily make up such a story about her brother if there were not some substance to it? After all, her book did acknowledge that Charles had been most kind to her and her daughter both before and after her alcoholic husband's death. He had given them a home in Avondale when they were in difficulty and largely dependent on him for support. And because of her residence for long periods at Avondale, she was closer to him in many ways than any other member of the family. The answer to the question has to take account of the fact that, as her book shows, she was highly imaginative, gossipy, egocentric, fanciful and exuberant where her knowledge of the facts was slightest, and wildly inaccurate on several points. Emily was the kind of person who was most easily convinced by, and came to believe in, her own version of events. It is now generally accepted that the Daisy episode happened only in Emily's vivid imagination.

The next sex scandal in Parnell's life, again like the Daisy story, did not surface publicly until still longer after his death. In this case the revelation of the Irish leader's alleged misconduct was made by Tim Healy. One of the ablest of Parnell's parliamentarians, his reputation was such that he was once described by Bismarck as the 'cleverest man in the British Parliament'.[16] Healy was also the most bitter, nasty and outrageous of Parnell's critics throughout the Split. He became the first Governor-General of the Irish Free State (1922–8), and in 1928, the year his term of office came to an end, his memoir entitled *Letters and Leaders of my Day,* was published. Although 38 years since the split and now in his seventies, Healy was still giving no quarter to the man he had once christened 'the Uncrowned King of Ireland'.

The ferocity of Healy's antipathies was legendary. He could never refrain from expressing in the strongest words his feelings about those with whom he disagreed; appearing to bask in the applause and smiles which his outrage and wit induced in the British Parliament and press. In an interview with the *Daily Express* in 1928, he said of de Valera: 'Jealousy, not patriotism, is the root of his position . . . He is a vain, shallow man without a shred of ability . . . He is nothing but a barren impostor'.[17] Unlike others of the anti-Parnellite camp – William O'Brien, Davitt, T. P. O'Connor, Dillon – time did not mellow Healy's anti-Parnellism. The Quaker anti-Parnellite MP, Alfred Webb, regretted that they had ever allowed Healy's 'spirit' to get mixed up in their campaign. He wrote: 'Subsequent events have proved that, not patriotism, but personal spite, and a hatred of all placed above him, was the moving spirit with Mr Healy.'[18] Webb's observation is interesting, if only because Healy himself was to acknowledge and assert that 'jealousy and envy' were 'the mainsprings of human action'.[19] Characteristics which, along with the enduring hostilities of the split, have to be taken into account in everything Healy wrote about Parnell.

So, in *Letters and Leaders*, Healy was only too ready to endorse Emily's Daisy story. He introduced it by stating that the cause of Parnell's rustication from Cambridge was in dispute. He wrote that Davitt, in his *Fall of Feudalism* – and, incidentally, wrongly citing the page reference as 'p. 207' instead of page 107 – attributed the rustication to a brawl, but that Parnell's sister told a different story which she regarded as 'the most impressive incident of his career . . . And from the family point of view, therefore, her account cannot be ignored.'

Coming from a legal expert – an esteemed King's Counsel – this was disingenuous, even insidious. It smacked of the forensics he had been used to at the bar – trying to make the best of a poor case. He ignored the evidence for Parnell's rustication which Barry O'Brien had given in his much acclaimed biography of Parnell published 30 years earlier. He ignored, too, John Howard Parnell's biography of his brother published in 1916 – nine years after Emily's – which also gave the brawl as the cause of Charles' sending down from Cambridge. Far from Emily's version being, as Healy would have his readers believe, 'the family point of view', her brothers, Henry Tudor and John Howard, held the better substantiated version.

Healy then proceeded to quote at length the most colourful extracts from Emily's Daisy story. Yet, he was fully aware that the authoress was an unreliable witness. Her book's weaknesses and inaccuracies had been generally recognised; Healy himself acknowledged that the *Irish Times* had dubbed it 'A Patriot's Sister's Mistake'. His offence, therefore, lay in adopting and circulating a defamatory story, whose authenticity he must have known to be highly questionable. But it suited his purpose, for the story was intended to strengthen the base of the sexual allegations his book would later make against his former Chief. And so he ended his quoting of the Daisy story with the verdict: 'Parnell's youth explains his manhood.'[20]

THE 'LIZZIE' SCANDAL

In the general election of April 1880, and shortly before he was elected chairman of the Party, Parnell worked hard – and successfully – to ensure that his own men, mainly his Land League colleagues, were chosen as candidates for the Irish constituencies. Patrick Egan and Tim Healy strongly resented Parnell's wish to adopt as a candidate the disreputable Edward St John Brenon. Brenon had a pretty wife, said Healy, 'so dainty that Parnell often went to Kingstown to dine with her while the election was in progress.' The insinuation against Parnell's character was blatant (although to cover himself in the case of Mrs St John Brenon, Healy added: 'She was a most virtuous woman'). Brenon was, shortly afterwards, expelled from the Land League because of an article he had published in a London magazine in which he 'foully and scandalously libelled the character of the ladies of the city of Dublin'.[21] Later, a judgment was given against him for defrauding a feeble-minded gentleman.

Immediately after the election something more scandalous still, according to Healy, was to befall Parnell. He left Dublin for Manchester before the parliamentary session began, and, Healy continued: 'There, a certain hotel was an Irish centre. The barmaid, whom I shall disguise as "Lizzie from Blankshire," was a gracious and amiable girl . . . Parnell often stayed at the hotel.' While Parnell was away, Shaw was again appointed Chairman of the Party, to which Healy comments: 'Dallying at Manchester during these important days, Parnell forgot ambition.' The innuendo is clear: Parnell's passion for the Lizzies of the world was far stronger than his concerns for Kathleen Ni Houlihan! Callanan has shown that Healy's accusation of Parnell's 'dallying' in Manchester, fails to take into account his energetic efforts (supported by the *Nation*) to have the meeting postponed from the 27 April as chosen by Shaw's supporters. Parnell wrote on the 25 April looking for an immediate conference with Shaw, saying that he left for England on the 26th and could not return before the 29th.[22]

Parnell dislodged Shaw as Chairman in a new election on 17 May 1880. This means that his 'dallying' at Manchester took place between mid-April (when the elections were over) and mid-May when he was back in Dublin for the election of the Chairman. The significance of placing Parnell in Manchester in this timeframe emerged nine months later on 13 February 1881.

The following is Healy's version of what transpired after the re-arrest of Davitt on 3 February 1881. The Land League executive decided to meet in Paris at the Hôtel Brighton, Rue de Rivoli, which was then kept by an Italian married to an Irishwoman, Ellen Dore. Those who gathered there included the MPs Biggar, Dillon, T. D. Sullivan, James O'Kelly and Healy himself, as well as Patrick Egan, Matt Harris and J. J. Louden. When Parnell had not turned up after a week they became extremely uneasy. O'Kelly, 'always alarmist', 'thought he must be either in the Tower or at the bottom of the Thames'. Healy, as Parnell's secretary, was asked whether he had any letters which might provide a clue to his whereabouts. Healy had opened Parnell's 'letters daily, yet of late . . . had reserved for [Parnell] himself packets coming in a woman's hand. A number of these had accumulated for a fortnight, and I brought them to Paris to give him.' The others pressed Healy to give one up for their scrutiny. After solemn debate it was proposed and carried that, 'in the national interest', Healy should hand over the letter. The decision was solely animated by concern for the cause of Ireland. Healy stipulated that its contents should be entrusted only to Dillon and Egan, upon which they retired to another room to open it. When they returned gloomily, they proposed that Biggar and Healy should go to London by the first train next morning to search for Parnell at an address taken from the letter. Biggar copied the address into a notebook. Healy, who so very reluctantly had handed over the letter in the first place, now refused to take it back. O'Kelly proposed that on reaching London they should set ex-detectives Druscovich and Meiklejohn to trace Parnell.

Next morning Biggar and Healy started out to catch the early train. As their cab reached the street from the courtyard, Parnell arrived in another cab. They turned back, and as they reached the door of the hotel, Parnell mounted hastily to a room. Healy ran upstairs and knocked at the door. Parnell half opened it and snarled 'What do you want?' Healy replied 'I'm glad to see you. We were anxious about you.' Without reply, Parnell closed the door in his face. 'It was the only act of rudeness in all our relations', Healy sadly noted. The decision to open the letter should not be harshly judged, said Healy. Parnell's chief partisan, O'Kelly, was foremost in demanding it. After the split, Parnell's opponents never revealed or made use of the incident; they confined themselves solely to the publicly known facts of the O'Shea case as the root of the trouble.

Later, Healy heard that Biggar had sent a friend – without consulting Healy – to the address in Holloway where the forlorn lady lodged. He reproached Biggar, who argued that he feared a scandal might break out if her applications for help were left unanswered. This was 'Lizzie from Blankshire', the barmaid from Manchester, found in a barely furnished garret, in bed with a baby. A likeness of Parnell, cut from the *Dublin Weekly News* was pinned to her bedcover. Though in want, she was staunch to the father of her child, and never complained. Her needs were provided for; and she was told where to apply should she require further help. 'This she never did, so Parnell must have made amends for his temporary neglect.'

Healy's story has too many errors and weak links throughout to compel conviction. From the start he is incorrect in implying that the colleagues he names were all waiting a week for Parnell: Dillon and Biggar were in London until mid-week; and Andy Kettle stated that he met up with Parnell at Calais and they travelled together to Paris.[23] That Parnell was already on the stairs before Healy got through the door of the hotel would have to mean either delay on Healy's part in returning to base or that Parnell hadn't stopped to register and collect his key. It is probable that it was Healy himself who volunteered the information that he had in his possession letters brought for Parnell; and he protests too much that he was the one most reluctant to open one of the letters. That they were 'solely animated' by concern for Ireland, that what they did was 'in the national interest', also has an overly defensive ring to it and has to be balanced against what would be natural curiosity about the private life of their mysterious leader. A gossip like Healy, who was already growing critical of Parnell, now had the excuse of anxiety over Parnell's safety for opening his private correspondence. (Ironically, Healy himself objected to the British authorities' opening of Land Leaguers' correspondence in transit through the post.)[24]

The decision to send Healy and Biggar to look for Parnell at the address in Holloway seems, to say the least of it, very odd indeed. For why would Lizzie write to Parnell if he were to be found at her address? Then the story about Biggar's friend getting entry to a garret where Lizzie lay in bed with her baby, complete with a sketch of Parnell from a Dublin newspaper, is as bizarre as it gets. And what happened to the opened letter which Healy says he refused to take back? Was it retained by Egan, or Dillon? Was it given to Biggar to help him locate the woman's address? Was it perhaps returned to Parnell with the rest of his correspondence, or was it destroyed? If ever discovered, the signature on it would determine the identity of the sender.

The proposal to engage the two ex-detectives to track down the absent Parnell raises its own ethical questions. Meiklejohn and Druscovich were disgraced ex-detectives of Scotland Yard: involved in 1877 in a sensational case of police corruption and bribery which had caused shock and public outrage; they were dismissed from the police, and sentenced to two years imprisonment – the maximum that could be imposed. The rationale behind the proposed hiring of such corrupt characters was to surface a few years later – Meiklejohn was then hired by William O'Brien, the editor of *United Ireland*, in the 'Castle Scandals' libel actions, brought by senior Dublin Castle officials for allegations made against them in *United Ireland*.[25] The allegations had been made in an unsigned article written by Healy. Speaking in parliament on 17 June 1884, Healy justified the employment of Meiklejohn on the grounds that a private individual in Ireland did not have at his back the resources and machinery of the state and the police which the government had; and further, the government did not hesitate to use men like Meiklejohn themselves, or those notorious conspirators in the Phoenix Park murders who were reprieved by the government for informing on their fellow conspirators. The employment of Meiklejohn, argued Healy, was a case of setting a thief to catch a thief.[26]

In her memoir Katharine O'Shea states: 'He [Parnell] now had all the parcels and letters he received sent on to me, so that I might open them and give him only those it was necessary for him to deal with.'[27] This was in the autumn of 1880 (that is, some months before the Paris meeting), the implication being that, despite O'Shea's sometimes erroneous dating of events, Parnell would hardly have so directed if some 'Lizzie' were writing to him.

The Healy story in all its theatrical detail, published 47 years after the event, when Healy, still bitterly hostile to Parnell, was in his seventies and the others present at the Paris meeting were dead, leaves too many unanswered questions to be fully convincing. Some five months before the Paris meeting, Healy, already curious about Parnell's private life, was wondering why he wanted to end a particular debate and go off somewhere else. In a letter to his brother of August 1880 Healy wrote: 'Why is this? There must be a lady in the case, else he would not be in such a hurry to leave the House as he has been, two or three times this week!'[28]

Healy's instinct was correct – Parnell's secret affair with Mrs O'Shea had just begun following their first encounter in July. So, had the letter opened in Paris come from Katharine O'Shea? Certainly there were many who believed it had. T. P. O'Connor, although not present in Paris, in his biography of Parnell published in 1891 (less than ten years after the Paris meeting) understood, no doubt from his colleagues who were present, that the letter had come from Katharine O'Shea, and was the first warning the Irish Party had of the tragic affair. Healy, by a non-too-subtle juxtaposition of paragraphs, falsely conveys the impression that O'Connor was referring to the Lizzie affair, although it is clear that his reference was to Katharine O'Shea when he wrote that despite

> the brutality sometimes of their political controversy . . . [the opening of the letter] was never communicated for years afterwards by the men who knew it, even to their intimate and close friends in the same party; and that the vast majority of the members of the party never heard of it at all.[29]

Michael Davitt, although in prison at the time of the Paris meeting, knew all of the participants intimately, also believed the letter had come from Mrs O'Shea. He wrote that the 'extreme step' was taken of 'opening the letters which *awaited him in the hotel* [my italics]' in the hope of finding a clue to Parnell's whereabouts. Davitt continued:

> The first letter that was read revealed the secret which afterwards worked his ruin. None of his most intimate associates had hitherto suspected the liaison in which he was found entangled. It was a painful discovery, for it was the first cloud that had

fallen menacingly over what had promised to be the most successful political career that had ever been carved out of brilliant and beneficial service to the cause of Ireland.[30]

Katharine O'Shea also maintained the opened letter came from her. She wrote, 'certain members of the Party opened one of my letters to Parnell. I make no comment.'[31] Could it have been that the sting in her '*I make no comment*' goaded Healy into his version of the episode? And certainly, under Parnell's precise instructions, she addressed at least five letters to him at the Hôtel Brighton, Rue de Rivoli, later that same month of February 1881.

One of Parnell's letters from the Hôtel Brighton to Katharine, dated 27 February 1881, contains the following very intriguing sentence: 'I have been warned from Dublin that there is some plot on foot against us which has been originated by information received from Cork, and you will guess the original source.'[32] Initial reading of this sentence might suggest that the 'us' refers to the Land Leaguers, and that the plot was a government one. In the same letter, however, Parnell said he thought the government's intention to arrest him (for something he had said in a speech in Clare) had now been abandoned. So did the 'us' mean Katharine and himself? And was the 'original source' from Cork, the identity of which Katharine would be able to guess, a veiled reference to Healy?

J. J. O'Kelly, who, according to Healy was Parnell's 'chief partisan' and the 'alarmist'[33] at the Paris meeting, had remained steadfast to Parnell during the split, and in 1895 on the fourth anniversary of Parnell's death stated in a newspaper article that Healy, 'this contemptible mountebank', had opened a private letter of Parnell's in Paris and circulated its contents 'among those he thought most likely to use the information to injure Parnell'.[34] He, too, believed the letter was from Mrs O'Shea.

The most extensive recent biographers of Parnell – F. S. L. Lyons and Robert Kee – were unconvinced by Healy's story. Lyons wrote that the opened letter was 'most probably' from Mrs O'Shea.[35] And Kee agreed that 'it seems likely' that it was from her and had been delivered to the hotel before Parnell's arrival.[36] In his earlier biography of Dillon, published in 1967, Lyons stated that 'The Holloway barmaid was almost certainly an invention of Healy's'. He added in a footnote, however, that Dillon's son, James, had mentioned to him 'that he had some recollection of his father saying that an illegitimate child was involved, though Mr Dillon thinks the address was Birmingham, not Holloway.' Lyons concluded: 'The mystery, therefore, remains'.[37] Nor had he moved far from that verdict ten years later when his *Charles Stewart Parnell* was published. In this he questioned the reliability of a story which had the bitterly, anti-Parnellite Healy as the only source, 'whose recollections', he said, 'are frequently unreliable'.[38] He wrote:

'Healy's virtues – intelligence, quickness, wit – were obvious. His vices – envy, malice, vanity and ruthless ambition – only later became apparent'.[39] Kee pointed out that by reading Hansard's Parliamentary Debates and the newspapers of that week 'a good part' of Healy's narrative (especially that section claiming that all of them were waiting a week for Parnell's arrival in Paris) can easily be shown to be untrue.[40]

Surprisingly, however, both Lyons and Kee totally ignored one very significant aspect of Healy's story. Lyons, like Davitt, assumed that the letter which his colleagues opened had arrived at the hotel for the absent chief. And Lyons goes on to make the very reasonable point:

> It is much more credible that Katharine should have written to this address than a barmaid who, even if she was not just a figment of Healy's imagination, was unlikely to have had the same knowledge of Parnell's extremely secretive movements.[41]

Even more explicit than Lyons, Robert Kee stated that the letter was: 'addressed to Parnell at the Hôtel Brighton'.[42] Both have overlooked Healy's categorical claim that, as Parnell's assistant, he had brought the letters with him from London to Paris. Healy wrote:

> Parnell had treated me with entire confidence as to his correspondence. I used to open his letters daily, yet of late I had, without a hint from him, reserved for himself packets coming in a woman's hand. A number of these had accumulated for a fortnight, and I brought them to Paris to give him.[43]

Healy's inaccuracies, his delight in a good story, his propensity to embellish and overstate, his enduring hostility to Parnell, and the fact he related his barmaid story 47 years after the event when he was 73 years old make it difficult to accept his reliability as a witness.

And yet, while allowing for all of this, it is also equally difficult to believe that he would stoop so low as to invent and publicise a story without any foundation in fact. None of the other eight (excluding Healy and Parnell) who are mentioned as being present on the occasion in Paris ever referred to the Lizzie episode. There is, however, some circumstantial support for Healy's central allegation that the letter was from a woman who was the mother of Parnell's child. The page proofs of Healy's book provide some further details. In this unpublished version (his editors undoubtedly wary of publishing names and details), Healy identifies Lizzie as having come from Shropshire; and the hotel in which she was a barmaid as the Wellington Hotel in Manchester, kept by Mr and Mrs John Barker. He was an English Catholic and she was Irish.[44]

Further tentative support for Healy's story comes from another quarter. The wealthy Henry Labouchere, journalist and politician on the radical wing of the Liberal party, was sympathetic to Home Rule. He maintained a close personal contact with the leading members of the Irish Party – especially with Healy. Like Healy, he was a malicious gossip, a sardonic wit and an incorrigible schemer. He also came to share with Healy an extreme dislike of Parnell and to underestimate Parnell's leadership qualities. During the political manoeuvrings in 1885–6 that preceded Gladstone's conversion to Home Rule, Healy and Labouchere, with Gladstone's son, Herbert, acting as intermediary with his father, worked together to undermine Parnell's strategy and leadership with schemes of their own for a Liberal-Nationalist alliance. The only thing that frustrated them was the respect that Gladstone senior had for Parnell's ability.

When, four years later, the O'Shea divorce scandal resulted in the Parnell Split, Labouchere, in December 1890, just before the Kilkenny by-election, provided Herbert Gladstone with a version of the Manchester barmaid story. He wrote that the anti-Parnellites were thinking of going public on the barmaid scandal. He claimed that in 1878 Parnell had seduced the barmaid at the Wellington Hotel, Manchester; lived with her in London and had a child with her. Several letters from her begging Parnell for assistance had found their way to Paris. Labouchere continues:

> It was decided his letters should be opened by Biggar, Barry and Healy . . . Barry went to see the girl in Camden town. She was absolutely without means, and appeared a very quiet respectable girl, and she was dying. Barry advanced money to her. But Parnell, having taken up with Mrs O'Shea would do nothing for her. She died.[45]

Certain elements of Healy's and Labouchere's versions are identical: the barmaid, the Wellington Hotel, the letter opened in Paris, the visit to the girl in London, the financial assistance given to her by one of Parnell's supporters. There are also pronounced differences in the two accounts. Labouchere says the seduction took place in 1878, whereas Healy implies it was in 1880. Labouchere claims that Parnell lived with her in London. Healy makes no such claim. Healy does not list John Barry among those present in Paris. Healy says that Biggar sent along a friend to look after the girl's needs. Labouchere identifies that friend as John Barry. Healy says she was in a garret in Holloway. Labouchere says she was in Camden Town. (Both locations are comparatively close in north-east London).[46] Healy had the elaborate story of the baby being in bed with her. No baby is mentioned in Labouchere's version. Like Labouchere, Healy might have been expected to make the most of the rumour that the girl, abandoned by Parnell, had died. Instead, he implies that she survived, and that Parnell must have made up for his temporary neglect.

A partial explanation for the differences in the two versions might well be that Labouchere was relating the story of the barmaid in 1890, four or five years after he could have heard it from his friend Healy in the mid-1880s, when they were both plotting against Parnell. Another explanation may be that the rumour only began to take wings privately, in the context of the O'Shea scandal and the bitter split, some ten or twelve years after the alleged seduction and its emergence in the opened letter in Paris; and by the time that Healy made it public in 1928, he was trying to ascribe to Parnell some of the worst vices of the landlord class.

John Barry, however, may well have played a much larger role in the whole development of the story than has been hitherto recognised. An ex-Fenian, Barry was the chief organiser and secretary of the Home Rule Confederation of Great Britain. A relation of Tim Healy, it was with him in Manchester that Healy stayed when he first went to England as a railway clerk. Barry became a partner in what was said to be the largest linoleum business in Britain. And when Healy moved to London to become a journalist for the *Nation* newspaper (run by the Sullivans, also cousins of Healy), he supplemented his income by doing clerical work for Barry's business. Healy and Barry were to remain political allies right through the Parnell Split. If anyone knew the hotels in Manchester, and indeed wherever else in England the Home Rulers held their conferences, it was Barry. That the girl in the story had worked as a barmaid in a Manchester hotel possibly originated with him. Besides, he was the only one who allegedly spoke with her.

None of this, however, brings us any closer to a solution of the mystery of Parnell's alleged barmaid. Nevertheless, it may be worthwhile considering a footnote to what remains an enigma. A communication from a lady in Northern Ireland claimed that Parnell, according to a strong oral tradition in her family, was her great grandfather. The story went that her great grandmother, Mary Crawford, while working for Parnell's mother became pregnant with Parnell's child. The child was brought up by Mary's family in Antrim, and given the family name of Robert Crawford. The family story added that the Parnells assisted financially in his upbringing.[47] Because of the lack of any documentary evidence, and the fact that some of what was claimed was highly unlikely the immediate reaction has been to dismiss the claim as not proven.

Mary Crawford was born in Tobergill, Donegore, Co. Antrim, on 2 February 1851, the fifth in a family of six (four boys and two girls). Her son, Robert, was born on 6 May 1879 – a date that slots in neatly enough with Labouchere's dating of the alleged seduction of the barmaid in 1878. The census of 1881 records the following details about Mary Crawford – year of birth: 1851; birthplace: Ireland; age: 30; occupation: kitchen-maid; marital status: unmarried; dwelling where living: the Neptune Hotel, Liverpool. These then, are the few facts that can be established about her early life. Anything else has to be – for the present at least – surmise and speculation.

A part of the tradition in Mary Crawford's family is that she had been a 'lady-in-waiting' to Parnell's mother. After the death of Parnell's father, Mrs Parnell and family moved out of Avondale and resided temporarily between 1862 and 1870 at 14 Upper Temple Street, Dublin. By 1870 she was residing in Paris and thereafter in America. Mary Crawford would have been eleven years old in 1862 and no more than eighteen in 1870. Mrs Parnell who engaged ostentatiously in the high social life of Dublin, London, Paris and New York would undoubtedly have boasted of a lady-in-waiting if she had been attended by such a person. Her daughter, Emily, would certainly have made the boast in her extravagant memoir. But there is no mention of any 'lady-in-waiting' in any record left by Mrs Parnell or Emily, or by the more modest John Howard. This does not rule out the possibility that Mary Crawford may have been a domestic in the Parnell household. But so far none of the records have revealed that Mary Crawford was ever in the employment of the Parnell family. And from what we know about her she would appear not to have travelled outside of Ireland and Great Britain.

It is not impossible that Mary, who was living and working as a kitchen-maid in the Neptune Hotel, Liverpool in 1881 could have served as a barmaid in the Wellington Hotel, Manchester in 1878. On the motion of John Barry, Parnell was elected president of the Home Rule Confederation of Great Britain at its annual convention at Liverpool on 27th and 28th August 1877. And it is known that Parnell visited the branches of that association in both cities from time to time. The 1878 annual convention of the Home Rule Confederation was held in Dublin in October of that year. While we do not know whether Parnell had ever met Mary Crawford, or even been aware of her existence, it cannot be dismissed that her shadowy figure might yet turn out to be Healy's Manchester barmaid.

Her family have some evidence to suggest that she had been living in Dublin since the 1890s. If this is the case, the Census of 1911 deepens the mystery surrounding her. There are two potentially relevant references to a Mary Crawford in that Census. In one of these she is described as a resident of No. 7 Marine Terrace, Kingstown. According to *Thom's Directory* this was a Young Women's Christian Institute and Home with a total of 14 residents. The head of the house was a Miss Potterton, described as honorary secretary and superintendent. Of the 14 residents, 11 were Church of Ireland, one Plymouth Brethren, one Presbyterian, and one Methodist. All were single, and of the 13 'boarders', 11 were domestics and two were nurses. Mary Crawford's occupation is given as 'matron (children's home)'; her age: 55;

place of birth: Co. Antrim; religion: Methodist. The second entry has Mary Crawford as a resident of No. 32 Clarinda Park West. The head of this house with four residents is an 80-year-old Elizabeth Pim. Two of the other residents are Roman Catholic and 'servants'. This Mary Crawford is aged 54, Presbyterian, born in Co. Antrim, and a 'nurse attendant'. Her relationship to the head of the house is 'domestic servant'. It seems too much of a coincidence that these two Mary Crawfords should be born in Antrim, of practically the same age and religion, and both nurses. Another coincidence is that Parnell's brother, John Howard, was living at No. 1 Clarinda Park East.

Where does this information on Mary Crawford and her family's tradition of the relationship with Parnell leave us? Perhaps it lends a little more credence to the central contention of Healy's story. But the enigma is still far from being solved. Mary Crawford's relationship with Parnell is no more than a possibility, a speculation that has yet to be tested against whatever further evidence may be unearthed. Ultimately, only a DNA test involving the surviving descendants of Mary Crawford's family and the descendants of Parnell's youngest sister, Theodosia (Paget), might answer the question. No doubt the unravelling of the mystery matters a great deal to the descendants of Mary Crawford. If the oral tradition in their family should turn out to be true, then they are the only direct descendants of Charles Stewart Parnell surviving, since his descendants through his two daughters with Katharine O'Shea appear to have died out. On the day of his arrest, 13 October 1881, he wrote to 'My own Queenie' telling Katharine not to fret because if anything should happen to her and 'our child', 'I must die childless.'[48] But, if Robert Crawford was his child, then he was the only son that Parnell had. Robert had five children, three girls and two boys. Currently there would appear to be about a dozen direct descendants in Northern Ireland and about twice that number in Australia. 'History', according to Carlyle, 'is but the biography of great men' – kings, military conquerors, leading statesmen and religious leaders. Since Carlyle's day, history has come to mean and include much more. It now also involves the so-called ordinary people – peasants as well as emperors, foot soldiers as well as famous generals. And barmaids or kitchenmaids like Mary Crawford have their place in history as well as, or even sometimes beside, the Charles Stewart Parnells and Tim Healys. Healy's barmaid story and his endorsement of the unfounded Daisy story of Parnell's Cambridge days have some relevance for the light they throw on the personalities of both Healy and Parnell. The alleged sexual scandals – whether true or false – emphasise the secretive, enigmatic private life of the Irish leader and the vindictive, unscrupulous nature of his chief accuser. However, in assessing the public career of Parnell and his contribution to the political history of Ireland and what Gladstone referred to as 'the splendid services rendered by Mr Parnell to his country',[49] the alleged scandals have less significance.

Parnell drew, and rigorously preserved, a dividing line between his private life and public career. In a rare reference to his private life, which, of course, had become public because of the divorce proceedings, he said to his supporters in Dublin:

> I tell you, fellow country-men, that when the day comes for measuring the amount of my shortcomings, and the amount of my opponents' shortcomings, the balance will not be against me.[50]

Judged alongside the reprehensible behaviour of Captain O'Shea or Tim Healy, Parnell's words, while not excusing his actions and misjudgement, are worthy of some attention. Parnell confessed before that same gathering in Dublin's Rotunda:

> I don't pretend to be immaculate. I don't pretend that I had not had moments of trial and of temptation; but I do claim that never in thought, in word, or deed have I been false to the trust that Irishmen have confided in me.[51]

Ultimately, the O'Shea divorce scandal, or the still unresolved allegation of the Manchester barmaid do not detract from the towering role and outstanding achievements of Parnell's public career. His vices may have been ordinary and commonplace. His virtues were extraordinary and rare.

Notes

1 Michael Davitt, *The Fall of Feudalism in Ireland* (London, 1904), p. 306.

2 Emily Monroe Dickinson, *A Patriot's Mistake: Reminiscences of the Parnell Family* (London, 1905), pp 49–59.

3 Ibid., p. 51.

4 Ibid., p. 53.

5 Ibid., p. 54.

6 Ibid., p. 55.

7 Ibid., p. 57.

8 Ibid., p. 59.

9 Ged Martin, 'Parnell at Cambridge: the education of an Irish nationalist', in *Irish Historical Studies*, vol. 19, no. 73 (Mar. 1974), p.77.

10 Ibid., pp 72–82.

11 Henry Harrison, *Parnell Vindicated: the Lifting of the Veil* (London, 1931), p. 432.

12 Martin, 'Parnell at Cambridge', p. 77.

13 R. F. Foster, *Charles Stewart Parnell: the Man and his Family* (Sussex, 1976), p. 109.

14 F. S. L. Lyons, *Charles Stewart Parnell* (London, 1977), p. 32.

15 Robert Kee, *The Laurel and the Ivy: The Story of Charles Stewart Parnell and Irish Nationalism* (London, 1993), p.39; pp 38–40.

16 Frank Callanan, *T. M. Healy* (Cork, 1996), p. 436.

17 Ibid., p. 625.

18 Alfred Webb, *The Autobiography of a Quaker Nationalist*, Marie-Louise Legg (ed.) (Cork, 1999), p. 77.

19 T. M. Healy, *Letters and Leaders of My Day* (New York, 1928), vol. I, p. 179.

20 Ibid., vol. I, p. 51.

21 Callanan, *Healy*, p. 52. For further information on Brenon, see Patrick Maume's entry on him in the *Dictionary of Irish Biography* James McGuire and James Quinn (eds).

22 Ibid., p. 53.

23 Kee, *Laurel and the Ivy*, pp 335–9.

24 Callanan, *Healy*, p. 637, n. 39.

25 For the 'Castle Scandals' and the role played by Meiklejohn in uncovering the homosexual ring among the officials, see ch. 6 above, Myles Dungan, 'Mr Parnell's Rottweiler: *United Ireland*, 1881–1891', pp 103–4.

26 *Hansard*, 3rd series, vol. 289, cols 705–6 (17 June 1884).

27 Katharine O'Shea, *Charles Stewart Parnell: His Love Story and Political Life* (London, 1914), vol. I, p. 151.

28 Healy, *Letters*, vol. I, p. 98.

29 T. P. O'Connor, *Charles Stewart Parnell: A Memory* (London, 1891), p. 133; Healy, *Letters*, vol. I, p. 110.

30 Davitt, *Fall of Feudalism*, p. 306.

31 O'Shea, *Parnell*, vol. II, p. 165.

32 Ibid., vol. I, p. 179.

33 Healy, *Letters*, vol. I, p. 110.

34 Quoted in Callanan, *Healy*, p. 54.

35 Lyons, *Parnell*, p. 150.

36 Kee, *Laurel and the Ivy*, p. 337.

37 F. S. L. Lyons, *John Dillon: A Biography* (London, 1968), p. 47.

38 Lyons, *Parnell*, p. 149.

39 Ibid., p. 108.

40 Kee, *Laurel and the Ivy*, pp 335–7.

41 Lyons, *Parnell*, p. 150.

42 Kee, *Laurel and the Ivy*, p. 337.

43 Healy, *Letters*, vol. I, p. 108.

44 Healy, *Letters and Leaders of My Day*, proofs, forty-four (quoted in Callanan, *Healy*, pp 52–3).

45 Callanan, *Healy*, p. 54.

46 A tradition in the Dillon family had her living in Birmingham (Lyons, *Parnell*, p. 149).

47 Correspondence in possession of the present writer.

48 O'Shea, *Parnell*, vol. I, p. 207.

49 Philip Magnus, *Gladstone: A Biography* (London, 1954 edn), p. 388; Lyons, *Parnell*, p. 494; John Morley, *The Life of William Ewart Gladstone* (London, 1903), vol. III, p. 437.

50 Jennie Wyse-Power, *Words of the Dead Chief* (Dublin, 2009 edn), p. 143

51 Ibid.

CHAPTER 10

The March of the Nation

Parnell's *Ne Plus Ultra* Speech

Pauric Travers

No man has the right to fix the boundary to the march of a nation (great cheering). No man has the right to say to his country: 'Thus far shalt thou go, and no further': and we have never attempted to fix the *ne plus ultra* to the progress of Ireland's nationhood, and we never shall (cheers).[1]

Parnell's *ne plus ultra* speech in Cork in January 1885 is among his most famous, or, to be more precise, those words from the speech which were later preserved on his monument unveiled on O'Connell Street in 1911 are the best remembered and most often quoted utterance of the Uncrowned King.[2] For successive generations of Irish nationalists the words came to encapsulate the Irish aspiration for independence and self-government, becoming what one historian has called 'the anthem of Irish national consciousness.'[3] Indeed, the words have struck a chord with independence movements elsewhere as they offer a glimpse of the promised land to those weighed down with the immediate struggle. Alex Salmond, for instance, leader of the Scottish Nationalist Party, at the opening of the new Scottish Parliament in 2004 cited Parnell's ringing declaration.[4]

Words once uttered and speeches once made are like literary texts – they become common property and take on a life of their own. Their original context is quickly forgotten and they are open to interpretation and reinterpretation in ways that might sometimes surprise their original author. Subtle context and nuance are often lost or forgotten, particularly when, as in this case, a few memorable sentences are taken out of context and reproduced in a different form, at a different time – and sometimes for a different purpose. Writing in the 1920s, Parnell's biographer St John Ervine complained that Parnell's original sentiments had been:

used by every crack-brained revolutionary who has flourished in Ireland since Parnell's death, but it may be enough to say that if Parnell had lived to be the first Prime Minister of Ireland, he would have clapped nearly all who make oratorical capital out of his famous passage into Kilmainham. It is one of those passages which appear to mean a great deal but mean, in fact, very little; but hundreds of professional Irishmen have used it for the befuddlement of the minds of thousands of their countrymen.[5]

St John Ervine's venom was directed in particular at Eamon de Valera – Parnell, he ventured, would have 'given uncommonly short shrift to Mexican gentlemen with a passion for metaphysical hair splitting'.[6]

Parnell's 'march of the nation' speech is a play in at least two acts. Act I opens, appropriately, in the Cork Opera House on 21 January 1885 with the address' maiden delivery; *dramatis personae* includes the Mayor of Cork and assorted local dignitaries, the Press, a few thousand cheering spectators and, of course, Parnell, with noises off from, among others, Gladstone, and assorted Fenians. Act II opens much later, in 1911, on O'Connell Street, Dublin with John Redmond as the principal protagonist and a new cast of characters associated with the unveiling of the Parnell Monument that enshrined Parnell's words. In a sense there is also a continuing postscript – as the monument with its peroration is the ultimate in performance art, there to be interacted with, interpreted, and reinterpreted by generations yet to come.

This chapter will seek to place the inscription on the Parnell monument in the context of the rest of Parnell's original Cork speech – the context of the moment in which the words were first uttered, and the very different context at the time when they were chosen for inscription on Saint-Gaudens' dramatic memorial. In particular, in St John Ervine's terms, it will explore what Parnell's words meant to Parnell, and why he was moved to utter them at that particular time.

Parnell in 1885 was thirty-eight and approaching the height of his political power. Elected to the House of Commons in 1875, he had emerged as a significant force during his leadership of the land movement. He was elected chairman of the Irish Parliamentary Party in May 1880; in 1881 he was arrested and imprisoned in Kilmainham Gaol; after the 'Kilmainham Treaty' and his release in May 1882, his main political energies were focused on the political issue of Home Rule and the newly established Irish National League. The period between then and 1885 was one of relative inactivity but was formative in terms of the political machinery and internal organisation of the Parnellite party: the selection of candidates, and their control once elected, was streamlined; and a strengthened party pledge for members was introduced in 1884. That year also saw the passing of the Third Reform Act which gave counties the same voting rights as boroughs – all adult, male householders and men who rented unfurnished lodgings to the value of £10 a year were now entitled to vote (but still leaving an estimated 40 per cent of men and all women disenfranchised). In Ireland, the Reform Act increased the electorate from 226,000 to 738,000.[7] This presented both a significant challenge and an opportunity to the Irish Party: the tide was flowing in the direction of more representative parties, so long as they could engage their new electorate and capture their allegiance. In the event, and despite the predictions of Gladstone, the Irish Party significantly increased its representation at the general election in 1885, winning 86 seats and holding the balance of power between Liberals and Conservatives. In the process, the social composition of the Irish Parliamentary Party shifted considerably.[8]

Parnell's visit to Cork in January 1885 was part of the long-term preparations for the general election expected later in the year and his speech should be read in that light. Although elected originally for Co. Meath, Parnell had moved to represent Cork in 1880. He had been initially touted as a candidate for Co. Cork but, having met with some opposition, he switched in confused circumstances to the city constituency. The choice of an urban constituency is interesting and may partly reflect an interest in the trades and manufactures, representatives of both of which were prominent during this visit. Cork was not previously a nationalist bastion – Joseph Ronayne, the obstructionist MP[9] with whom Parnell had been friendly had repeatedly told him that it would be impossible for nationalists to win both seats in the city. Parnell was duly returned along with a moderate Home Ruler. He was also elected for Mayo and Meath but opted to sit for Cork City.[10]

Although he described himself as having 'planted the banner of Irish Nationality in the city of Cork' and pledged to defend it[11], Parnell was an infrequent visitor to his constituency in the years which followed – visiting Cork in March and April 1880, October 1880, December 1882, July 1883, January 1885, December 1890 and March 1891 at the height of the split.[12] By the end of 1884, there were mutterings within nationalist circles generally about his political inactivity which may or may not have prompted a short tour of Wicklow and Tipperary in early January when he spoke in Arklow, Bansha, Thurles and Clonmel. The Tipperary visit was aimed at quelling local opposition to John O'Connor of Cork, Parnell's preferred candidate for an impending election there. 'Long John' O'Connor was secretary of the Land League in Cork, a senior member of the IRB and had played an active part in the negotiation of the so-called 'new departure'. He had been persuaded by Parnell of the value of the constitutional route and Parnell had agreed his candidacy with Archbishop Croke.[13] In refuting accusations of carpet-bagging, Parnell told a meeting in Thurles that: 'When I went to Meath I was told that I was not a Meath man . . . When I went to Cork, no one there said that

I was not a Cork man.' Parnell's reply was that 'The question is not whether you belong to this county or to that, but whether you are a good Irishman.'[14] In the event, Tipperary nominated the Corkman.

Parnell's 1885 Cork visit was as an elected Member of Parliament; giving an account of his stewardship and seeking a renewed mandate for himself and his Party. If he had any concerns about the welcome he might receive, he was quickly reassured – the excitement and enthusiasm of his reception was unquestionable. The *Irish Times* conceded that it was 'very enthusiastic' while the *Freeman* judged it 'the most cordial and enthusiastic ever given by a great constituency to its very best honoured representative'. Remembering Tipperary, it also noted that 'no strain of discord was heard' and 'the threatening shadow of division or disunion chased away from gallant Tipperary never once overcast fair Cork.'[15] This emphasis on the lack of 'discord' and 'disunion' is telling and reflected a concern, evident in Parnell's speech, to balance different constituencies and interests.

Parnell had travelled from London to Cork, via boat and train. Somewhat unusually, he appears to have travelled alone.[16] Several hundred supporters met the mail train at noon, only to find that Parnell was not on board. An even larger gathering of some thousands were there to greet the afternoon train at 3.30. An official reception committee and a delegation from the Cork trades were officially admitted to the station but, in spite of the efforts of the railway officials, the platform was stormed and Parnell's appearance was greeted with ringing cheers. A procession was rapidly formed with members of the Young Ireland Society and several bands (including the Blackpool, the Butter Exchange, the Tailors' and the Barrack Street). Then came the Mayor's carriage carrying Alderman Madden, Parnell and John Deasy MP (who had been elected for Cork City in 1884), followed by other carriages carrying the ever-present John O'Connor MP, and the High Sheriff, Mr Wycherly. According to one account, the crowd in their enthusiasm removed the horses from the Mayor's carriage and drew it themselves through the city *en route* to the Mardyke residence of M. J. Horgan TC, solicitor and Parnell's election agent, where Parnell was staying.[17] The streets were thronged with people who 'abandon[ed] themselves to unrestrained enthusiasm.'[18] Horgan's young son John Joseph, who watched the dramatic scene from his nursery windows, confessed that he was more impressed by the bands than by Parnell who spoke to the crowd briefly.[19]

Appropriately enough, given its dramatic nature, the main event of Parnell's visit to Cork took place that evening at the Cork Opera House. Originally the Athenaeum when it was opened in 1855 on a site adjacent to the Royal Cork Institution (now the Crawford Municipal Art Gallery), it was renamed Munster Hall in 1875 and following extensive reconstruction in 1877 became the Cork Opera House. It had a capacity of approximately

3,000 and was full to the rafters for Parnell's address. An all-ticket affair, it was a sell-out well in advance. The theatre was thronged more than an hour before the proceedings were to begin; the two circles were full and the private boxes were occupied, with many ladies noted as being present. The orchestra pit was occupied by the Press who attended in large numbers, while the stage was occupied by 'some of the leading men of Cork' including the High Sheriff, aldermen, MPs, businessmen and clergy from city and county. The Mayor, Alderman Madden, presided. At the back of the stage a gas illumination proclaimed: 'C. S. Parnell' surmounted by a harp and shamrock, also depicted in gas jets.

When Parnell and his colleagues appeared on stage he was greeted by a prolonged standing ovation, the entire audience cheering and waving hats and handkerchiefs before singing 'God Save Ireland'. Resolutions of support for, and confidence in, their two MPs (Parnell and John Deasy), in Parnell's leadership and in the Irish Parliamentary movement were then proposed, seconded and adopted before Parnell was called on to speak. In introducing him, the Mayor explained that Parnell was at a great disadvantage having left his sick bed where he had lain for three days, and had been travelling since seven o'clock the previous evening: they were all 'greatly obliged to him that he has come at all, considering the great cold he is suffering from.' To which a voice from the crowd was heard to interject: 'He is a sick Moses'.

Parnell, on rising, was greeted with another prolonged ovation, lasting several minutes. He told his audience that he had indeed been feeling ill and had doubted when leaving London whether he would be able to complete his journey. But the closer he came to Ireland, the better he felt; and the nearer he came to Cork, the better still so that when he arrived among them he felt fully restored. Clearly whatever his alleged deficiencies as a public speaker, Parnell could do *plámás* with the best of them. Nonetheless, he did crave their indulgence indicating that he would be keeping his remarks much shorter than normal.

The first section of his speech consisted of a short reflection on the period since his first election for Cork, a restatement of the principles of independent opposition in parliament, a defence of his achievements and a justification of the faith which had been placed in him. Parnell then linked this to the extension of the franchise which would guarantee an end to 'rule by the oligarchy' in Cork forever. The emphasis on the relationship between the Parliamentary Party and the wider nationalist movement, and their different but mutually dependent roles, was a preoccupation of Parnell's political speeches; and at this time, the huge increase in the electorate added greater immediacy.

In the main body of his speech, Parnell laid out briefly in turn the policy of the Party on the land question, the rights of labourers, the promotion of

---

manufactures and on national self-government. While the latter attracted subsequent attention, Parnell's statements about easing the burden of rent on farmers, his emphatic assertion of the rights of labourers, the need for promotion of Irish industry and the necessity for farmers and labourers to buy Irish products even where they were more expensive than cheaper imports were forthright and challenging and attracted both positive and critical contemporary comment. *The Times* of London condemned the suggested interference with free trade and predicted that an Irish resort to bolstering industry through a preference for Irish goods might draw a reaction against Irish agricultural produce in Britain.[20] In Cork, Parnell's balancing of different economic interests won some favour, in particular his espousal of both labour and manufacturing interests. This was reflected in the range of delegations which he met during his visit. Part of his itinerary during this brief visit was a tour of Rushbrook and Passage Docks in Cork Harbour. Parnell had been active in his support for attempts to revive shipbuilding there and had attracted support from both business interests and the Cork trades as a result.

Of course, it is Parnell's remarks on the national question which attracted most attention at the time and since. Barry O'Brien described Parnell as beating the 'tocsin of war . . . in a speech which cheered the heart of every Nationalist in the country.'[21] The language was strong and militant, and the openness to wherever the march of the nation might lead was not explicitly qualified. That is certainly how the London *Times* read the speech, concluding that Parnell's programme posed a threat to the long-term security of the United Kingdom. Parnell, it said, 'declines to forecast the future so far as to state either by what means this restitution will be brought about or the extent to which the "rights" are to go but his hints are tolerably clear.' Then, after quoting the *ne plus ultra* declaration, it concluded: 'a plainer hint at total separation could hardly be uttered. It is just as well that we should know where we stand; and Mr Parnell may claim our gratitude for telling us so plainly where he and his followers . . . are intending to go.'[22]

The longer term verdict of historians is rather different: Lyons speaks of 'calculated ambiguity'; Alan O'Day of 'studied ambiguity' to deal with an awkward situation; Richard Aldous of 'an inspirational yet purposely imprecise declaration of intent'.[23] Oliver MacDonagh, among others, has pointed out that the peroration about not fixing boundaries to the march of the nation follows immediately on from a limitation for the current generation to the restoration of Grattan's Parliament.[24] Paul Bew in his recent assessment concludes that Parnell 'would have been embarrassed by the fact that the speech was later used to justify the most exaggerated forms of nationalism.'[25] The speech is a great illustration of Parnell's much used device of rhetorical flourish, combined with less conspicuous reservation and implicit qualification. It is clear that Parnell in the Opera House was speaking to multiple audiences: moderate and radical nationalist, Liberal and Conservative, Irish and English. So it was necessary to convey mixed, or rather, multiple messages. Facing into a general election, the watchword among nationalists was unity. Parnell had devoted a good deal of attention in the previous years to wooing Fenians and ex-Fenians. 'Long John' O'Connor, sitting beside him on the stage was a considerable catch who later claimed to have brought other erstwhile Fenians into the ranks of the Parnellites. And O'Connor, as he quickly made clear, was very happy with Parnell's words.[26] Equally, Parnell was also speaking to the leaders of the two main British political parties, indicating (as he had done earlier in the month at Clonmel), that he was available to treat on a measure, however limited, but that was without prejudice to the longer term national aspirations.[27]

While Parnell may have left some ambiguity as to what he believed in himself – as opposed to what was achievable at that moment – there was no ambiguity as to his views on how his movement should and would proceed for the foreseeable future. That much is plain, particularly from the last paragraph of the speech which is rarely quoted but which repays closer attention. Parnell called for all nationalists to do everything possible 'to obtain for Ireland the fullest measure of her rights' while not giving up 'anything which the future may put in favour of our country'. He concluded: 'We shall not do anything to hinder or prevent better men who may come after us from gaining better things than those for which we now contend (prolonged applause).'[28]

What is also plain, and what is conceded by Lyons in his article 'The Political Ideas of Parnell', is that Parnell did not see the restoration of Grattan's Parliament as being a final solution to the question of national self-government.[29] Both MacDonagh and Lyons have questioned Parnell's frequent reference to Grattan's Parliament, pointing out that its independence was limited and its powers more constrained than Parnell acknowledged. While this is true, and while Parnell did have a preoccupation with Grattan's Parliament, it would be a mistake to see its restoration as anything more for Parnell than a symbolic expression of a measure of self-government, not unlike the term 'Home Rule' itself.[30]

Why did Parnell speak *these* words at *this* time? In the weeks before the speech, Joseph Chamberlain and Captain O'Shea had both been involved in privately floating schemes for local government reform in Ireland, which in Chamberlain's plan at least, would involve some devolution of political powers to an Irish board. Parnell's Cork speech may be read in general terms as his response to this alternative to Home Rule.[31] But one other significant piece of context has been largely forgotten. It relates to an article by Lord Monteagle, published in the English Liberal organ, the *Pall Mall Gazette*, on the evening of 20 January 1885, just as Parnell was about to depart for Ireland. The article was reprinted in the *Freeman's Journal*, the following day, when he was *en route* to Cork via Dublin. The *Gazette* had recently taken the radical step of supporting the principle of Home Rule for Ireland. In a response entitled 'A Liberal Policy for Ireland', Lord Monteagle took issue with this development and argued instead for a policy originally suggested by Gladstone – the delegation of certain functions from an over-worked Imperial parliament to local bodies, not only in Ireland but throughout the United Kingdom. This, he argued, would be 'the true Liberal platform . . . [and] it would go a long way towards satisfying the legitimate demands of the Irish people.'[32] At the heart of Monteagle's perceptive critique was the argument that the *Gazette* had not defined Home Rule and neither had Parnell. It was, he said, 'a commonplace of politics that every theory turns on the definition of the judiciously vague term.' Monteagle admitted that Isaac Butt, back in 1870, had attempted to define Home Rule on federalist lines but the news-papers had been too preoccupied with the Franco-Prussian war to take much notice. Parnell, in contrast:

> has taken good care never to commit himself in such a fashion. And however much one may distrust his aims or disapprove of his methods, I cannot but admire the skill and coolness of head with which he has avoided raising the question in any form that should be tangible to English politicians. 'Home Rule' is perfect as a party cry, especially for an Opposition; but regarded as a policy, it has a facility and a plausibility which should make statesmen beware.[33]

Monteagle pointed out that federalism would not be acceptable to advanced nationalists or to Fenians, and argued that there was no middle ground between local government and ultimate separation. Parnellite Home Rule would, he predicted, lead to separation.

Monteagle was a liberal landlord, grandson of Thomas Spring Rice, from Co. Limerick, the first Baron Monteagle and former Whig Chancellor of the Exchequer. He had hitherto adopted the maxim that the less landlords such as himself had to say about politics the better. This made his intervention now of more significance, as did the fact that he admitted that some conces-sion would ultimately have to be made. Although he did not mention it, there is little doubt that Parnell was aware of Monteagle's article: the passage on self-government in the Cork speech reads like a direct retort. The *Freeman* said as much the next day in an editorial comment. Referring to Monteagle's complaint about Parnell's lack of definition, it said:

> we think that Mr Parnell was sufficiently explicit for his lordship – as he certainly was for his audience last night . . . passing contemptuously by the plasters and local

emollients under the name of County Board Government and other reforms which he would at the same time accept and use, he gives the key to his policy when, urging the people to push on self-reliantly and sagaciously, he presumes on no finality, but is confident that by degrees the full measure of constitutional rights and National Self-Government will be won.[34]

Here then is the official nationalist gloss on Parnell's words. They were intended as a retort to Monteagle as well as an answer to nationalist critics on the left of his own party and outside. It also suggests that an interpretation of the speech as a masterpiece of 'studied ambiguity' is not an adequate or sufficient verdict.

After the rhetorical heights of Parnell's speech, the remainder of the proceedings in the Opera House were inevitably something of an anticlimax. Parnell was followed by John Deasy, the junior member for the city, whose remarks focussed on the more mundane business of Castle government, nominations to the magistracy and state jobs. John O'Connor MP, a somewhat reluctant speaker called upon by popular demand, promised that if a large measure of self-government was not achieved in the next parliament, he would resign his seat and tell his Tipperary constituents that they needed to resort to methods other than constitutional. And Fr Eugene Sheehy PP, Rockcorry, lauded the unprecedented unity of priests and people behind Parnell and, referring to Parnell's earlier remarks, ventured that Parnell was not only renewed and reinvigorated physically but 'morally' by being away from England and in the bosom of the people of Cork.[35]

Next day, Thursday 22 January, the recuperative effects of the Cork air were evidently wearing off: Parnell found himself 'so much exhausted and indisposed after the fatigue of travelling . . . and speaking', that 'under advice he remained during the day within doors at the residence of Mr M. J. Horgan.'[36] This necessitated the postponement of the planned visit to Rushbrook and Passage Docks, but he felt well enough to receive callers who included the Mayor, Deasy and O'Connor, Sir John Arnott and Ludlow Beamish and Fr Sheehy. In the evening a dinner attended by sixty guests was hosted in his honour by the Mayor at the Victoria Hotel. At about ten in the evening the dinner was interrupted by the arrival outside of six bands and a very large crowd. Parnell did not feel well enough to speak but the crowd was addressed by the Mayor, John Deasy and John O'Connor, who said that if Parnell was not able to speak 'it was because his health had been impaired and his body had been shattered by his efforts in opposing misrule in Ireland'. He continued:

Mr Parnell knew well that the citizens of Cork formed no small part of the patriotic sentiment of Ireland, and that they were accorded . . . the title of rebel Cork (cheers), and rebels they would ever remain to be until the last shred of British tyranny had been trodden under foot by a united and determined people, resolved to win their rights, and not to lower their banner until those rights were won fully and completely and entirely (continued cheering).[37]

On the following morning, Parnell 'though not yet restored to robust health, found himself . . . much better after his comparative rest' the previous day and started out at 11.00 am to fulfil various engagements. These included meetings with separate deputations from the Cork Board of Guardians and the Cork Ratepayers' Protective Association on the reform of the Irish poor-laws – their main concerns were the Cork ratepayers having to 'support paupers from all parts of Munster' as well as those returning through Queenstown from England and America. He then travelled by special train to the Cork Harbour Company's Docks at Passage, accompanied by Sir John Arnott, chairman of the Dock's Company, and a deputation from the Cork trades. He was met by the local band and large crowds, and was presented with an address from the local tradesmen and working men of the town and another from the Queenstown Town Commissioners. Parnell then toured the docks and in his remarks displayed close familiarity with their problems, reminding his audience of his commitment to the development of Irish industry generally and that he had canvassed on behalf of the Docks' Company for British Admiralty shipbuilding contracts. At the refreshments which followed a toast was proposed for Parnell's health.[38]

That evening Parnell visited Queen's College, Cork and later delivered a lecture at the South Mall Assembly Rooms under the auspices of the Cork Young Ireland Society. Over the stage where Parnell spoke were the words 'Young Ireland', again in gas illumination. A message was read from the President of the Society, William O'Brien MP before Parnell delivered his lecture. This event was the occasion for a well-known anecdote about the Chief. The subject of the lecture – Ireland and her Parliaments – had only been finalised the previous day. M. J. Horgan later recalled for Barry O'Brien, that Parnell had told him that he did not really know anything about Irish history and asked him for books to read. The lecture was due to start at 8.00p.m., and according to Horgan, Parnell rose from dinner at 7.45, took the books, pen and paper into another room and began to prepare the lecture. An hour later he was finished and proceeded to the hall where he began to speak at 9.15, an hour and a quarter late (although the local press reported Parnell arrived at 8.45). Horgan was nervous for him and feared he would break down – he need not have worried. Parnell was cheered from beginning to end and impressed Horgan with his 'majesty' which 'dwarfed all round him'.

Afterwards, Parnell's own verdict was 'I think I got through very well'.[39]

From the very extensive newspaper accounts, Parnell's lecture was rather more substantial than Horgan's account would suggest. Given what we know about its preparation one can only conclude that Parnell's knowledge of history was more detailed than he had admitted. The choice of subject – which was largely Parnell's – and its scope and content are also instructive in relation to the interpretation of the Opera House speech given that he had announced the restitution of Grattan's Parliament as the immediate national demand. In the lecture Parnell argued that the reform of the franchise and the progress of the demand for a restoration of an Irish Parliament made it vital that the younger generation knew something of the history of that Parliament. Having apologised for his lack of preparation, Parnell began his treatise with Henry VIII's Irish parliament of 1541, then traced the fortunes of the three Elizabethan parliaments of 1560, 1570 and 1585; the seventeenth-century parliaments of 1613, 1661 and 1689; and finally the loss and restoration of the independence of the Irish parliament in the eighteenth century. In relation to Grattan's Parliament, he argued that while it suffered from 'many defects in its actions and franchises . . . [it] had a constitution of a very sufficient character' and one which would have enabled it to reform itself and respond to changing circumstances. He suggested Ireland had 'prospered' during the 18 years of its existence and, had it survived, Catholic emancipation would have come earlier, the franchise would have been extended and the oppression of the tenantry and other horrors would have been avoided. The thrust of his position was that Ireland's claim was not for something new but for a restoration of what had been taken from it through 'bribery and corruption'. Echoing his words at the Opera House, he said:

> We stand on unapproachable ground. We are entitled to ask for that which has been stolen from us by means which nobody now seeks to defend for a moment shall be restored to us (applause). We might, perhaps, be unwise if we went further than that demand – we should certainly be foolish if we asked for anything less (loud cheers).[40]

From Cork, Parnell travelled to Limerick and then Clare where he delivered stirring addresses in Ennis and Miltown Malbay. As one might expect, these addresses focussed mainly on the land issue. The *Freeman's* editorial declared that with 'withering scorn he poured words like red-hot shot on the persecutors of the Irish peasantry.' It continued, commenting on Parnell's distinctive style: 'Half the secret of the Irish leader's electric power lies in the feeling that there is within him a reserve force which he struggles to repress rather than to manifest.'[41] Before speaking at Miltown Malbay, Parnell turned the sod on the West Clare Railway (which opened two years later in July 1887), accompanied by the principal contractor, William Martin Murphy. Unfortunately Percy French was not present to immortalise Parnell's visit in song, but a silver spade presented by Murphy to mark the event is now preserved in the Clare County museum.

In the run-up to the 1885 election and in the debate on Home Rule which followed, Parnell's stirring words at Cork gained some currency, providing an answer to critics of both his moderation and his radicalism. They were included by Jennie Wyse-Power in her selection of his speeches, *Words of the Dead Chief*, first published in 1892 and featured in Barry O'Brien's, *Life of Charles Stewart Parnell* which was published in 1898.[42] It may well have been O'Brien who suggested to John Redmond their inclusion on the Parnell Monument, he was certainly consulted about the inscription. The story of the monument is a paper in its own right.[43] The foundation stone was laid in 1899 but the completed monument by American sculptor, Augustus Saint-Gaudens, was not unveiled until October 1911. In the meantime, there was high drama, intrigue, financial irregularities, transatlantic misunderstandings and bickering, embarrassment, fire and farce.[44]

Initiated by John Redmond in 1898, the project was characterised by conflict, confusion, and inefficiency. The original Monument Committee consisted of Lord Mayor Daniel Tallon, Count Plunkett, Dr J. E. Kenny, Edward Blake MP, Redmond and Thomas Baker (manager of the *Irish Independent*) who acted as secretary. As the project dragged on and Baker died, new members joined. The preferred location was outside the Irish Parliament on College Green, but this was the site of the Thomas Moore statue. The committee offered to move the Moore statue but the Corporation refused and instead offered a site on Upper Sackville Street, near the Rotunda Hospital. The unveiling of the foundation stone on 8 October 1899 was the occasion of bitter division with boycotts by anti-Parnellites, bishops and clergy and fist fights involving fervent republicans annoyed that the proposed Wolfe Tone statue was being put on the back burner.[45] In his speech, Redmond vociferously rejected the allegation that the initiative was a Party one and argued that it should become a symbol for unity.

From the outset, the project was beset with financial difficulties. Redmond, Dr Kenny and the Lord Mayor visited the United States in 1899 to collect funds but only managed to raise around $6,000. A contract sum of $40,000 had originally been suggested by Saint-Gaudens but this was later re-negotiated to $25,000 with $2,500 for architectural works.[46] As the project dragged on, there were bitter complaints from Saint-Gaudens about non-payment of money due; and reciprocal threats from the committee to terminate the contract when no progress was evident. At one point, Baker travelled to New York, Vermont and New Hampshire to confront Saint-Gaudens and in 1904 Redmond visited.[47] There were other problems too. In 1903, Saint-Gaudens contracted cancer and the following year a fire destroyed his studio in Cornish, New Hampshire. Among the works lost was the cast for his Parnell statue. 'More than all the rest of my losses in the fire', he wrote, 'I regret, as an Irishman, the loss of the Parnell statue'.[48] Undaunted, he resumed work and completed the statue but died shortly after it was shipped to Ireland in 1907. The statue was displayed for a time at the Royal Hibernian Academy in an unsuccessful attempt to raise funds for the architectural works necessary to complete the monument.

While the commissioning of Augustus Saint-Gaudens was intended partly to encourage funding from Irish America, he was the pre-eminent American sculptor of the nineteenth century.[49] His work included military memorials to American heroes such as Admiral Farragut in Madison Square, New York; Colonel Shaw (commander of the 54th Regiment Massachusetts, the first African-American unit to fight in the Civil War) in Cornish, New Hampshire; Abraham Lincoln in Chicago and General Sherman in Manhattan. Saint-Gaudens' approach to the commission was painstaking. Although he was reluctant to visit the site in person, he had a scale replica of the location and surrounding buildings constructed and solicited photographs and clothes from Katharine O'Shea and Parnell's tailor.[50] He told Redmond that he wished to keep the monument 'as simple, impressive and austere as possible, in keeping with the character of the Irish cause as well as of Parnell'.[51] The statue is a bronze figure about 8ft standing beside a table and set against a triangular obelisk column.[52] Parnell is depicted in frock coat with one hand resting on the table and the other extended dramatically. Saint-Gaudens didn't like 'towering chimneystacks' so popular in eighteenth and nine-teenth century memorials – his Parnell is unmistakeably a contemporary politician rather than a military or classical figure. There is a resemblance to Saint-Gaudens' *Standing Lincoln* monument in Chicago. Judith Hill compares the monument favourably with the nearby O'Connell monument by John Henry Foley, particularly as it 'demonstrated a willingness to search for a new form of expression.'[53]

When, on 1 October 1911, the monument was finally unveiled, the procession was the largest seen in Dublin for many years, with almost seventy bands and numerous representative bodies and trades' societies taking part.[54] In his speech Redmond posed the rhetorical question: where were the belittlers of Parnell's greatness now? Up there on the platform behind him was the caustic answer from Arthur Griffith and his newspaper *Sinn Féin*.[55]

The words from the Cork speech emblazoned on the monument attracted significant attention. It was by no means certain that these words would be chosen, or indeed, any quotation from Parnell. Several options were considered, including tributes suggested by Barry O'Brien and Thomas Baker.[56] One of these read:

> He was a tower of strength to the Irish people
> In making them
> Strong by unity
> Effective by Discipline
> And
> Respected by Wise and Courageous Action.
> The Justice of Ireland's claims
> Was Made
> Manifest to the World
> And
> Their Full Concession Rendered Inevitable

Another suggested variation was:

> He was
> A Tower of Strength to the Irish Race
> In making his Fellow Countrymen
> Powerful by Unity
> Effective by Discipline
> Respected by Wise and Courageous Counsel
> And
> Invaluable in Policy
> Whereby
> The Justice of his Country's claims for National Autonomy
> Was made
> Manifest to the World
> And
> The concession of Self Government
> Rendered
> Inevitable

It would be tempting to conclude that on the eve of the Home Rule bill in 1911, Redmond's choice of inscription was prompted by similar considerations and circumstances to Parnell in 1885. Redmond, no less than Parnell, had to balance what was immediately achievable with long-term aspirations. However the chronology for such a neat conclusion is askew – while the monument was not unveiled until October 1911, the inscription was decided between September 1905 and February 1906. It is more likely, therefore, that

Redmond was influenced in his choice of inscription by the discussions going on in relation to devolution of modest powers to an Irish council – a step towards Home Rule but one far short of the demand for self-government.[57]

Warre B. Wells, one of Redmond's earliest biographers, noted that the inclusion on the monument of Parnell's 'somewhat trite remark that "no man could fix boundaries to the march of a nation" drew charges against Redmond of being a "separatist"'. However, in refutation, Wells cited Redmond's own words, 'Separation is impossible; and, if it were not impossible, it is undesirable.'[58] Redmond's most recent biographer, Dermot Meleady, remarks more perceptively that

> For Redmond the Parnell memorial was a means of simultaneously vindicating and bidding goodbye to his own stance of the past decade, of slipping off the ties that had bound him to the 'Parnellism' of the 1890s while making the full legacy of Parnell – or a mythologised version of it – the property again of all nationalists.[59]

It is certainly the case that the monument – and in particular the inscription – helped make Parnell's legacy the property of all nationalists whether moderate constitutionalists like Redmond or physical force radicals like Patrick Pearse. In his pamphlet *Ghosts*, Pearse summoned the 'pale and angry ghost of Parnell to stand beside the ghosts of Tone and Davis and Lalor and Mitchel', the four main begetters of Irish separatism.[60] For Pearse, Parnell had 'a separatist instinct', citing the Cork speech as evidence. Through his role in erecting the monument, John Redmond could claim credit for re-establishing Parnell as a national rather than a sectional figure but the ultimate achievement was Parnell's. Political speeches are by their nature fleeting and time-bound; Parnell's speech in 1885 in the Cork Opera House is not – it is dynamic. Central to the speech is the notion of continuity and change over time, with each generation facing the recurrent issue of national self-government in its own way. It is that which keeps Parnell's words relevant for succeeding generations.

Notes

1   *Cork Examiner*, 22 Jan. 1885; *Freeman's Journal*, 22 Jan. 1885. See also Jennie Wyse-Power, *Words of the Dead Chief* (Dublin, 2009 edn), pp 101–2.

2   Parnell himself echoed his own words on a number of occasions, most notably at Listowel on 13 Sept. 1891, shortly before his death. Wyse-Power, *Words*, pp 169–72.

3   Alan O'Day, 'Parnell: Orator and speaker', in D. George Boyce and A. O'Day, *Parnell in Perspective* (London, 1991), p. 213.

4   Launching the Scottish independence referendum campaign at the SNP conference on 24 Oct. 2011, Alex Salmond said: 'On the way to Inverness I noticed an outdoor company called 'naelimits'. No limits is a beautiful idea, and somehow it carries more punch in Scots. Nae limits to your ambition, your courage, your journey Nae limits sums up the spirit of freedom which many of us take from our magnificent landscape, and which we wish for our society and politics. This same spirit was reflected in the words of Charles Stewart Parnell: 'No man has the right to fix the boundary of the march of a nation; no man has the right to say to his country, "Thus far shall thou go and no further".' No politician, and certainly no London politician, will determine the future of the Scottish nation. Slugger O'Toole blog, 24 Oct. 2011, accessed 15 Nov. 2011. See also 'Shaping Scotland's Future', speech by First Minister Salmond, TCD, 13 Feb. 2008 at www.scotland.gov.uk/News/This-Week/Speeches/First-Minister.

5   St John Ervine, *Parnell* (London, 1925), pp 219–20.

6   Ibid., p. 220.

7   Brian Walker, 'The Irish electorate, 1868-1915', *Irish Historical Studies*, vol. XVIII, no. 71, Mar. 1973, p. 391.

8   For a brief elaboration of these points, see Pauric Travers *Settlements and Divisions: Ireland 1870–1922* (Dublin, 1988), pp 44–5.

9   Joseph Ronayne (1822–76), engineer and railway proprietor was MP for Cork City from 1872 to 1876.

10   Paul Bew, *C. S. Parnell* (Dublin, 1980), pp 36–7; Mr Murphy, a moderate Home Ruler won the other seat. M. J. Horgan, Parnell's election agent, claimed that the nomination of Parnell was originally a Tory initiative aimed at splitting the Liberal vote and allowing the Conservative to slip in. R. Barry O'Brien, *The Life of Charles Stewart Parnell* (London, 1898), vol. I, pp 214–18.

11   Wyse-Power, *Words*, p. 45; Parnell's speech at the Opera House, *Freeman's Journal*, 22 Jan. 1885.

12   For Parnell and Cork see 'Mr Parnell's Connection with Cork', *Cork Daily Herald*, 6 Oct. 1891.

13   F. S. L. Lyons, *Charles Stewart Parnell* (London, 1978 edn), p. 252; Owen McGee, *The IRB* (Dublin, 2005), pp 77, 131. For more on O'Connor, see above ch. 7 'Defending the Cause' above.

14   R. Barry O'Brien, *Parnell* (London, 1898), vol. II, p. 37.

15   *Irish Times*, 22 Jan. 1885; *Freeman's Journal*, 22 Jan. 1885.

16   *Irish Times*, 22 Jan. 1885, remarked that Parnell travelled 'unaccompanied'. The account of the visit which follows is based on the coverage in the *Cork Examiner, Freeman's Journal* and *Irish Times*, 22–27 Jan. 1886.

17   John J. Horgan, *Parnell to Pearse* (Dublin, 2009 edn), p. 28.

18   *Freeman's Journal*, 22 Jan. 1885.

19   Horgan, *Parnell to Pearse*, p. 28.

20   Quoted in *Irish Times*, 23 Jan. 1885.

21   R. Barry O'Brien, *Parnell*, vol. II, p. 38.

22   Quoted in *Irish Times*, 23 Jan. 1885.

23   Lyons, *Parnell*, p. 261; O'Day, 'Parnell: orator and speaker', pp 213–16; Richard Aldous, *Great Irish Speeches* (London, 2007), p. 42.

24 Oliver MacDonagh, *States of Mind: A Study of Anglo-Irish Conflict, 1780–1980* (London, 1983), p. 60.

25 Paul Bew, *Enigma: A New Life of Charles Stewart Parnell* (Dublin, 2011), p. 118.

26 McGee, *The IRB*, p. 138.

27 For the Clonmel speech, see *Nation*, 17 Jan. 1885. Some months after the Cork speech, Parnell told an audience in Wicklow that while it would be impossible to guarantee that Home Rule would lead to separation, it would weaken the demand for it as separatism was a product of misgovernment. Pauric Travers, 'Reading between the Lines: the Political Speeches of Charles Stewart Parnell', in Donal McCartney and Pauric Travers, *The Ivy Leaf: The Parnells Remembered* (Dublin, 2006), p. 62.

28 *Cork Examiner*, 22 Jan. 1885.

29 F. S. L. Lyons, 'The Political Ideas of Parnell', *Historical Journal*, vol. 16, no. 4 (Dec. 1973), p. 764.

30 Ibid., p. 764; MacDonagh, *States of Mind*, p. 60.

31 Lyons, *Parnell*, pp 269-71; Paul Bew, *Enigma*, pp 117–19. On the central board scheme, see C. H. D. Howard, 'Joseph Chamberlain, Parnell and the Irish "Central Board" Scheme, 1884–1885', *Irish Historical Studies*, vol. VIII, no. 32 (Sept. 1953), pp 324–61.

32 *Pall Mall Gazette*, 20 Jan. 1885; *Freeman's Journal*, 21 Jan. 1885.

33 Ibid.

34 *Freeman's Journal*, 22 Jan. 1885.

35 Ibid.

36 Ibid., 23 Jan. 1885.

37 Ibid.

38 Ibid., 24 Jan. 1885.

39 Ibid.; Horgan, *Parnell to Pearse*, p. 29; R. Barry O'Brien, *Parnell*, vol. II, pp 39–40.

40 *Freeman's Journal*, 24 Jan. 1885.

41 Ibid., 27 Jan. 1885.

42 Wyse-Power, *Words*, p. 101; R. Barry O'Brien, *Parnell*, vol. II, pp 38–9.

43 See Timothy J O'Keefe, 'The art and politics of the Parnell monument', *Eire-Ireland*, xix, no. 1 (Spring, 1984), pp 6–25; Sean Rothery, 'Parnell Monument: Ireland & American Beaux Arts', *Irish Arts Review*, 4, no.1 (Spring, 1987), pp 55–7; Judith Hill, *Irish Public Sculpture: A History* (Dublin, 1998); Gary Owens, 'Nationalist Monuments in Ireland: Symbolism and Ritual c. 1870–1914', in Raymond Gillespie and Brian P. Kennedy, *Ireland: Art into History* (Dublin, 1994); Brian Fallon, *Irish Art 1830–1990* (Belfast, 1994).

44 The account which follows is based on the correspondence in the Parnell Monument and other files in the Redmond Papers in the National Library of Ireland (hereafter NLI), Mss 9006, 15,167(2); 15,239; 15,241(10),15,249; 15, 256; 15, 268.

45 The foundation stone of the Wolfe Tone statue had been laid in 1898. On the 'determined stand' of republican groups against the Parnell monument, see John Mallon to Under Secretary, 1 Aug. 1899; and on the disturbances at the laying of the foundation stone, see Chief Commissioner Jones to Under Secretary, 9 Oct. 1899. National Archives of Ireland, Dublin Metropolitan Police Papers, Ms 3/794/14, files 5290 and 5343.

46 Augustus Saint-Gaudens to Thomas Baker, 29 Jan. 1900. Redmond Papers, NLI, Ms 15,167(2). Saint-Gaudens estimated that the project would take four or five years.

47 See report by Baker to Redmond, 3 June 1903. Redmond Papers, NLI, Ms 15,167(2).

48 *New York Daily News*, quoted in Archive Consultants, *History of Monuments: O'Connell Street Area* (Dublin City Council. 2003), p. 19.

49 Saint-Gaudens was born in Charlemont Street, Dublin in 1848, son of a shoemaker from Gascony and daughter of Mary McGuiness from Ballymahon, Co. Longford. The family emigrated when he was six months. Lawrence William White, 'Saint-Gaudens, Augustus', in *Dictionary of Irish Biography* James McGuire & James Quinn (eds), pp 721–3.

50 Saint-Gaudens to Mrs C. S. Parnell, 2 Dec. 1904. Redmond Papers, NLI, Ms 15,167(2).

51 Saint-Gaudens to Redmond, 22 Oct. 1902. Redmond Papers, NLI, Ms 15,241(10).

52 Saint-Gaudens originally intended to use a pyramid but this was changed as the Wellington memorial used a pyramid.

53 Hill, *Irish Public Sculpture*, p. 114.

54 Dublin Metropolitan Police report, 2 Oct. 1911, National Archives of Ireland, CO 904/13. For the unveiling of the monument, see Pauric Travers, 'The Thurible as a Weapon of War: Ivy Day at Glasnevin, 1891–1921', in McCartney and Travers (eds), *The Ivy Leaf* (Dublin, 2006), p. 152.

55 *Irish Times* 2 Oct. 1911; *Freeman's Journal*, 2 Oct. 1911; *Sinn Féin*, Oct. 1911.

56 Baker to Redmond, 29 Sept. 1905. Redmond Papers, NLI, Ms 15,167(3). Other possible inscriptions can be found in Ms 15,268. Saint-Gaudens suggested inclusion of some words in Irish. These were chosen following consultation with P. W. Joyce and Eoin MacNeill and read: *Go soirbigid Eire da clan.*

57 On devolution and the subsequent Irish Council bill, see Travers, *Settlements and Divisions*, pp 67–9; 76–8.

58 Warre B. Wells, *John Redmond: A Biography* (London, 1919), pp 95–6.

59 Dermot Meleady, *Redmond: The Parnellite* (Cork, 2008), p. 315.

60 Patrick Pearse, *Political Writings and Speeches* (Dublin, 1924), pp 241–5.

CHAPTER 11

Parnell's Manifesto 'To the People of Ireland', 29 November 1890

Context, Content and Consequences

Donal McCartney

Following the lurid revelations of the O'Shea divorce scandal, a public meeting was held in Dublin at which a proposal by Justin McCarthy, vice-chairman of the Irish Party, seconded by Tim Healy, was passed unanimously. It declared that: '. . . in all political matters Mr Parnell possesses the confidence of the Irish nation', and the meeting 'rejoices at the determination of the Irish Parliamentary Party to stand by their Leader'.[1]

In Britain, however, Gladstone was under intense pressure from his nonconformist supporters and party advisers to end his alliance with the convicted Irish adulterer. Reacting to this pressure, he wrote a letter to John Morley, to be shown to Parnell before the Irish Parliamentary Party met to elect its leader. The vital part of this letter read:

> . . .notwithstanding the splendid services rendered by Mr Parnell to his country, his continuance at the present moment in the leadership would be productive of consequences disastrous in the highest degree to the cause of Ireland . . . [It] would not only place many hearty and effective friends of the Irish cause in a position of great embarrassment, but would render my retention of the leadership of the Liberal Party, based as it has been mainly upon the prosecution of the Irish cause, almost a nullity.[2]

Gladstone had also authorised Justin McCarthy to convey his views to the Irish leader. Gladstone's messages, however, were not delivered before the Parliamentary Party had re-elected Parnell. The failure of the various messengers to deliver was hardly surprising given Parnell's aptitude for concealing his tracks and for making himself inaccessible whenever it suited. Morley met Parnell by chance on his way from re-election, read him Gladstone's letter and urged that a temporary retirement, at the least, was indispensable. Parnell replied that he had no intention of retiring, temporarily or perman-ently. Then, as if he had already prepared his next move, added: 'Of course Mr Gladstone will have to attack me . . . He will have a right to do that . . . It will put him straight with his Party.'[3]

A furious and impetuous Gladstone decided to publish his letter imme-diately. And what in a private communication had been a genuine and well-meaning piece of friendly advice was transformed into a public and hostile act of intervention. The Irish Party and people were presented with a stark choice: Parnell's resignation or no Home Rule. To imagine that Parnell had not already been planning how to deal with the leadership crisis resulting from the divorce scandal, is to belie all that we know about his reputation as a cool and calculating strategist. With no intention of stepping aside, his best plan was to have the Irish people and Party endorse his leadership. All demands from Britain for his resignation could then be denounced as unacceptable intervention in the rights of the Irish people to choose their own political leaders, and condemned as an attempt to destroy the indepen-dence of the Irish Party. This was the context in which Parnell delivered his famous Manifesto, as well as the reasoning behind its argument.

With his leadership already endorsed at the public meeting in Dublin, and his re-election as leader by the Party members in London, it could be said that the battle was going according to Parnell's plan, and that Gladstone by attacking him publicly had fallen into Parnell's trap. Gladstone's letter had, however, also created consternation in the ranks of the Irish Party, and it became clear that formidable opposition to Parnell was hardening among his colleagues. So, in the home in London of Dr J. G. Fitzgerald, MP for Longford South, Parnell wrote the document which he entitled 'To the People of Ireland'. It was the longest piece ever penned by him.

For convenience, the Manifesto may be divided into two major sections. The first section is an attack on Gladstone; the second section attacks John Morley, who after Gladstone was the member of the Liberal front bench most committed to Home Rule. It begins defiantly:

> The integrity and independence of a section of the Irish Parliamentary Party having been apparently sapped and destroyed by the wirepullers of the English Liberal Party, it becomes necessary for me, as Leader of the Irish nation, to take counsel with you, and, having given you the knowledge which is within my possession, to ask your judgement upon a matter which now solely devolves upon you to decide.
>
> The letter of Mr Gladstone to Mr Morley, written for the purpose of influencing the decision of the Irish Party in the choice of their Leader, and claiming for the

Liberal Party and their leaders the right of veto upon that choice, is the immediate cause of this address to you, to remind you and your Parliamentary representatives that Ireland considers the independence of her members as her only safeguard within the constitution, and above and beyond all other considerations whatever. The threat in that letter, repeated so insolently on many English platforms and in numerous British newspapers, that unless Ireland concedes this right of veto to England she will indefinitely postpone her chances of obtaining Home Rule, compels me, while not for one moment admitting the slightest probability of such loss, to put before you information which until now, so far as my colleagues are concerned, has been solely in my possession, and which will enable you to understand the measure of the loss with which you are threatened unless you consent to throw me to the English wolves now howling for my destruction.[4]

The Manifesto then claims to reveal details of Gladstone's Home Rule proposals as outlined in the private meeting between the two leaders at Hawarden a year earlier. Allegedly, Gladstone told Parnell that: (a) it would be necessary to reduce Irish representation in the imperial Parliament from 103 to 32; (b) that an Irish parliament would not be given the power of solving the agrarian difficulty, and that Gladstone was not prepared to pressurise his colleagues to do so; and (c) that control of the Irish constabulary and all appointments to the judiciary would be left with Westminster for a number of years. No way, wrote Parnell, would he consent to the reduction in the number of Irish MPs before full and satisfactory legislative independence had been won.

Parnell claimed that his private interviews with Morley had convinced him that, quite apart from Home Rule, the Liberals could not be trusted either on land purchase or the plight of the evicted tenants. He also asserted that Morley had asked him whether he would be willing to become Chief Secretary of Ireland or allow another member of his Party to take the position when the Liberals returned to power. Morley had also suggested filling one of the law offices of the Crown in Ireland with a legal member of the Irish Party (this was understood as a swipe at Tim Healy by Parnell). Parnell replied that he could not agree to forfeit in any way the independence of the Irish Party, nor any of its members; that he would on no account renege on the trust the Irish people had placed in him on this issue of independence. The Manifesto finished with a flourish:

Sixteen years ago I conceived the idea of an Irish Parliamentary Party independent of all English Parties. Ten years ago I was elected the leader of an independent Irish Parliamentary Party. During these ten years that Party has remained independent, and because of its independence it has forced upon the English people the necessity of granting Home Rule to Ireland. I believe that Party will obtain Home Rule, only provided it remains independent of any English Party. I do not believe that any action of the Irish people in supporting me will endanger the Home Rule cause, or postpone the establishment of an Irish Parliament, but even if the danger with which we are threatened by the Liberal Party of to-day were to be realised I believe that the Irish people throughout the world would agree with me that a postponement would be preferable to a compromise of our National rights by the acceptance of a measure which would not realise the aspirations of our race.

The Manifesto was a powerful appeal to nationalist Ireland. It vibrated with echoes of the defiant speeches characteristic of the man who had conducted the Land War; created the dynamic Party machine; and led his people within sight of the promised land of legislative independence. It was also an appeal to the people, over the heads of a wobbling Party. He had often insisted that they, the people, must select only men of determination and integrity as their representatives, men who would reject all dictation from England; be dependent only on Irish public opinion; hold themselves 'aloof from all English parties' and 'refuse to accept any situation until it is in the power of the Irish people . . . to give to their faithful servants suitable reward.'[5]

The Manifesto was especially significant, not only in what it said, but also in what it had left unsaid. Not a word was uttered about that which lay at the heart of the whole controversy – the divorce scandal. Parnell had once observed that it was 'a favourite device with politicians' when dealing with an accusation, not to deny it, but to talk about something else.[6] His own Manifesto was along those very lines. And as such it was an audacious, diversionary tactic worthy of the political general he was. The objective was to shift the debate away from the question of his moral unfitness to lead Ireland because of the O'Shea scandal; and to focus attention instead on the issue of dictation from Gladstone, and on renewed attempts by English politicians to sap the integrity of Irish MPs. There was no denying the strength and cleverness of his device. Mary Gladstone described it as 'defiant' and 'devilish'.[7] It was characterised in one prominent British newspaper as 'diabolically clever'.[8] And Randolph Churchill expressed the view that it was a 'masterpiece' because it had raised the issue from the question of the divorce scandal to the level of a big political debate.[9]

But had Parnell overplayed his hand? For one who had a reputation for clarity and of not using one word more than was necessary, the section on Morley's attitude to the land question and the evicted tenants was particularly long and complex. And although it embraced plenty of passionate language, there were no trademark Parnellite sound bites (if we exclude 'English wolves howling for my destruction'). It had none of the elevating patriotism of the 'No man has the right to fix the boundary to the march of the nation' speech. It had none of the inspirational call to arms of his Land League days with its mantra: 'Keep a firm grip of your homesteads'. Nevertheless, it was arguably the address that had the most critical effect on his political career.

Gladstone and Morley immediately denied the accuracy of Parnell's version of their private interviews with him. What gives credibility to Gladstone's denial was the fact that directly after their interview at Hawarden in December 1889, Parnell, speaking privately and publicly had expressed extreme satisfaction with the outcome. Addressing the Liverpool Reform Club, he had referred to Gladstone as 'your great leader' who was ready to 'terminate the strife of centuries'.[10] Likewise the Liberal leader had written in his diary after the Hawarden meeting: 'He is certainly one of the very best people to deal with that I have ever known'.[11] The Manifesto had acknowledged that the interviews with Gladstone and Morley had been private and confidential. Gladstone now pointed out that even if Parnell had given a true account, the breaking of the seal of confidentiality rendered any further political cooperation with Parnell impossible. He was no longer the man with whom business could be done.

The Irish Party now had to choose between Parnell and Gladstone. Over the years the Party, moulded by Parnell, had grown in strength and self-confidence. As it tended to outgrow its creator, it became more comfortable with the Liberal-Nationalist alliance – an alliance that had been forged by Parnell himself and which Michael Davitt described as 'the chief triumph of his political career'.[12] In Ireland, however, many had come to trust Gladstone too. 'No Irish Nationalist', wrote Barry O'Brien, 'was more determined to establish a Parliament in Ireland than was the Liberal leader.'[13] A majority in the Party regarded the Liberal-Nationalist alliance as a priority. And now Parnell with his Manifesto was seen to be abandoning his own creation – the 'Union of Hearts'. If the price to be paid for preserving that alliance was the deposition of Parnell, so be it. Healy led the charge, and exploiting the inconsistencies in the document, made the telling point that either Parnell's earlier enthusiastic expressions at Liverpool of satisfaction with the Gladstone interview were false, or his Manifesto was false. And if Gladstone's proposals were at the time so unsatisfactory, why in the meantime had Parnell kept silent on the issue?

One of the deadliest blows to Parnell came from the leaders of the Plan of Campaign, then on a major fundraising tour of America. On that six-man delegation were John Dillon, William O'Brien, Tim Harrington, T. P. O'Connor, T. D. Sullivan and T. P. Gill. Immediately after the divorce case, and like their Party colleagues at home, they – with the exception of Sullivan – cabled their strong support for Parnell. Hot on the heels of Gladstone's letter, however, all – with the exception of Harrington – with equal forcefulness urged Parnell to retire. After the publication of the Manifesto they declared that on no account would they ever serve again under the leadership of the man who could issue such a document. They repudiated his 'insulting language'; and insisted on the necessity of maintaining the Liberal alliance. As far as the most senior and influential members of the Party were concerned, the Manifesto had backfired on Parnell.

Until the publication of the Manifesto, the bishops had remained silent on Parnell's leadership. Archbishops Walsh of Dublin and Croke of Cashel, hitherto Parnell's most outspoken supporters among the hierarchy, now called for his removal, which they claimed, would maintain 'our honourable alliance' with the Liberals; preserve the unity of the Party; ensure victory at the elections; and make Home Rule certain. Walsh described the Manifesto as 'an act of political suicide' which would bring disaster upon Ireland. Then, while the Party famously debated the leadership in Committee Room 15, the body of bishops issued an Address to the clergy and laity. Parnell, it declared, had been convicted of one of the greatest offences known to religion and society: 'Surely Catholic Ireland . . . will not accept as its leader a man thus dishonoured, and wholly unworthy of Christian confidence.'[14]

The argument now shifted away from the political, on which Parnell with the Manifesto had pinned his hopes, and back to the issue of his private morality. Throughout the campaign in Ireland, Healy and his clerical allies never wearied of condemning Parnell chiefly on moral grounds. Yeats was not altogether wrong: 'The bishops and the Party/ That tragic story made'.

For, if Parnell was to retain the leadership he had to keep the Party, under pressure from the people, on his side; and at the same time hope that the clergy would remain silent on the political question and not use their powerful influence with the people against him. With the Church, the Party, the contemporary public attitude towards sexual morality, and changed political and social circumstances now massively arrayed against him, he found himself – armed only with the blunted weapon of the Manifesto – in an epic battle against overwhelming odds. The outcome was that his appeal, 'To the People of Ireland', failed.

Parnell conceded that Gladstone did mean to establish some sort of Home Rule, but said he would be satisfied with any kind: he was an old man in a hurry who could not wait. As for himself, he was young and could 'afford to wait' for an Irish parliament whose structure would last. He added: '. . . if we do not get it this year or next I can wait for half a dozen years; but it must be a real Parliament when it comes.'[15] Home Rule, he asserted, would not come in Gladstone's time; and none of his likely successors cared enough to risk anything for it. They would bow to nothing but power – the power of an independent, united Party. Parnell said he would pull the country together again in five years. He was dead within a matter of months. When Gladstone did return as Prime Minster in 1892 he introduced his second Home Rule

Bill. It passed the House of Commons by 34 votes; but was thrown out by the House of Lords by 378 votes. Six months later, at the age of 85, Gladstone resigned.

Parnell had been deposed to save the Liberal-Nationalist alliance and Home Rule. But in spite of all the predictions of his opponents, clerical and lay, Home Rule was never to materialise. Parnell had been sacrificed – and still Home Rule was lost. And in the process the Party was torn apart. Only gradually would it dawn on the people to whom the Manifesto had been addressed that the fall of Parnell had left the country bereft of any politician with the charisma, defiance, tenacity and skill of the dead Chief. And all that Ireland had received in return was the myth of its tragic and romantic hero.

Notes

1 *Freeman's Journal*, 21 Nov. 1890.

2 John Morley, *The Life of William Ewart Gladstone* (London, 1903), vol. III, p. 329.

3 Ibid., vol. III, pp 331–2.

4 *Freeman's Journal*, 29 Nov. 1890. The text is given in full in F. S. L. Lyons, *The Fall of Parnell, 1890–91* (London, 1960), vol. I, pp 320–6; in Katharine O'Shea, *Charles Stewart Parnell: His Love Story and Political Life* (London, 1914), vol. II, pp 166–74; and in R. Barry O'Brien, *The Life of Charles Stewart Parnell* (London, 1910), pp 481–7.

5 See for example his speeches at Navan, 8 Apr. 1880; at Fintona, 2 Sept. 1881; at the 'Eighty Club', 8 Mar. 1889 all in Jennie Wyse-Power, *Words of the Dead Chief* (Dublin, 2009 edn),   pp 44, 62–3, 134–5.

6 At Plymouth, 27 June 1886 in Wyse-Power, *Words*, p. 114.

7 Quoted in Frank Callanan, *The Parnell Split, 1890–91* (Cork, 1992), p. 25.

8 Ibid.

9 P. J. Walsh, *William J. Walsh Archbishop of Dublin* (Dublin, 1928), p. 415, citing *Life of Randolph Churchill*, vol. II, pp 437–8.

10 Quoted in Robert Kee, *The Laurel and the Ivy: the Story of Charles Stewart Parnell and Irish Nationalism* (London, 1993), p. 533.

11 F. S. L. Lyons, *Charles Stewart Parnell* (London, 1978 edn), p. 450.

12 Michael Davitt, *The Fall of Feudalism in Ireland* (London, 1904), p. 644.

13 R. Barry O'Brien, *Parnell*, pp 490–1.

14 For the Bishop's Address see Walsh, *William J. Walsh*, pp 419–20. See also ch. XVI 'The Parnell Crisis' ibid. for Archbishop Walsh's handling of the leadership issue; and Mark Tierney, *Croke of Cashel: The Life of Archbishop Thomas William Croke, 1823–1902* (Dublin, 1976), ch. xii, 'The Parnell Crisis, 1890–91' for Archbishop Croke's attitude.

15 Barry O'Brien, *Parnell*, p. 540.

Index